Past Multistate Performance Test Questions and Point Sheets

MPT

In Re Barnett
In Re Rose Kingsley
Reynolds v. Preferred Medical Partners
In Re Clarke Corporation
Bennett v. Sands
Rivera v. Baldisari
State v. Miller
Graham Realty Inc. v. Chapin
Wells v. Wells
State v. Tweedy
In Re Al Merton
GVP Non-Disclosure Agreement

© AmeriBar Bar Review 2006 (as to parts not copyrighted NCBE)
AmeriBar Bar Review • Phone (800) 529-2651 • Fax (800) 529-2652

FILE

In re Barnett

The Open Housing Center

Education, Information & Advocacy

To: Applicant

From: Kellis Parker, Director of Litigation

Date: February 24, 2005

Re: Barnett Assignment

Matt and Sarah Barnett have come to us seeking representation regarding the housing discrimination they feel occurred during their attempt to rent an apartment at 91 Woodland Avenue here in Kingsfield, Franklin. Their initial inclination is to pursue this matter before the Franklin Commission on Human Rights.

Matt and Sarah want to bring an action and seek relief against Tony Gordon, the owner of the apartment building. Please draft a memorandum to me that explores in detail how the facts support our claims that

(1)   Tony Gordon violated §§ 107(a) *and* 107(b) of the Franklin Administrative Code; and

(2)   Matt and Sarah are *each* entitled to bring an action to recover substantial damages from Tony Gordon.

The Open Housing Center

Education, Information & Advocacy

To: Kellis Parker, Director of Litigation

From: Marianne P. Relman

Date: February 10, 2005

Re: Matt Barnett: Interview Notes

I interviewed Matt Barnett today. He feels that he and his family were discriminated against in their attempt to secure an apartment at 91 Woodland Ave., Kingsfield.

Over the last month, Matt and Sarah have been actively looking for a new home for their family. They have three children: Casey (15), Nicole (11), and Sammy (5). Matt is white, 42 years old, and the assistant manager of a restaurant in the Point Pleasant section of Kingsfield. He has been married to Sarah for 17 years. She is dark skinned and was born and raised in England.

Two weeks ago, Matt noticed a flier stapled to a telephone pole outside the restaurant he manages. The flier described a spacious three-bedroom apartment in a two-family brownstone in the Point Pleasant section of Kingsfield (only blocks away from Matt's restaurant) that was renting for $1,000 per month. I made a copy of the flier, which Matt has seen on "lots of" poles since the incident.

Matt called the number on the flier and spoke to Tony Gordon, who described himself as the owner of the building. Matt made an appointment to see the apartment on his lunch hour the next day. Gordon took Matt's home phone number. Gordon told Matt that Gordon would leave a key to the apartment with his sister, Helena Pall, who lives in the other unit in the building, and that Matt could take a look. Gordon lives elsewhere.

That night, Matt told Sarah about the appointment. They were both excited because they had been looking for a place with more room. Their current apartment is in Dunlop Square. Though the apartment is in good condition, it is small (two bedrooms—all of the kids now share one bedroom) and there is no place for the kids to play except the sidewalk and street (Dunlop Square was originally an industrial area that has gradually shifted to residential use). Now that the kids are getting older, having only one bathroom has become a problem; the local schools are not ranked highly by the Board of Education; and both Matt and Sarah must use public transportation to get to work, which takes them each about 30 minutes each way. The rent on their current apartment is $800. However, they can afford to pay more rent now that Sarah has begun working for the Kingsfield Legal Aid Society, in the criminal defense division. They can afford to pay as much as $1,200 per month in rent, but apartments in their price range are not plentiful.

Matt went alone to see the apartment the next day, and he picked up the key from Helena Pall. Pall was cordial. She had been expecting Matt because her brother Tony had told her about the appointment. Matt described the apartment as "a palace compared to our current place." It has three large, sunny bedrooms and a study that Pall said had been used by the former tenant as a fourth bedroom. There is a sunken living room, which opens through French doors into a nice-sized dining room. The kitchen is more than adequate. There are two bathrooms. Matt said that the apartment was "perfect for kids." He returned the key to Pall and left.

Matt was excited when he returned home that evening, as was Sarah after hearing Matt describe the apartment. That night, Matt called Gordon and made an appointment to take Sarah to see the apartment the next evening after work. Gordon had already picked up the key from Pall, but told Matt he would drop it off again the next day.

The next evening when Matt and Sarah went to see the apartment, they arrived on time and rang Pall's doorbell. There was no answer. They waited on the stoop for another minute and rang again. This time, Pall came to the window and said, "Sorry, it's been rented," and walked away.

Disappointed and feeling a little put out, Matt and Sarah returned home. Later that evening, Sarah answered the phone. It was Gordon, who was calling to see whether they wanted the apartment. Sarah said that she and Matt had gone to see the apartment but were turned away by Pall. Gordon apologized, saying that his sister must have been "confused." He asked if they would visit again and when Sarah agreed, they arranged to see the apartment the next evening.

The next evening when they returned, Matt and Sarah picked up the key from Pall, looked at the apartment, and then dropped off the key with Pall. Pall was not rude, but was not nearly as cordial as she had been when Matt visited the apartment alone. Sarah said it was a great apartment, and Pall said, "Yes it's certainly worth the $2,500 monthly rent." Matt said the flier stated that the rent would be $1,000 per month. Pall insisted that he was mistaken. Sarah looked aghast. Matt said he knew immediately what was going on, took Sarah by the hand, and stormed out of the building.

Matt was sure they had been denied the apartment because the owner did not want to rent to what appeared to him to be an interracial couple. Sarah conceded that he might be right but wanted to be sure. When they arrived home, Matt was too angry to go inside and went for a long walk.

Sarah called Gordon and told him what had transpired and requested an explanation. Gordon told her that the apartment had been rented to someone else.

The next day, Sarah arranged for a "test" to confirm that the apartment was available and to verify the original rent amount. Matt suggested that we talk with Sarah about that.

Matt said that this has been an ordeal and has hit his family "like a bombshell." He is very upset, has started smoking again, and his ulcers have "flared up, big time," requiring him to see his doctor, who "doubled" the strength of his ulcer medicine. In addition, Sarah seems constantly angry. The kids are aware of what is going on and are upset as well. Matt said that the worst part was when his youngest son, Sammy, came to him and suggested that Matt and Casey (his light-skinned older brother) take the new apartment and that he (Sammy) would find another place with Sarah and Nicole, who is dark skinned as well. Matt was on the verge of tears as he related this incident to me.

Matt said that he and Sarah don't want to have anything to do with Tony Gordon or his apartment. However, they want "justice" and would like to "make sure that Gordon understands the pain he has caused" and that they want to "do something that prevents him from doing this again to anyone else."

HOME SWEET HOME

3 bedrooms in a large newly renovated two-family brownstone. Features large, modern kitchen with all appliances, spacious living room, dining room, small study, and 2 full bathrooms.

Central a/c, working fireplace, hardwood floors, lots of windows, recessed lighting, crown molding, walk-in closets, and private deck/patio overlooking landscaped backyard with garden. Street parking available.

Monthly Rent: $1,000
Contact Tony Gordon (owner) at (608) 555-4291

The Open Housing Center

Education, Information & Advocacy

To: Kellis Parker, Director of Litigation

From: Marianne P. Relman

Date: February 18, 2005

Re: Sarah Barnett: Interview Notes

Sarah is an impressive woman with an interesting history. After years of working as a classical violist and part-time music teacher, Sarah (age 40) recently graduated from Kingsfield School of Law and is working as an attorney with the Kingsfield Legal Aid Society. She is dark skinned, was brought up in England, and speaks with an English accent. She emigrated to the U.S. in her late teens and, shortly after her marriage to Matt, became a U.S. citizen.

She related her sense of outrage with regard to her final phone conversation with Gordon, and with what she called Gordon's "blatant lie." After Pall told her and Matt the rent was $2,500 per month, Sarah called Gordon to find out what was going on. Gordon told her, "Sorry, I just rented the apartment to an old family friend. But if you'd like, I'll put your name on file in case something else opens up at one of my other properties." Sarah said she hung up without responding. She is embarrassed that she even called Gordon and wishes that she had displayed the anger she now feels toward him. In our time together, she seemed more demoralized than angry. At one point she said, "We work hard and try to do things right. I thought that if we played by the rules we would be rewarded. I see that this is not the case."

Following this phone discussion with Gordon, she withdrew, feeling alternately angry and depressed. She found it difficult to face her work responsibilities and missed a day of work. She is not getting much sleep, has lost 5 pounds, and cannot muster the enthusiasm for work that she had only a short time ago. She has also begun seeing a psychotherapist to deal with her anger and depression. Neither she nor Matt has resumed a search for a new place. "What's the use?" she says.

She mentioned a "test" that her friend Brian performed at her request. Brian Donnelly works in Sarah's office. The day after her final conversation with Gordon, she phoned Brian from home, explained what had happened, and asked if he would call Gordon to see whether the apartment was available and, if so, at what rent. Brian called Gordon that day. He spoke to Gordon's assistant, who informed Brian that she thought the apartment was still available and that the rent would be $1,000 per month.

Like Matt, Sarah would like to litigate this matter.

LIBRARY

In re Barnett

FRANKLIN ADMINISTRATIVE CODE

TITLE 8, CIVIL RIGHTS: CHAPTER 1. COMMISSION ON HUMAN RIGHTS.

§ 101. Policy.

In the State of Franklin, there is no greater danger to the health, morals, safety, and welfare of the state and its inhabitants than the existence of groups prejudiced against and antagonistic to one another because of their actual or perceived differences. It is therefore the intent of the Legislature to end discrimination in housing based on the actual or perceived race, creed, color, national origin, gender, age, occupation, disability, sexual orientation, marital status, or alienage or citizenship status of such person or persons, or because children are, or may be, residing with such person or persons. The Franklin Commission on Human Rights established hereunder is given general jurisdiction and power to eliminate and prevent discrimination from playing any role in actions relating to housing.

§ 102. Definitions.

* * * *

2.   The term "person aggrieved" shall mean any person who has suffered injury as a result of an unlawful discriminatory practice.

3.   The term "injury" includes loss of housing and related amenities and services, and economic, emotional, physical or other harm.

4.   The term "unlawful discriminatory practice" includes only those practices specified in § 107.

* * * *

7.   The term "national origin" shall, for the purposes of this chapter, include "ancestry."

* * * *

10. The term "housing accommodation" includes any building or portion thereof which is used or occupied or is intended, arranged or designed to be used or occupied as the residence or sleeping place of one or more persons.

* * * *

21. The term "alienage or citizenship status" means: (a) the citizenship of any person, or (b) the immigration status of any person who is not a citizen or national of the United States.

* * * *

§ 107. Unlawful Discriminatory Practices—Housing accommodations.

In all housing accommodations, it shall be unlawful for the owner, lessee, or managing agent of, or other person having the right to sell, rent or lease or approve the sale, rental or lease of a housing accommodation to do any of the following on the basis of the actual or perceived race, creed, color, national origin, gender, age, occupation, disability, sexual orientation, marital status or alienage or citizenship status of such person or persons, or because children are, or may be, residing with such person or persons:

(a) To refuse to sell, rent, lease, approve the sale, rental or lease, or otherwise deny to or withhold from any person or group of persons a housing accommodation or;

(b) To discriminate in the terms, conditions or privileges of the sale, rental or lease of any such housing accommodation.

* * * *

§ 109. Petition.

Any person aggrieved by an unlawful discriminatory practice may petition this Commission for a hearing and determination.

* * * *

§ 120. Decision and Order.

If, upon all the evidence at the hearing, the Commission finds that a respondent has engaged in any unlawful discriminatory practice, the Commission shall issue an order requiring the respondent to cease and desist from such unlawful discriminatory practice and to take affirmative action to effectuate the purposes of this chapter including:

(a) Directing the sale, rental or lease, or approving the sale, rental or lease of housing accommodations;

(b) Directing the payment of compensatory damages to the person aggrieved by such practice or act, including damages for emotional distress;

(c) Imposing a civil penalty of not more than fifty thousand dollars ($50,000) where the Commission finds the respondent's actions were willful, wanton or malicious. Any civil penalties recovered pursuant to this chapter shall be paid into the general fund of the State.

(d) Requiring the respondent to participate in training regarding the requirements of the law;

(e) Monitoring the respondent's future housing practices; and

(f) Directing the payment of costs and reasonable attorneys' fees to the prevailing party.

Rosa v. Brusco

Franklin Court of Appeal (2001)

This is an appeal from an order of the Franklin Commission on Human Rights ("the Commission") that found petitioners guilty of discrimination on the basis of race in denying rental of an apartment to a black woman.

Petitioner Angelina Brusco is the owner of the premises located at 309 West Street in Kingsfield, and petitioner Louis Brusco is her son and manager of the building. Petitioner Brusco Fuel Oil Co., Inc., is a fuel oil company that is alleged also to be a managing agent of the premises.

In July of 2000, Eneida Rosa, a black female law student at Kingsfield School of Law, attempted to rent an apartment in the subject building. The uncontroverted statements of Rosa and a white friend, Gail Gregory, indicate that Rosa was the victim of discriminatory treatment by Yvonne Lomelino, who said she was a rental agent for the landlord. She offered to rent the apartment to Gregory. She did not, however, offer to rent the apartment to Rosa even though it was apparently available, and she discouraged Rosa from filling out an application form. Although Lomelino ultimately accepted Rosa's application for the apartment with a check for one month's rent, her application was rejected, and the apartment was rented to someone else.

Rosa filed a complaint with the Commission. The Commission held hearings and found Angelina and Louis Brusco and the Brusco Fuel Oil Co. responsible for discriminatory conduct against Rosa and awarded Rosa damages.

The Bruscos and the company do not dispute the discriminatory treatment of Rosa. However, they deny liability on the ground that they are not responsible for the conduct of Lomelino, who, they insist, is not authorized to act as their agent either under § 107 of the Franklin Administrative Code or by general common-law principles of agency. They contend that the determination of the Commission is not supported by substantial evidence.

Although Lomelino identified herself as the rental agent, job titles are not dispositive on the question of whether an agency relationship exists. Instead, we look to the facts of each case. Here, evidence given at the hearing indicated that Lomelino was authorized to show apartments, had keys to the apartments, and had the initial authority to determine whether to submit applications for further consideration to the manager and owner. These facts create an agency relationship between Lomelino and the Bruscos. The responsibilities exercised by Lomelino establish that her actions are imputed to the owner and manager. The Commission was justified in finding that

Angelina Brusco, as owner of the building, and Louis Brusco, as manager, were responsible for the discriminatory actions of Lomelino. The failure of the Bruscos to monitor the performance of their agent cannot be a valid defense. Those who discriminate are not likely to do so openly.

Regarding Brusco Fuel Oil Co., there is no substantial evidence supporting the Commission's finding that the company was also a managing agent of the premises and thus responsible for discriminatory practices by the rental agent. The fact that Louis Brusco was employed at the company and, therefore, could be reached for inquiries and complaints at the telephone number of the company can in no way be interpreted as giving a management role to the company itself. Moreover, the testimony that Louis Brusco would, on occasion, send a company workman over to the subject building to make emergency repairs is not sufficient to show that the company did anything other than conduct a fuel business. The record is devoid of evidence that Brusco Fuel Oil Co. was in any way an owner, operator, or managing agent of the property, or that the company played any role in the discriminatory actions.

Accordingly, the Commission's order is vacated as it relates to Brusco Fuel Oil Co. and in all other respects affirmed.

Sethi v. Austin

Franklin Court of Appeal (2000)

This is an appeal from an order of the Franklin Commission on Human Rights finding George Austin liable for an unlawful discriminatory practice. The Commission awarded Anjali Sethi $15,000 in compensatory damages for mental anguish. Although an award of compensatory damages in a nominal amount was warranted, we conclude that the Commission abused its discretion in fixing the amount of the compensatory award for mental anguish at $15,000.

The Commission could reasonably conclude, from this record, that housing discrimination on the basis of color and national origin in violation of the Franklin Administrative Code was established. Sethi is a dark-skinned woman with a pronounced Indian accent. The evidence adduced at the hearing showed that Austin told Sethi in a telephone conversation that the house was no longer available even while he continued to advertise it in a local newspaper and was showing the house and negotiating its sale with others.

A claim for compensatory damages may be based entirely on mental anguish, as is the case here. When that is the case, the award must be supported by competent evidence concerning the extent of the injuries and a showing that a sufficient causal connection exists between the respondent's illegal acts and the complainant's injuries. Awards may be made on the basis of complainant's testimony alone. There is no requirement for either expert medical testimony or lay corroboration, though both are permitted.

Here, the compensatory damage award was based solely upon Sethi's conclusory testimony that she was "upset and outraged" by Austin's actions. This testimony was unsupported by details and incidents from Sethi's life that could have painted a vivid picture of the injuries caused by the discrimination. That picture could show, for example, changes in the victim's relationships with family, friends, or coworkers, or changes in the victim's activities of daily living such as eating, working, sleeping, and recreation. Though not required in every case, trial records that support substantial awards frequently include a comparison between a complainant's life before and after the discriminatory incident, tracking changes in interests, self-perception, and attitude toward the future.

Here the record supports an award of compensatory damages in a nominal amount. However, there is insufficient evidence to support the Commission's order as to the amount of damages awarded to Sethi. We remand for further proceedings.

POINT SHEET

In re Barnett

In re Barnett

DRAFTERS' POINT SHEET

In this performance test item, the Open Housing Center represents Matt and Sarah Barnett, a married couple who experienced housing discrimination. Matt is white. Sarah is dark skinned and was born and raised in England. Matt saw a flier advertising an apartment that seemed perfect for his family at an affordable price in a desirable neighborhood. He visited the apartment and was shown it by Helena Pall, the sister of the owner, Tony Gordon. Later, Matt and Sarah returned together. At that point, things started to happen that made it clear to Matt and Sarah that the apartment owner would not rent to what appeared to him to be an interracial couple.

Matt and Sarah now want to pursue their remedies before the Franklin Commission on Human Rights. The applicable statute is Title 8 of the Franklin Administrative Code, which sets forth the unlawful discriminatory practices and defines who is an "aggrieved person."

The File contains the instructional memorandum from the Director of Litigation, notes of separate interviews with Matt and Sarah, and the flier that advertised the apartment.

The Library contains excerpts from Title 8 of the Franklin Administrative Code and two cases bearing on the subject.

The task for applicants is to draft a memorandum explaining how and why Gordon violated two specific subsections of the statute and whether Matt and Sarah can each bring an action to recover substantial damages from Gordon for violating the law.

The following discussion covers all of the points the drafters intended to raise in the problem. Applicants need not cover them all to receive passing or even excellent grades. Grading is entirely within the discretion of the graders in the user jurisdictions.

I.   Overview: Applicants' work product should resemble an office memorandum to a supervising attorney and should reference the facts and legal materials as appropriate. The instructional memorandum is intentionally specific and is intended to force an analysis of the facts as to each type of violation (§ 107(a) *and* § 107(b)) and avoid answers that bunch them together into a single, fungible violation. Applicants are told to use the facts and the law to reach the conclusions that

- Gordon violated § 107(a):
    - This section makes it unlawful to refuse to rent, lease, or otherwise deny or withhold a housing accommodation based on race, color, or national origin.

- As to this part, applicants must conclude that, as an owner of the property, Gordon is within the class of people who can be liable under the Code and that his liability arises from his refusal to rent to Matt and Sarah on the basis of Sarah's actual or perceived race, color, or national origin.
  - Sarah's race and ethnicity are intentionally veiled. That she is "dark skinned," was raised in England, and speaks with an English accent are suggestions that applicants have to address.
- Gordon violated § 107(b):
  - This section makes it unlawful to discriminate in the terms and conditions of a rental or lease of a housing accommodation.
  - As to this part, applicants must set forth the argument that there was an agency relationship between Gordon and his sister, Pall, because it was Pall's communication of the excessively high rent that resulted in a discriminatory term and condition.
- Matt and Sarah are each entitled to bring an action against Gordon:
  - As to this part, applicants will have to conclude that both Matt and Sarah are "persons aggrieved" under § 102.2 of the Code in that they suffered injuries as a result of Gordon's discriminatory practices. Injuries are defined in § 102.3 to include "loss of housing and related amenities and services, and economic, emotional, physical, and other harm."
- As "persons aggrieved" under § 102 of the Code, Matt and Sarah are entitled to recover damages against Tony Gordon for the injuries they have suffered as a result of Gordon's discriminatory practices in an amount more than nominal because they have available detailed and nonconclusory evidence of the harm he caused.

The call of the question focuses on *Gordon's* liability and not that of his sister, Pall. Except to the extent that it is necessary to discuss whether the acts committed by Pall can be imputed to Gordon under the agency principles set forth in the *Rosa v. Brusco* case, discussions about Pall's *own* liability are off point.

II. Gordon's violation of § 107(a): The best approach for applicants is to parse § 107, apply the facts to each component, and conclude that Gordon committed a violation when he told Sarah that he had already rented the apartment to an old family friend.

- Section 107 breaks down as follows:

- Among the persons who can commit an unlawful discriminatory practice is an "owner."
    - Gordon is clearly the owner of the apartment at 91 Woodland Avenue.
        - The fliers advertising the apartment list him as the apartment's owner. He also described himself as the apartment's owner to Matt during their initial telephone conversation.
- The discriminatory practice must relate to a "housing accommodation."
    - The apartment is obviously a housing accommodation as defined in § 102.10—that is, it is a portion of a building designed to be occupied as a residence.
    - The Barnetts wanted to rent it to use as their residence.
- The discriminatory act under subsection (a) is, in this case, the refusal to rent the apartment on the basis of an *actual or perceived* protected characteristic.
- Under the facts of this case, the *actual or perceived* characteristics upon which Gordon based his refusal to rent to the Barnetts are the race, color, and possibly national origin of Sarah.[1]
    - Under § 102.7, "national origin" includes "ancestry," so, to the extent that Gordon perceived that Sarah was dark skinned, it is a reasonable inference that he might have thought she was of African or Indian ancestry.
- This is the component to which applicants must apply the facts as set forth in the interviews with Matt and Sarah in order to support the claim that Gordon violated § 107(a).
    - Gordon never actually saw Sarah, but there is a strong inference (approaching a certainty) that he was told by his sister, Pall, that Sarah was dark skinned.
        - When Matt and Sarah visited the apartment together the first time, Pall saw them through the window and said, "Sorry, it's been rented," and walked away.

---

[1] It is unlikely that any other protected characteristics – e.g., citizenship or marital status – come into play. Gordon could probably have figured out that Sarah had an English accent (and therefore could have "perceived" that she was British) when he spoke to her on the phone the first time, and he still expressed an interest in renting to her. Although it might be argued that the perception of a "mixed marriage" status might have played a part in the refusal to rent, that goes to race or color, not marital status.

- It was obviously not already rented because later that evening, Gordon phoned, spoke to Sarah, and asked if the Barnetts wanted the apartment and said that his sister must have been "confused."

- Gordon asked them to visit the apartment again. Up to then, Gordon was willing, indeed anxious, to rent the apartment to them.

- It was probably after Pall's initial contact with Sarah that she told Gordon that Sarah was dark skinned. When Matt and Sarah returned the next evening, Pall told them that the rent was $2,500, not $1,000 as stated in the flier.

- Later that next evening, when Sarah called Gordon to ask for an explanation of why Pall had communicated the inflated rent figure, Gordon told her that he rented the apartment to an old family friend.

- Gordon's comment that he had already rented the apartment to an old family friend when in fact it was probably still available to Brian Donnelly, Sarah's colleague, is evidence that Gordon discriminated against the Barnetts in violation of § 107(a).

- Although the pretextual increase in the rent is the basis for the violation of § 107(b)—discrimination in terms and conditions (*infra*)—it is also evidence of discrimination under § 107(a) in that it was intended to discourage the Barnetts after Gordon evidently learned that Sarah was dark skinned.

- The irresistible inference is that, having just learned that Sarah was dark skinned, Gordon discriminated against her and Matt on a prohibited basis.

  - In any case, it is abundantly clear that Gordon had changed his mind about renting to the Barnetts when he spoke to Sarah the second time, and that can only be attributable to his having learned that she was dark skinned.

- The apartment thereafter remained on the rental market—Matt continued to see the fliers advertising it at $1,000 per month, and Sarah's colleague, Brian Donnelly, did a "test" by calling Gordon. Brian spoke to Gordon's assistant who told him that she thought the apartment was still available for $1,000 per month.

- Accordingly, the circumstantial evidence supports a conclusion that Gordon violated § 107(a).
  - *Cf. Austin v. Sethi*, where, based on similar circumstantial evidence, the court found housing discrimination.
  - It does not matter whether Sarah was *actually* a person of color or of another race or nationality.
    - What matters is that the evidence strongly supports a conclusion that Gordon *perceived* her to be a person of color or of another race or nationality.
    - Discrimination based on such a perception constitutes a violation of the Franklin Administrative Code.

III. Gordon's violation of § 107(b): The predicates for application of § 107—that is, that Gordon was an "owner" of a "housing accommodation"—are present for the application of subsection (b) as well:

- Gordon was an "owner";
- The discrimination relates to a "housing accommodation"; and
- Because of Sarah's dark skin, Gordon acted on a "perception" of Sarah's race, color, or national origin.
- There is, however, an additional component that applies to subsection (b):
  - The prohibited discrimination relates to the "terms, conditions, or privileges" of the rental.
  - In the context of this case, the discriminatory "term or condition" is the amount of rent changing from $1,000 per month to $2,500 per month, according to Pall.
  - The monthly rental amount was advertised on the fliers as $1,000, but when Matt and Sarah visited the apartment the second time, Pall told them that the monthly rent was $2,500.
    - Based on the communication from Pall to the Barnetts, Gordon was offering the apartment to them for $2,500 per month but to everyone else at $1,000.
      - The fact that the fliers continued to advertise the $1,000 rental and Donnelly's "test" are evidence supporting this conclusion.
- However, Gordon himself never communicated the increased rent to the Barnetts.

- In order to hold Gordon accountable for a violation of subsection (b), it is necessary to conclude that Pall acted as his agent and that Pall's acts are imputed to Gordon.
    - The facts and holding in *Rosa v. Brusco* provide the authority for applicants to argue persuasively that Pall was Gordon's agent for these purposes.[2]
        - It does not matter that Pall was not Gordon's employee and did not have some kind of "agent" job title. Under *Rosa*, it is the parties' actions that determine whether an agency relationship exists.
        - Pall was entrusted with the key to give to interested parties.
            - In the first telephone conversation with Matt, Gordon told him that he would leave the key with Pall, his sister.
        - Pall was expecting Matt and gave him the key.
        - After Matt and Sarah's first encounter with Pall, Gordon said Pall must have been "confused" and asked if they would visit again.
            - This suggests he specifically authorized Pall to give the Barnetts the key and allow them to see the apartment.
        - Importantly, Pall first communicated the increased rent amount to the Barnetts just after they finished their tour of the apartment.
            - She had to have spoken to Gordon after their first visit to get the key from him for their second visit.
            - Applicants can infer that the mention of the rent increase originated with Gordon and that he instructed Pall to tell the Barnetts the rent was $2,500. She was thus acting on Gordon's specific instructions.
    - Accordingly, while not as clear-cut as in the *Rosa* case, there is evidence to support the conclusion that Pall was Gordon's agent and that, therefore, Gordon violated subsection (b) by discriminating against the Barnetts in the terms and conditions on which he offered to rent based on his perceptions of Sarah's race, color, or national origin.

IV.   Matt and Sarah are each a person aggrieved: The analytical framework for determination of this issue is that Matt and Sarah are each a "person aggrieved" and, as such, are entitled to the protection of the Code.

---

[2] The fact that Pall may be independently liable for a violation is irrelevant. The call of the question asks only for a discussion of *Gordon's* liability.

- Section 109 allows any "person aggrieved" to petition the Commission (the adjudicative body established to enforce the Code) for a determination.
  - The Commission is authorized to issue a determination and order, which includes damages and other relief. § 120.
  - Section 102.2 defines a "person aggrieved" as one who has suffered injury from an unlawful discriminatory practice.
  - Section 102.3 defines "injury" to include "loss of housing and related amenities and services, and economic, emotional, physical, and other harm."

V. Matt and Sarah suffered cognizable injuries as the result of Gordon's violations.

- They both suffered the loss of "housing and related amenities."
  - Clearly, both of them, along with their family, lost the housing—Gordon didn't rent to them, stating the apartment was already rented.
  - They also lost related amenities, when compared to the current apartment: the backyard for the children to play in, the extra bedroom and study, the two bathrooms, and the ideal location.
- Matt and Sarah also suffered out-of-pocket losses in that Matt had to get treatment from his doctor and double the strength of his ulcer medicine, and Sarah began psychotherapy and missed a day of work.
- The aggravation of Matt's ulcer also qualifies as physical harm within the meaning of § 102.3.
- Importantly, both Matt and Sarah have suffered emotional injury upon which they can each base a claim for substantial compensatory damages.
  - Section 120(b) allows the Commission to direct payment of compensatory damages for emotional injury.
  - *Sethi v. Austin* holds that a claim for compensatory damages may be based entirely on proof of mental anguish.
    - Moreover, awards may be made based on the aggrieved party's testimony alone. *Id.*
  - The facts amply demonstrate that Matt has suffered compensable emotional injury in more than a nominal amount:
    - The interviews with Matt and Sarah show an estrangement between them as a result of Gordon's actions;

- Matt's relations with his children have become strained, and his emotional reaction to the remarks of one of his children gives credence to the depth of the injury;
- Matt has started smoking again; and
- He has not had the energy or inclination to renew his search for a new place to live.

- All of this is directly traceable to Gordon's violations and, since Matt's injury is the direct result of Gordon's discriminatory practices, Matt is a "person aggrieved" and can recover damages from Gordon, the perpetrator of the discrimination.

- The facts also demonstrate that Sarah has suffered compensable emotional injury in more than a nominal amount:
  - Following the incident, she withdrew and was angry and depressed;
  - She lost her enthusiasm for her new job and missed one day of work;
  - She has had trouble sleeping;
  - She has lost five pounds; and
  - She and Matt have given up searching for a new place.

- Again, as with Matt, all these injuries stem from Gordon's violations, and thus make Gordon potentially liable to Sarah.

FILE

In re Rose Kingsley

Burke & Clements, LLP
Attorneys at Law
4333 Skillman Avenue
Dixon, Franklin 33133

MEMORANDUM

February 22, 2005

TO:	Applicant
FROM:	Thomas Burke
RE:	*In re Rose Kingsley*

We represent Rose Kingsley, a local lawyer, in a fee dispute with Karen Greene, another local lawyer. Recently, Kingsley received $1 million as her fee for settling the $3 million Moreno case that Kingsley and Greene worked on. A few days ago, Kingsley received a letter from James Kuntz, an attorney representing Greene, demanding a portion of Kingsley's fee from the Moreno case.

Please draft a memorandum analyzing the following issues:

    (1) whether Greene was a partner or an associate of Kingsley for purposes of Rule 200 of the Franklin Rules of Professional Conduct; and

    (2) whether the requirements of Rule 200 have been met by the fee-splitting agreement between Kingsley and Greene and the communication with Moreno.

In each part of the memorandum, you should incorporate the relevant facts, analyze the applicable legal authority, and explain how the facts and law affect our client's obligations.

TRANSCRIPT OF THOMAS BURKE'S INTERVIEW
WITH ROSE KINGSLEY
February 21, 2005

Burke: Ms. Kingsley, when you phoned yesterday, you said you had some sort of fee problem with another lawyer?

Kingsley: Yes, that's right. Her name is Karen Greene. I have this letter from a lawyer representing her, demanding a fee of $300,000 out of a $1 million fee I obtained from a client, with a threat of litigation if I don't pay. Here's the letter and two enclosures.

Burke: Why don't you tell me what it's all about.

Kingsley: Sure. I have a solo practice here in Dixon, with a small office and a secretary and a legal assistant. I do a lot of personal injury work on the plaintiffs' side. About three years ago, I agreed to represent Janice Moreno, who had a personal injury claim against Graham-Hadley, Inc.

Burke: Graham-Hadley is that big aerospace company just outside of Dixon, right?

Kingsley: That's the one. Graham-Hadley used hazardous substances such as TCE—that's trichloroethylene—from the late 1940s into the 1980s. Throughout that period, there were accidental TCE spills. Those spills polluted the ground water, and that pollution caused various cancers and birth defects. Ms. Moreno developed a rare form of cancer.

Burke: And the fee problem?

Kingsley: Well, I entered into a retainer agreement with Ms. Moreno providing that I would advance all costs and would receive as my customary contingency fee 33 percent of any recovery I might obtain for her.

Burke: Yes, that's customary.

Kingsley: Well, soon I realized that I needed help. I'd done a great deal of personal injury work, but none involving pollution of the sort present here. I had to deal with issues of hydraulics and hydrology, well sampling, contamination plumes, and so on.

Burke: And that's where Karen Greene came in?

Kingsley: Right. Karen had worked as a mechanical engineer for some time before she went to law school. She told me she was trying to start a practice, working out of her home. I asked her whether she would like to work with me on a temporary basis on the Moreno case, primarily to do preliminary investigation and to conduct and respond to any discovery, and she accepted.

Burke: You wanted her to do the investigation and discovery because of her engineering background?

Kingsley: Yes. Karen was familiar with the technical matters or could quickly become familiar with them.

Burke: What about supervision?

Kingsley: On the legal side, I supervised Karen since she was a new lawyer. But on the technical side, I relied on her expertise. I can't really say that I supervised her much. I had to leave her a relatively free hand because she was the engineering expert and I was not.

Burke: Did Karen deal directly with Ms. Moreno?

Kingsley: Rarely outside of my presence. A number of times, we met with Ms. Moreno together. Occasionally, Karen and Ms. Moreno would talk on the phone. Since I was the only attorney of record, I insisted that Karen have no face-to-face contact with Ms. Moreno except with me or through me. I'd gotten into unpleasant situations in years past as a result of irregular client contacts, and I wanted to avoid that.

Burke: And the fee agreement?

Kingsley: I entered into a fee agreement with Karen, providing that I would pay her 30 percent of whatever fee I might receive from the Moreno case.

Burke: What happened after Karen accepted your offer?

Kingsley: I temporarily made room for her in my office to work on the Moreno case. She used my staff and facilities solely for the Moreno matter, and worked part-time as needed on the Moreno case.

Burke: Tell me about the case.

Kingsley: Okay. I brought an action on Ms. Moreno's behalf against Graham-Hadley. For about two years things went well with Karen. My deal with Karen was that she would work on the Moreno matter as much as I needed her to. The problem was that she was at the same time trying to build her own practice and work out of her home. She got upset because the Moreno case was taking up more of her time than she wanted to devote. Also, she had the feeling we were going to lose the case. So, she left.

Burke: At the time she left, how much of her work on the Moreno case was left to do?

Kingsley: Well, discovery was pretty much done and we were getting ready for trial. I didn't need her to do any more. I managed to try the case without her.

Burke: Did she *refuse* to do any more work on the case?

Kingsley: Not really. After she left, I just never called and asked her to do any more. We parted company on good terms, and she moved out of my office. She had devoted 600 hours to the case before she left, and I'd been paying her all along $50 per hour under our agreement. As I said, I was under a lot of pressure then. I don't want to seem greedy, but I've already paid her $30,000, and she's the one who quit. But before I can even think about whether I'm willing to give her any more, I need to know from you whether I'm bound to pay her 30 percent of my recovery.

Burke: Well, how much was your fee?

Kingsley: I obtained a jury award of $6 million against Graham-Hadley, settled with Graham-Hadley for $3 million in advance of judgment, and received my fee of $1 million.

Burke: All with much publicity in the Dixon press.

Kingsley: Right. Publicity that led to this demand letter.

Burke: Karen's lawyer goes out of his way to assert that your fee agreement with Karen complies with Franklin's rule on fee-splitting. Let me ask you this: Did you disclose the arrangement to Ms. Moreno and obtain her consent?

Kingsley: I sent Ms. Moreno a letter informing her that I had engaged Karen to assist me on the case and that this arrangement wouldn't affect the amount of any fee she might have to pay me. I asked her to sign and mail back a copy acknowledging receipt. This is the letter Ms. Moreno signed and returned to me. I sent a copy to Karen as well.

Burke: Did you send Ms. Moreno a copy of your agreement with Karen?

Kingsley: No, but I have a memo from Karen saying that Karen explained it to her and Ms. Moreno said it was okay with her.

Burke: Did Karen ever question whether your letter and Ms. Moreno's acknowledgment satisfied the Franklin fee-splitting rule?

Kingsley: No, Karen never raised the issue, even though, as I said, I sent her a copy.

Burke: I'm sorry, but I have to get to court soon. Can we set up a meeting in a couple of days, say on the 23rd, to discuss this matter again, after I have done some research?

Kingsley: Sure. The demand letter deadline is February 28, so I'd like to have some idea how to respond as soon as possible.

Burke: Okay, I'll get back to you very soon.

* * * *

Kane, Reynolds & Kuntz, LLP
Attorneys at Law
1710 Shrub Oak Boulevard
Dixon, Franklin 33137

February 18, 2005

Rose Kingsley, Esq.
Law Office of Rose Kingsley
1110 Wooden Valley Road, Suite 3
Dixon, Franklin 33133

Re: Karen Greene

Dear Ms. Kingsley:

We represent Karen Greene, who as you know was counsel with you on behalf of Janice Moreno in *Janice Moreno v. Graham-Hadley, Inc.*

We have learned that under your Retainer Agreement with Ms. Moreno, you received $1 million as your fee.

We hereby demand that you pay Ms. Greene $300,000 as her fee in accordance with the Fee Agreement into which you and Ms. Greene entered on October 17, 2002. A copy of the Fee Agreement is enclosed.

The Fee Agreement complies fully with Rule 200 of the Franklin Rules of Professional Conduct governing fee-splitting between lawyers. As you know, Ms. Moreno consented to the Fee Agreement between you and Ms. Greene. (See the enclosed letter.)

If you fail to pay Ms. Greene the $300,000 you owe her within 10 days of the date of this letter, we will pursue this matter.

Very truly yours,

James F. Kuntz

Enc.

FEE AGREEMENT

The Law Office of Rose Kingsley (Kingsley) was retained on April 5, 2002, by Janice Moreno (Moreno) to represent her with respect to any claim she might have for personal injury against Graham-Hadley, Inc.

Kingsley was retained under the terms of a retainer agreement that provides, among other things, that Kingsley shall receive 33% of any recovery Kingsley might obtain for Moreno.

Kingsley hereby engages Karen Greene (Greene) to assist in Kingsley's representation of Moreno by performing a preliminary investigation, conducting and responding to discovery in any ensuing action, and doing any and all other tasks and projects agreed upon. Greene acknowledges that she has received a copy of the retainer agreement referred to above.

Kingsley and Greene further agree that Kingsley shall pay Greene 30% of whatever fee Kingsley receives from Moreno. Greene shall be paid $50 per hour for hours worked on the Moreno case. All sums paid for these hours will be deemed an advance on the 30% Greene is entitled to receive under this agreement.

Kingsley and Greene further agree that this instrument shall be governed by, interpreted under, and enforced in accordance with the law of the State of Franklin.

Date: October 17, 2002

The Law Office of Rose Kingsley

_____

Rose Kingsley

_____

Karen Greene

The Law Office of Rose Kingsley
1110 Wooden Valley Road, Suite 3
Dixon, Franklin 33133

October 23, 2002

Janice Moreno
4142 Northern Boulevard
Dixon, Franklin 33137

Dear Ms. Moreno:

I have engaged Karen Greene, a lawyer licensed to practice in Franklin, to assist me in representing you with respect to your claim against Graham-Hadley, Inc., specifically to perform a preliminary investigation, conduct and respond to discovery in any ensuing action, and do any and all other tasks and projects agreed upon. My engagement of Ms. Greene will have no effect on the amount of any fee that you may become obligated to pay me pursuant to our retainer agreement of April 5, 2002.

Please sign and date one of the two enclosed copies of this letter and return it to me in the enclosed stamped envelope. Please retain the other copy for your files.

Very truly yours,

Rose Kingsley

I hereby acknowledge that I have received this letter, and have read and understood its contents.

_____
Janice Moreno

Dated:

cc: Karen Greene

MEMORANDUM

TO: Rose Kingsley
FROM: Karen Greene
DATE: November 1, 2002
RE: Moreno Case—Phone Conversation

When you were out of the office on October 30, Ms. Moreno called to go over some of the details of the case. She mentioned the letter you sent her on October 23, 2002; she said she was confused about what it meant. I explained to her my 30% arrangement with you, and she said she now understands and that it's perfectly okay with her.

LIBRARY

In re Rose Kingsley

Franklin Rules of Professional Conduct

RULE 200. Financial Arrangements Among Lawyers

A lawyer shall not divide a fee for legal services with a lawyer who is temporarily engaged and who is not a partner or associate of the lawyer unless: (1) the client has consented in writing thereto after a full disclosure has been made in writing that a division of fees will be made and the terms of such division; and (2) the total fee charged by all lawyers is not increased solely by reason of the provision for division of fees and is not unconscionable.

OFFICIAL COMMENT

Rule 200 does not require that the division of fees be in proportion to services performed by each lawyer or on the basis that each lawyer assumes joint responsibility. However, Rule 200 is stricter than most other state rules regarding client disclosure and consent. Its purpose is to protect the client to the maximum extent possible.

Chambers v. Kay

Franklin Court of Appeal (2002)

This case centers on the application of Rule 200 of the Franklin Rules of Professional Conduct regarding fee-splitting arrangements between a lawyer and a temporarily engaged lawyer. Attorneys Arthur Chambers and Philip Kay had separate law practices in Sanderville. They had individual office letterheads. They had separate professional addresses and did not list each other as associates or partners in any documents.

Chambers paid Kay $200 per month to use a conference room in Kay's office for depositions and client meetings. Chambers used Kay's office telephone service, law library, and postage and copy machines. Chambers also maintained files and a computer in Kay's office, rented a monthly space in the building parking lot, and was listed as a co-tenant on the building directory. Kay assisted Chambers with his work on a few cases. Additionally, Kay's staff regularly provided assistance to Chambers with case-related documents.

At Kay's request, Chambers began serving as co-counsel in a sexual harassment action that Kay had previously filed on behalf of his client, Maggie Dees. Chambers' responsibilities in the case included maintaining the files, conducting discovery that Kay assigned to him, conferring with Dees in the office, and appearing as co-counsel on her behalf at pretrial hearings. Both Chambers and Kay were listed in the Dees case pleadings as her counsel. Chambers, however, continued to work on other cases he had at the time.

During discovery in the Dees case, a dispute arose between Chambers and Kay over the disclosure of certain documents and Chambers' alleged efforts to persuade Dees to settle. Kay soon notified Chambers by letter that Chambers was removed effective immediately from the Dees case with Dees' approval. Kay's letter offered Chambers compensation in accordance with the following fee-splitting arrangement: In the event the case was settled before depositions, "16.5% of the fee called for under my agreement with Ms. Dees, which is 40% of the monies recovered"; thereafter, an "increase to 28%" of the fee specified under the agreement with Dees. In response, Chambers sent a letter accepting Kay's offer. In an apparent attempt to comply with Rule 200, Kay sent a letter to Dees informing her of his fee-splitting agreement with Chambers, but never sought or obtained her consent, either oral or written.

Kay eventually obtained a large judgment for Dees and got a substantial fee for himself. Kay then wrote to Chambers abrogating the fee-splitting agreement between them. This letter contained an offer to compensate Chambers for his services in the Dees case in the amount of $200 per hour for the total number of hours specified in his prior billing statement. Chambers declined Kay's offer and initiated this action against Kay, alleging breach of contract based on their fee-splitting agreement. Kay predicated his defense on the asserted unenforceability of the agreement. The trial court granted Kay's motion for summary judgment, determining that the agreement failed to comply with Rule 200 and therefore was unenforceable.

On appeal, Chambers concedes that the fee-splitting agreement was not properly consented to by the client, and therefore he can only recover for breach of contract if the relationship between Kay and him was that of a partner and an associate.[1]

We do not believe that Kay and Chambers' relationship was that of partner and associate within the meaning of Rule 200. For purposes of the rule, an associate is a lawyer who works *for*, rather than *with*, another lawyer.

In determining whether a temporarily engaged lawyer works *for* another lawyer and is therefore an associate for purposes of Rule 200, or works *with* the other lawyer and is therefore *not* an associate, we consider the totality of the circumstances, including the other lawyer's supervision and, in particular, the compensation of the temporarily engaged lawyer. At one end of the continuum are those cases where the presence of close supervision and non-contingent compensation (e.g., salary) most clearly indicate that the temporarily engaged lawyer works *for* the other lawyer. At the opposite end are those situations where the presence of loose supervision and contingent compensation (e.g., a sum dependent on the outcome of the litigation) clearly indicates that the temporarily engaged lawyer works *with* the other lawyer. Most cases—like the present one—fall somewhere in between.

Factors that bear on our evaluation of how closely a temporarily engaged lawyer is supervised include the following: both direct and indirect control of the representation, including litigation strategy; oversight of the temporarily engaged lawyer in legal and factual aspects of a case; control over the working environment; and the relationship with the client. Here, Kay's supervision of Chambers in the Dees case was not especially close. While the work was performed in Kay's office, with the assistance of his staff and at his direction, and Kay retained sole control over the course of the litigation, Chambers was allowed to conduct discovery, to appear in court on Dees' behalf, and was listed with Kay on case pleadings as Dees' counsel. These facts favor the conclusion that Chambers was working *with*, as opposed to *for*, Kay. However, the degree of supervision is far from dispositive. As in any given case, the contributions of the lawyers involved will vary according to the elements of the case and each lawyer's individual strengths and areas of expertise.

---

[1] The Chambers-Kay relationship was not that of partners within the meaning of Rule 200. Generally speaking, a partnership is an association of two or more persons to carry on, as co-owners, a business for profit, connoting co-ownership in partnership property, with a sharing in the profits and losses of a continuing business. Here, no evidence suggests that Chambers and Kay acted as co-owners of a law firm or law office, or that they contemplated sharing in the profits and losses of a continuing business engaged in the practice of law.

Accordingly, the more indicative evidence of the parties' relationship is the compensation agreement between the lawyers. In this case, Kay and Chambers agreed that Kay would be compensated solely on a contingent basis, specifically, as a percentage of any contingent fee that Kay might receive from Dees. This agreement to compensate Kay on a contingent basis by splitting any fee recovered in the Dees litigation, combined with the relatively loose supervision of Chambers by Kay, leads us to conclude that Chambers was not Kay's associate for purposes of Rule 200. Therefore, the fee agreement is unenforceable.

Affirmed.

Margolin v. Shemaria

Franklin Court of Appeal (2000)

This breach of contract action arises out of a fee-splitting agreement between two law firms and their lawyers.

The issue crucial to the resolution of this case is the enforceability of the fee-splitting agreement under Rule 200 of the Franklin Rules of Professional Conduct. By its terms, Rule 200 prohibits the splitting of a fee between lawyers who are not related as partners or as partner and associate unless the client has consented in writing to the fee-splitting arrangement after a full disclosure of the arrangement has been made in writing and the total fee charged by all lawyers is not increased solely by reason of the arrangement and is not unconscionable. As stated in the Official Comment, the purpose of Rule 200 is to protect the client to the maximum extent possible.

Plaintiff Elyse Margolin's complaint alleged that Margolin referred a case to defendant Joseph Shemaria in consideration for his oral agreement to: (1) provide Margolin with 50% of any fee received by Shemaria in conjunction with Shemaria's representation of the referred client; (2) provide the referred client with written disclosure of the fee-splitting agreement; and (3) obtain the referred client's written consent thereto. According to the complaint, Shemaria received $450,000 as his fee from the referred client, and he refused to pay Margolin any part of it. Shemaria's answer to the complaint alleged as an affirmative defense the unenforceability of the fee-splitting agreement for noncompliance with Rule 200.

The trial court granted Shemaria's motion for a directed verdict based on the unenforceability of the agreement.

In her appeal, Margolin contends that Rule 200 should not prevent her from sharing in the fee because the rule's client-protection purpose was satisfied, inasmuch as evidence at trial showed that the referred client had received oral disclosure of the fee-splitting agreement between Margolin and Shemaria, and had given oral consent thereto.

We find that Rule 200's client-protection purpose was in fact not satisfied. The rule is a bright-line rule. Its purpose is client protection *to the maximum extent possible*. That purpose is satisfied only by *full* compliance with the rule's written-disclosure and written-consent requirements. Just as a client has a right to know how his or her attorney fees will be determined, he or she also has a right to know the extent of, and the basis for, the splitting of such fees by two or more lawyers. Knowledge of these matters helps assure the client that he or she will not be charged unwarranted fees just so that one lawyer has sufficient compensation to be able to share fees with another lawyer. Disclosure of these matters to the client must be in writing because the client should not be expected to mentally retain such information throughout the pendency of the case.

Written disclosure has the additional benefit of ensuring that the lawyers themselves truly agree to the exact terms of the fee-splitting agreement, thus making it less likely that they will have a disagreement between themselves that will lead to litigation or potentially affect the client in a negative manner. Moreover, written disclosure makes it less likely that the lawyers will wittingly or unwittingly change the terms of the agreement during the pendency of the case. Requiring the client's written consent impresses on the client that he or she has the right to give or withhold consent.

Although she does not dispute any of these points, Margolin nevertheless argues that requiring full compliance with the written-disclosure and written-consent requirements will adversely affect many lawyers. That does not matter. The purpose of the rule is not *lawyer* protection, but *client* protection *to the maximum extent possible*.

Margolin, as a lawyer, is presumed to have known that the rule requires actual written disclosure to, and actual written consent by, the client. Margolin could have protected herself by providing the referred client with the required written disclosure and obtaining the required written consent.

Although we do not condone Shemaria's breach of his fee-splitting agreement with Margolin, we must hold the agreement unenforceable for noncompliance with Rule 200, in

order to protect the client to the maximum extent possible.

Affirmed.

POINT SHEET

In re Rose Kingsley

In re Rose Kingsley

DRAFTERS' POINT SHEET

In this performance test item, the client, Rose Kingsley, is a lawyer who temporarily engaged another lawyer, Karen Greene, to help her conduct discovery in a technically complex toxic tort case. Kingsley and Greene entered into a fee-splitting agreement under which Kingsley agreed to pay Greene 30 percent of whatever fee Kingsley eventually obtained in the toxic tort case. Kingsley and Greene subsequently had a falling out, and Greene quit. When Kingsley settled the toxic tort case and recovered a fee of $1 million, Greene demanded 30 percent of Kingsley's fee—$300,000. Kingsley has consulted applicants' firm for advice on whether she is bound to pay Greene the $300,000.

The central issue is whether the Kingsley-Greene fee-splitting agreement is enforceable under Rule 200 of the Franklin Rules of Professional Conduct, which prescribes certain requirements for the enforceability of fee-splitting arrangements between lawyers. Rule 200 requires some very specific disclosures to the client, but does *not* apply if the lawyers who are splitting the fees are partners or stand in the relation of partner and associate to one another.

Applicants' task is to draft an objective memorandum to the supervising partner analyzing whether Greene was a partner or an associate of Kingsley for purposes of Rule 200 and, if not, whether the fee-splitting agreement between Kingsley and Greene and the correspondence between Kingsley and Moreno comply with Rule 200's written disclosure and written consent requirements.

The File contains a transcript of an interview between the supervising attorney and Kingsley, a demand letter from Greene's attorney, the Kingsley-Greene fee agreement, a letter from Kingsley to the affected client, Janice Moreno, and Greene's memorandum to Kingsley regarding the client's understanding of their arrangement. The Library contains Rule 200 and accompanying comments and two cases that bear on the subject.

The following discussion covers all of the points the drafters intended to raise in the problem. Applicants need not cover them all to receive passing or even excellent grades. Grading is entirely within the discretion of the graders in the user jurisdictions.

I.   Overview: Applicants' work product should resemble a memorandum from one attorney to another. Applicants are told that both arguments in the two-part memorandum should set out the relevant facts, analyze the authorities, and explain how the facts and the law affect Kingsley's obligation to Greene.

- It is not expected that the memorandum contain a separate statement of facts, but it is essential that applicants use the facts to support their analysis.
- Better applicants will write cogent headings preceding each of the two issues assigned by the supervising attorney.
  - The headings set forth below are examples only and not to be taken by the graders as *the prescribed* headings.
- Rule 200 essentially exempts from the disclosure requirements lawyers who are partners or who stand in the relation of partner and associate to one another.
  - The fact that Greene was "temporarily engaged" would not prevent her from satisfying this requirement.
    - But applicants should conclude that under the facts of this case Greene was neither a partner nor an associate of Kingsley.
- Once it is established that Rule 200 applies because there was no partner or partner/associate relationship, its strict disclosure and consent requirements apply.
  - There must be a *full, written* disclosure to the client that
    - states that a division of fees will be made; and
    - describes the terms of the division.
  - Also, the circumstances must be such that
    - the total fee will not be increased solely because of the fee division; and
    - the total fee arrangement is not unconscionable.
  - The client must have consented *in writing* to the arrangement after the required disclosure.
- Applicants should discuss each of these components, particularly the full, written disclosure to the client and the client's consent in writing.

II. The Client Disclosure and Consent Requirements of Rule 200 Apply to the Kingsley-Greene Fee Agreement Because Kingsley and Greene Were Neither Partners Nor Partner and Associate.

- As a preliminary matter, applicants should state that the Kingsley-Greene fee agreement is a fee-splitting arrangement that comes within the purview of Rule 200.
  - They can reach that conclusion by analogy to the fee-splitting arrangements addressed in the two cases in the Library—that is,

- the agreement refers to the basic 33 percent fee arrangement between Kingsley and the client (Moreno); and
- Kingsley agrees to pay Greene 30 percent of whatever fee Kingsley eventually recovers from Moreno.
- Thus, the Kingsley-Greene agreement *splits* the Moreno fee.
- Applicants should also recognize that Greene was *temporarily engaged* by Kingsley, a fact that brings Rule 200 into play—that is, Rule 200 applies *only* to a fee-splitting arrangement with a temporarily engaged lawyer who is not a partner or associate of the other lawyer.
  - In the interview and in the Kingsley-Greene fee agreement, it is clear that Greene was hired to work only on the Moreno case, which was of limited duration.
- **Kingsley and Greene Were Not Partners.**
  - As the court observes in the footnote in *Chambers v. Kay*, a partnership is an association of two or more persons to carry on a business as co-owners, for profit, with a profit/loss sharing arrangement.
    - In the present case, the facts lead to the opposite conclusion—that is, that Kingsley and Greene were *not* partners.
    - From the interview with Kingsley, it is clear that:
      - Greene was a newly admitted lawyer looking for work;
      - Greene had special expertise in engineering that Kingsley needed for this *one particular* case;
      - Kingsley asked Greene to "*work with me on a temporary basis.*"
    - The Kingsley-Greene fee agreement states that "Kingsley . . . engages Greene to *assist*" in the Moreno case and to perform certain specified tasks.
    - There is nothing in the relationship that suggests that Greene would "carry on" Kingsley's business or share generally in the profits and losses.
    - Therefore, they were not partners.
- **Kingsley and Greene Were Not Partner and Associate.**
  - The *Chambers v. Kay* case furnishes the legal framework for analyzing whether Greene was an associate of Kingsley.
    - Note: Kingsley was a solo practitioner and thus not technically anyone's partner. For purposes of the analysis in this case, the term "partner" should

be taken to mean that Kingsley was the "owner" of her law office and Greene's "supervisor."

- *Chambers v. Kay* draws the distinction that, for purposes of Rule 200, an associate is a lawyer who works *for* rather than *with* another lawyer.
- *Chambers* sets up a totality-of-the-circumstances test for determining whether a temporarily engaged lawyer is an associate:
  - Whether the temporarily engaged lawyer works under the supervision of the other lawyer.
    - Note: Analysis of this "with or for" factor probably comes down *against* Kingsley, but applicants can also receive credit if they present a well-reasoned argument that Greene worked *with* rather than *for* Kingsley.
  - Supervision consists of such things as:
    - Direct or indirect control of the client representation and control over the client.
      - There is no doubt here that Kingsley controlled the client relationship—she told Greene that she (Greene) was not to deal with Moreno except with or through Kingsley.
    - Oversight of the legal and factual aspects of the case.
      - Although Kingsley furnished some guidance on the legal aspects of the case, she gave Greene a "relatively free hand" on the technical side because Greene had the expertise and Kingsley did not.
      - Thus, applicants could note that Kingsley did not exercise close supervision on the matters for which Greene was hired to be responsible.
    - Authority over the case.
      - Again, it is clear that Kingsley retained control over how the case was to be litigated.
    - Control over the working environment.
      - All the work was done in Kingsley's office with her equipment and facilities. Therefore, she had control of the working environment.

- However, the degree of supervision is far from dispositive on the question of whether a temporarily engaged lawyer is an associate for the purposes of Rule 200. Often, the more indicative evidence of the parties' relationship is how the temporarily engaged lawyer is to be paid. (*Chambers v. Kay*)
  - Payment on a contingent basis, as opposed to a salary, weighs heavily *against* a finding that the temporarily engaged lawyer is an associate.
  - The facts here show that Greene was to be paid on a *contingent* basis.
  - The Kingsley-Greene fee-splitting agreement provides that Greene will receive "30% of whatever fee Kingsley receives from Moreno."
    - Note: The correct focus is on the Kingsley-Greene agreement. Applicants who focus on the Kingsley-Moreno contingency fee agreement have missed the point.
- Although Greene was to receive $50 per hour for work on the Moreno case—which *sounds* like a non-contingent form of compensation—applicants should recognize that the hourly pay was to be advanced against the ultimate 30 percent contingency fee that Greene was to get if Kingsley prevailed in the Moreno case.
- Since Greene was to be paid on a contingent basis and such compensation scheme weighs heavily against a finding that the relationship is one of partner and associate, applicants should conclude that Greene was *not* an associate of Kingsley. Thus, Rule 200 applies, and the inquiry turns to whether there was a proper disclosure to the client and, if not, what the effect is.

III. Whether the Requirements of Rule 200 Have Been Met by the Fee-Splitting Agreement Between Kingsley and Greene and the Communication with Moreno.

- The necessary components of the consent and disclosure requirements of the Rule are:
  - There must be a *full, written* disclosure to the client that
    - states that a division of the fees will be made,
    - describes the terms of the division; and
  - The client must have *consented in writing* to the arrangement after the required disclosure.
  - Also, the circumstances must be such that
    - the total fee will not be increased solely because of the fee division, and

- the total fee is not unconscionable.
- The last part of the requirement can be disposed of easily:
  - It is clear from the facts that the total fee will not be increased by reason of Kingsley's agreement with Greene.
    - The total fee owed by Moreno will remain at 33 percent of the recovery in the lawsuit.
  - Also, applicants can take it as a given that 33 percent is a reasonable fee and not unconscionable.
    - See the supervising attorney's remark in the interview: "That's customary."
  - Note: Better applicants will recognize that these components (no fee increase and not unconscionable) are independent and need not be set out in the written disclosure.
    - But, it is no problem if applicants discuss them in terms of things that must be in the written disclosure.
- However, the letter of October 23, 2002, from Kingsley to Moreno is deficient in several respects.
  - It does not state that a division of the fees will be made.
    - It informs Moreno only that Kingsley has engaged Greene to perform part of the work.
  - It does not describe any fee division between Kingsley and Greene.
  - Because of the first two deficiencies, there was not full disclosure and, therefore, Moreno could not have given effective consent.
  - In any event, Moreno's signature was merely an *acknowledgement* of what the letter contained.
    - It is not, as required by Rule 200, a *consent* after full disclosure.
- The November 1, 2002, memo from Greene to Kingsley does not "cure" the deficiencies in the Kingsley letter to Moreno.
  - While Greene states in the memo that she explained to Moreno the 30 percent arrangement between Greene and Kingsley, the fee-splitting arrangement was still not reduced to writing so that Moreno could read and sign it.

- Applicants might mention that, because of Moreno's phone call, Greene had notice that the written description of the fee agreement was not clear to Moreno.

- Accordingly, the written disclosure is insufficient, and the Kingsley-Greene fee agreement is unenforceable.
    - At this point, applicants should look to the *Margolin v. Shemaria* case to explain that Rule 200 is a bright-line rule.
        - The Rule requires the strictest adherence to its terms and is designed to confer "client protection *to the maximum extent possible.*"
        - See also the Official Comment to Rule 200.
        - Unless there is compliance with the letter of the Rule, the fee-splitting agreement is unenforceable—period.
        - It does not matter that such a policy will adversely affect many lawyers.
            - It is a *client* protection rule and not a lawyer protection rule.
        - As a lawyer, Greene is *presumed* to know the rule, and she could have corrected the deficiencies in the letter to Moreno.
            - Applicants should address the point that appears in the interview that Kingsley did not want Greene dealing with Moreno.
            - Nevertheless, Kingsley gave Greene a copy of the October 23, 2002, letter to Moreno. Greene should have attempted to discuss the deficiencies with Kingsley and ensure that the client disclosure and consent properly complied with Rule 200.
- Thus, notwithstanding what seems to be an unjust result for Greene and a windfall to Kingsley, the case law interpreting Rule 200 makes it crystal clear that the faulty client disclosure and consent renders the fee-splitting agreement unenforceable.
    - Applicants should note that Greene received $30,000 for the work she did.
        - See Kingsley's statement in the interview, "I've already paid [Greene] $30,000."
        - The facts show that Greene worked 600 hours for which Kingsley paid her $50 per hour, which would have been an advance against the 30 percent contingency, in accordance with the fee agreement.

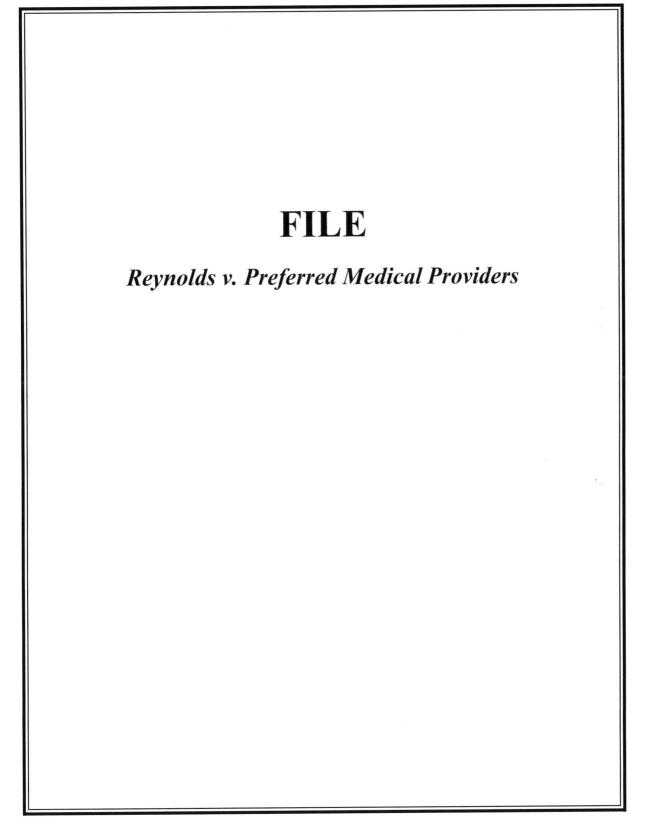

FILE

Reynolds v. Preferred Medical Providers

Allen, McBride & Lagos LLP
Attorneys at Law
1251 Bay Street
Margot Bay, Franklin 33501
(555) 424-0900

MEMORANDUM

To: Applicant
From: Arthur McBride
Date: February 22, 2005
Subject: *Reynolds v. Preferred Medical Providers*

Our client, Rowena Reynolds, is the daughter and sole heir of John Reynolds. John Reynolds died last year of complications from a kidney ailment. In 1995, John enrolled in a health insurance program called Elder Advantage, a type of Medicare plan. This insurance plan was issued by Preferred Medical Providers (Preferred), a health maintenance organization (HMO). The insurance plan is not an employer-sponsored plan governed by ERISA. During the last two years of his life, John and Rowena tried to persuade Preferred and its in-house medical evaluators to authorize and pay for a recently developed kidney therapy. Even though John's physician recommended the treatment, Preferred refused to authorize it.

We recently filed a multi-count complaint in the Franklin state district court against Preferred for damages for wrongful death, medical malpractice, willful misconduct, intentional infliction of emotional distress, and elder abuse. We requested a trial by jury.

John Reynolds' Elder Advantage contract includes a clause requiring subscribers to arbitrate disputes arising under the plan rather than file a lawsuit. The Franklin Medical Insurance Contract Act (MICA), § 63.1, regulates disclosures concerning arbitration requirements in a health care plan.

Preferred acknowledges that the arbitration clause in its Elder Advantage contract violates MICA § 63.1 because the disclosure regarding arbitration did not appear immediately above the signature line. However, Preferred's attorney, William Caldwell, claims that two federal statutes, the Federal Arbitration Act and § 1395mm of the Medicare Act, preempt MICA, and that the Reynolds case therefore must be resolved through arbitration, not litigation. Our position is that another federal statute, the McCarran-Ferguson Act, overrides the Federal Arbitration Act, and that § 1395mm of the Medicare Act does not preempt state regulation.

Please draft for my signature a letter to Preferred's attorney rejecting his arbitration demand and explaining:

> 1. Why the Federal Arbitration Act does not preempt MICA § 63.1; and
> 2. Why § 1395mm of the Medicare Act does not preempt MICA § 63.1.

Belle, Bruce & Caldwell LLP
Attorneys at Law
473 Bayliss Court, Suite 8500
Margot Bay, Franklin 33501
(555) 870-4566

February 21, 2005

Arthur McBride
Allen, McBride & Lagos LLP
1251 Bay Street
Margot Bay, Franklin 33501

Re: *Reynolds v. Preferred Medical Providers*

Dear Mr. McBride:

We have received from our client, Preferred Medical Providers ("Preferred"), the complaint you filed on behalf of Rowena Reynolds and her deceased father, John Reynolds.

On July 15, 1995, Mr. Reynolds enrolled in Elder Advantage, a Medicare HMO insurance plan offered by Preferred that provided to Medicare recipients substantial additional benefits. By enrolling, Mr. Reynolds agreed to submit all disputes arising under the plan to final and binding arbitration.

We are aware that Preferred's arbitration disclosure in the Elder Advantage contract does not strictly comply with the requirements of § 63.1 of the Franklin Medical Insurance Contract Act ("MICA") regarding the language and placement of arbitration clauses in health care plans. However, Preferred's marketing materials, including its enrollment contract, were timely and properly submitted to the Secretary of Health and Human Services as required by the Medicare Act, 42 U.S.C. § 1395mm(c)(3)(C), as it existed in 1995, at the time Mr. Reynolds enrolled. That section of the Medicare Act, as well as the Federal Arbitration Act, 9 U.S.C. § 1, *et seq.*, preempt § 63.1 of MICA. *See Casaro v. Super Sub Associates,* 15th Cir. (1996).

On behalf of Preferred, we hereby demand that you agree to submit the Reynolds matter to arbitration pursuant to the Elder Advantage plan. If you do not agree, we will file a motion to compel arbitration, which we are quite confident the court will grant. We will also seek an award for costs and expenses of the motion. If I do not receive your agreement to arbitrate this matter within 10 days of the date of this letter, I will file the appropriate motion.

Very truly yours,

William L. Caldwell

Excerpt from Transcript of Recorded Interview with Rowena Reynolds

May 24, 2004

* * * *

Attorney: Yes, Rowena, I'm sorry about your dad. What happened?

Reynolds: Well, his kidneys just gave out. We tried for almost two years to get his health care plan to authorize a state-of-the-art treatment that Dad's own doctor, Alex Moskovitz, was recommending.

Attorney: What health care plan did John have?

Reynolds: Preferred Medical Providers. When Dad turned 65, he signed up for Medicare and Elder Advantage.

Attorney: How does Elder Advantage work?

Reynolds: It's a health insurance plan. Preferred advertises itself as an HMO. It contracts with the government to manage and administer claims and benefits under the Medicare program. Elder Advantage members pay a monthly premium, and Preferred furnishes the medical services through hospitals and doctors Preferred contracts with.

Attorney: Whom did you deal with at Preferred, and what reasons did they give you for not authorizing the treatment?

Reynolds: The main guy was a Dr. Phillips, but I got the run-around and kept getting referred to other "claims evaluators," who just said they'd look into it and get back to me. Not even Dr. Moskovitz could get an answer. Piecing it together, it seems their excuse was that it was a new, unproven treatment and far too expensive. It wasn't "scheduled" on the Elder Advantage list of authorized treatments, so they just wouldn't okay it. Just about the time we thought they might agree to it, Dad died.

* * * *

Attorney: Okay. I know you want to sue Preferred. Let me look into it and I'll get back to you on what I think the best approach is. I think a jury will be very sympathetic to your situation.

LIBRARY

Reynolds v. Preferred Medical Providers

Franklin Medical Insurance Contract Act (1985)

§ 63.1.   Binding arbitration included as contract term; required disclosures

Any health care plan that includes terms that require binding arbitration to settle disputes and that restrict or provide a waiver of the right to a jury trial shall include a disclosure displayed immediately above the signature line provided for the individual enrolling in the health care plan. The disclosure shall appear in at least 10-point bold red type in substantially the following language:

NOTICE: BY SIGNING THIS CONTRACT YOU ARE AGREEING TO HAVE ANY DISPUTE ARISING UNDER THIS CONTRACT DECIDED BY NEUTRAL ARBITRATION AND YOU ARE GIVING UP YOUR RIGHT TO A JURY OR COURT TRIAL. SEE [THE APPLICABLE SECTION] OF THIS CONTRACT, WHERE THIS WAIVER OF YOUR RIGHTS IS FULLY SET FORTH.

Federal Arbitration Act, Title 9 United States Code (1947)

§ 2: Validity, irrevocability, and enforcement of agreements to arbitration

A written provision in any contract evidencing a transaction involving interstate commerce to settle by arbitration a controversy thereafter arising out of such contract or transaction, or the refusal to perform the whole or any part thereof, or an agreement in writing to submit to arbitration an existing controversy arising out of such contract, transaction, or refusal, shall be valid, irrevocable, and enforceable, save upon such grounds as exist at law or in equity for the revocation of any contract.

McCarran-Ferguson Act, Title 15 United States Code (1945)

§ 1012: Regulation by State law; Federal law relating specifically to insurance

(a) State regulation: The business of insurance, and every person engaged therein, shall be subject to the laws of the several States which relate to the regulation or taxation of such business.

(b) Federal regulation: No Act of Congress shall be construed to invalidate, impair, or supersede any law enacted by any State for the purpose of regulating the business of insurance . . . unless such Act specifically relates to the business of insurance. . . .

* * * *

Medicare Act, Title 42 United States Code

(As amended, 1993)

42 U.S.C. § 1395mm

* * * *

(c) Enrollment in plan; duties of organization to enrollees

(3) * * * *

(C) The Secretary of Health and Human Services may prescribe the procedures and conditions under which an eligible organization that has entered into a contract with the Secretary under this subsection may inform individuals eligible to enroll under this section with the organization about the organization, or may enroll such individuals with the organization. No brochures, application forms, enrollment contracts, or other promotional or informational material may be distributed by an organization to (or for the use of) individuals eligible to enroll with the organization under this section unless

(i) at least 45 days before its distribution, the organization has submitted the material to the Secretary for review and

(ii) the Secretary has not disapproved the distribution of the material. The Secretary shall review all such material submitted and shall disapprove such material if the Secretary determines, in the Secretary's discretion, that the material is materially inaccurate or misleading or otherwise makes a material misrepresentation.

Casaro v. Super Sub Associates

United States Court of Appeals for the Fifteenth Circuit (1996)

This case involves an arbitration clause in a standard form agreement for the operation of a Super Sub sandwich shop in Barber's Junction, Olympia. The arbitration provision appears on the fourth page of the agreement and states, "Any controversy or claim arising out of or relating to this contract or the breach thereof shall be settled by arbitration."

Franchisee, Paul Casaro, filed suit in U.S. District Court against the franchisor, Super Sub Associates (Sub), for an alleged violation of the franchise agreement. Sub moved to stay the action and to compel arbitration of the dispute. The trial court granted the motion and issued an order to compel Casaro to submit to binding arbitration.

The Federal Arbitration Act, 9 U.S.C. § 2, declares written provisions for arbitration "valid, irrevocable, and enforceable, save upon such grounds as exist at law or in equity for the revocation of any contract." However, state law, Olympia Code § 4-321.5, declares an arbitration clause unenforceable unless "notice that the contract is subject to arbitration is typed in underlined capital letters on the first page of the contract." The arbitration clause in this case does not comply with that provision.

Sub argued successfully in the trial court that the Federal Arbitration Act preempts the Olympia statute. We agree with Sub and affirm the trial court's order compelling arbitration.

In determining whether a federal statute preempts state law under the Supremacy Clause of the United States Constitution, it is necessary to examine the intent of Congress in enacting the statute. Generally, there are two possibilities, described as "field" preemption and "conflict" preemption.

Field preemption arises when, either because of the specific words of the statute or by necessary implication, it can be discerned that Congress intended to occupy the field to the exclusion of any state regulation of the field. In cases where the federal regulation purports to affect a field historically within the police powers of the states, the party asserting preemption has a particularly heavy burden to establish that preemption was the clear and manifest purpose of Congress.

Conflict preemption arises when it is alleged that there is a direct conflict between the federal statute and the state regulation. In such a case, the conflict requiring preemption must be such that the conflict makes compliance with both the federal and state regulations impossible.

In the present case, we need not venture into the area of conflict preemption because it is clear and manifest that in the Federal Arbitration Act Congress fully intended to occupy the field to the exclusion of any contrary or inconsistent state regulation such as Olympia Code § 4-321.5.

The Federal Arbitration Act establishes a broad principle of enforceability of arbitration agreements and § 2 provides for revocation of such agreements only upon "grounds as exist at law or in equity for the revocation of any contract." Thus, if state law governs issues concerning the validity, revocability, and enforceability of contracts *generally*, that law may be applied to invalidate arbitration agreements without contravening the Federal Arbitration Act. For example, generally applicable state laws that prohibit arbitration of disputes in contracts procured by fraud, duress, or unconscionability are not preempted by the Federal Arbitration Act.

However, courts may not invalidate arbitration agreements under state laws applicable *only* to contractual arbitration provisions. Congress precluded states from singling out arbitration provisions for suspect status, requiring instead that such provisions be treated exactly like other contract provisions.

Here, the Olympia law focuses only upon arbitration provisions contained in otherwise valid agreements. It imposes a special notice requirement not applicable to contracts generally. Such a statute, which contravenes the Federal Arbitration Act's broad principle of enforceability, is directly at odds with the Federal Arbitration Act and is therefore preempted by the Federal Arbitration Act.

Affirmed.

Smith v. ModernCare of Franklin

Franklin Court of Appeal (2001)

Plaintiff, Rulon Smith, filed an action against ModernCare of Franklin seeking damages for injuries sustained as the result of ModernCare's alleged failure to provide promised benefits, including the failure to timely authorize or extend needed treatment by health providers. ModernCare responded with a motion to compel arbitration, which was granted by the district court on the ground that the Federal Arbitration Act preempts the application of a Franklin statute that imposes a special notice requirement for health care contracts containing arbitration provisions.[1]

Smith appealed this court, seeking to vacate the trial court's order granting the motion to compel arbitration.

Smith was an employee of Addison County, which entered into a group health insurance contract with ModernCare, a Health Maintenance Organization (HMO), for the benefit of its employees. The four-page enrollment agreement signed by Smith in 1994 when he joined the group plan contained an arbitration provision on the second page. It set forth in bold print and in detail that ModernCare used binding arbitration to resolve all disputes arising under the plan; that enrollment in the plan constituted the agreement of the subscriber to submit all claims to final and binding arbitration before a neutral arbitrator; that

the subscriber understood and agreed that he/she was giving up the right to a trial by jury in any such dispute; and it referred the subscriber to the page and paragraph in the Evidence of Coverage booklet furnished to each subscriber where the arbitration agreement was set forth.

The sentence immediately above the signature line on the subscription agreement stated, "My signature below is an acknowledgement that I have read this Subscription Agreement and the Evidence of Coverage booklet, and that I understand and agree to all the terms and conditions set forth therein."

Section 63.1 of the Franklin Medical Insurance Contract Act (MICA) requires as a condition of the validity of an agreement to submit disputes to arbitration under a health care plan that a statutorily prescribed disclosure appear in at least 10-point bold red type *immediately* above the signature line.

The Franklin Legislature's goal in imposing this special notice requirement was to pointedly call the attention of health plan subscribers to the fact that, by agreeing to arbitration, they would be giving up extremely important civil and constitutional rights. At a time when they may be vulnerable, this notice gives subscribers a final opportunity to consider whether they truly want to trade those rights for a quicker, but probably less remunerative, resolution of disputes affecting their health and welfare.

---

[1] The Federal Arbitration Act is relevant in this case because health care programs inherently involve transactions in interstate commerce.

ModernCare, citing the decision of the 15th Circuit Court of Appeals in *Casaro v. Super Sub Associates* (1996), asserts that MICA § 63.1 is preempted by the Federal Arbitration Act. As the court stated in *Casaro,* "The Federal Arbitration Act, 9 U.S.C. § 2, declares written provisions for arbitration 'valid, irrevocable, and enforceable, save upon such grounds as exist at law or in equity for the revocation of any contract.'"[2] The court found that an Olympia statute contravened the Federal Arbitration Act because, in focusing only upon arbitration provisions contained in otherwise valid agreements, it imposed a special notice requirement not applicable to contracts generally.

The Franklin statute in the present case, MICA § 63.1, also focuses only upon arbitration provisions in contracts and imposes a special notice requirement not applicable to contracts generally. At first blush, § 63.1 suffers from the same infirmity as did the Olympia statute in *Casaro*. However, what was not dealt with and decided in *Casaro* is the effect of the federal McCarran-Ferguson Act, 15 U.S.C. § 1012 *et seq*. (McCarran-Ferguson).

In enacting McCarran-Ferguson, Congress clearly intended to reserve to the states the regulation of the business of insurance. It provides that:

> No Act of Congress shall be construed
> to invalidate, impair, or supersede any
> law enacted by any State for the pur-

pose of regulating the business of insurance . . . unless such Act specifically relates to the business of insurance. . . .

Accordingly, if MICA, of which § 63.1 is a part, is a state law relating to the business of insurance, no federal law that purports to preempt MICA can do so unless the federal law is also a law that *specifically* relates to the business of insurance.

The Federal Arbitration Act is obviously not a federal law that specifically relates to the business of insurance. It is a law of general applicability. Thus, the only way the Federal Arbitration Act can have the preemptive effect urged by ModernCare is if MICA is not a state law regulating the business of insurance.

The issue to be resolved, therefore, is whether MICA § 63.1 constitutes a regulation of insurance within the meaning of McCarran-Ferguson.

In *SEC v. National Securities, Inc.* (1969), the United States Supreme Court emphasized that, whatever the exact scope of the statutory term, the focus of McCarran-Ferguson is upon the relationship between the insurer and its policyholders. Insurance inherently involves spreading the risk between the insurer and its insureds. HMOs, such as ModernCare, are engaged in providing a service that is the equivalent of traditional health insurance. The only distinction between an HMO and a traditional health insurer is that the HMO provides medical services directly, while a traditional insurer does so indirectly by paying for the services. In both, however, the

---

[2] The Federal Arbitration Act is applicable in state courts as well as federal courts. *Southland Corp. v. Keating* (U.S. Supreme Court, 1984).

policyholder pays a fee for a promise of medical services in the event that he or she should need them. It follows that HMOs are in the business of insurance.

The remaining question is whether the state law at issue is an "insurance regulation." In order to be an insurance regulation, a law must not just have an impact on the insurance industry, but must be directed toward that industry. MICA § 63.1 regulates the language and terms of the policies that HMOs and other health insurers may offer in Franklin. Health insurers that want to use mandatory arbitration must provide certain disclosures in the documents issued to their plan enrollees, use certain language, and place the disclosures in a certain way. In protecting the insureds, the state has exercised its power through § 63.1 to regulate the performance of an insurance contract.

We conclude that ModernCare is engaged in the business of insurance and that the state law, MICA § 63.1, does regulate the business of insurance within the meaning of McCarran-Ferguson. Therefore, McCarran-Ferguson prevents the Federal Arbitration Act, a federal statute of general application that does not specifically relate to the business of insurance, from being used to preempt the state law. As a result, ModernCare's arbitration clause may not be enforced because of its failure to satisfy the specific requirements imposed by MICA § 63.1.

Accordingly, we vacate the order compelling arbitration and remand to the trial court with instructions to enter an order consistent with our decision.

THE CONGRESSIONAL RECORD
March 12, 1993

Report of the Conference Committee on the Bill Proposing Amendments to the Medicare Act

We convene to reconcile the differences between the Senate and House bills.

* * * *

The current Medicare law provides for the delegation of Medicare health insurance benefit administration to Health Maintenance Organizations (HMOs) that contract with the Secretary of Health and Human Services (Secretary) to do so. Such HMOs are authorized to manage benefit requests by Medicare beneficiaries.

* * * *

The Medicare Program confers upon the Secretary broad powers to safeguard the public interest by prescribing the procedures and conditions under which an HMO may market its programs and inform and enroll potential beneficiaries. It prohibits an HMO from distributing misleading and deceptive information and sending brochures, application forms, enrollment contracts, and other promotional materials (marketing and informational materials) without first submitting them to the Secretary. An existing provision of the Act, § 1395mm(c)(3)(C), requires submission of all such materials to the Secretary for review and approval.

The House and Senate disagreed during their separate deliberations on whether the review and approval power granted to the Secretary under § 1395mm(c)(3)(C) should be exclusive. In reconciling these differences, we conclude it would be an unnecessary incursion on the states' traditional police powers to regulate public health to preclude concurrent state and federal regulation of the HMO Medicare benefits marketing and informational materials. Congress previously has stated its intent to minimize federal intrusion in the traditionally state-regulated area of medical services for the elderly. Accordingly, the Committee resolves that the Secretary should not be the sole regulatory voice in the matter, recognizing that states may differ on the measure of protection they wish to provide for their elderly residents, who are vulnerable to misleading and deceptive practices. This Committee also recognizes the likelihood of more rigorous and comprehensive state standards for HMO providers and values them, as long as such standards do not impede compliance with federal standards.

The federal regulation of marketing and informational materials, as set forth in § 1395mm(c)(3)(C), satisfies the federal government's interest in preventing deception, and permissible state regulation allows the states to append whatever additional protections they deem appropriate, especially in the area of ensuring that senior citizens are fully informed of their rights before they commit themselves to a plan of insurance upon which their very survival may depend.

POINT SHEET

Reynolds v. Preferred Medical Providers

Reynolds v. Preferred Medical Providers
DRAFTERS' POINT SHEET

In this performance test item, applicants' law firm represents Rowena Reynolds. Her deceased father, John Reynolds, was a participant in Elder Advantage, a Medicare health insurance plan issued by Preferred Medical Providers (Preferred), a Health Maintenance Organization (HMO).

During the two years before Mr. Reynolds died, he suffered from a kidney ailment. His primary care physician had recommended that Mr. Reynolds be given a newly developed treatment, but Preferred's medical evaluators refused to authorize and pay for it, asserting that it was new, unproven, and too expensive. Mr. Reynolds died as a result of the kidney ailment.

Rowena Reynolds filed a suit in Franklin state court to recover damages for a variety of torts and demanded a jury trial. Preferred's attorney, William Caldwell, wrote a letter demanding that Reynolds submit the dispute to arbitration pursuant to an arbitration clause contained in Mr. Reynolds' Elder Advantage enrollment contract. Preferred's theory is that the Federal Arbitration Act and the Medicare Act preempt a provision of the Franklin Medical Insurance Contract Act (MICA) that requires very specific language and placement of the arbitration clause in any health insurance plan contract. Preferred's arbitration clause does not appear "immediately above the signature line" as required by MICA § 63.1.

Applicants' task is to draft a letter to Preferred's attorney rejecting his demand to arbitrate, explaining why the Federal Arbitration Act and the Medicare Act do not preempt MICA § 63.1. The File contains a short excerpt from a recorded interview with Ms. Reynolds and a letter from Preferred's counsel. The Library contains MICA § 63.1, the federal statutes, an excerpt from the Congressional Record, and two cases.

The following discussion covers all of the points the drafters intended to raise in the problem. Applicants need not cover them all to receive passing or even excellent grades. Grading is entirely within the discretion of the graders in the user jurisdictions.

I.   **Overview:** The task is to write a letter to Preferred's attorney rejecting his demand to submit to arbitration, explaining why the Federal Arbitration Act and the Medicare Act do not preempt § 63.1.[1]

- The work product should resemble in form and content a letter to opposing counsel.

    - It should contain legal citations as appropriate and references to the facts as needed.

    - It need not contain a separate statement of the facts.

  - The discussion section of the letter should be divided into headings preceding each of the major arguments in the discussion.

    - The case involves a largely legal argument, although there are *some* facts that should be incorporated.

- The issues that applicants must address are set forth in Preferred's letter and the call memo: (1) that the Federal Arbitration Act preempts MICA § 63.1 and (2) that § 1395mm of the Medicare Act also preempts § 63.1. The decision tree is as follows:

  - Section 63.1 requires that the arbitration clause appear "immediately above the signature line."

    - Preferred's enrollment contract does not comply. (Preferred concedes this.)

  - MICA § 63.1 is a Franklin (state) law that relates to the regulation of the business of insurance within the meaning of McCarran-Ferguson.

  - Thus, the Federal Arbitration Act, which is a law of *general* application, does not preempt § 63.1.

    - That is because McCarran-Ferguson prevents any federal law that does not itself *specifically* relate to the business of insurance from impairing or superseding any state law that does.

  - However, McCarran-Ferguson does not have the same non-preemption effect on the Medicare Act.

    - That is because the Medicare Act *is* a federal law that relates *specifically* to the business of insurance.

  - Whether the Medicare Act preempts MICA § 63.1 is determined by making the traditional preemption analysis—that is, whether Congress intended to preempt state laws that regulate the form and content of Medicare marketing materials.

---

[1] The drafters of this test item recognize that in this much-litigated area courts in various jurisdictions have sometimes ruled that the Medicare Act *does* preempt state laws such as MICA § 63.1. It is equally true that other state courts have ruled that there is no preemption. This test item is based on the latter construct.

- Section 63.1 is an exercise of the states' police powers (public health), which makes the burden of asserting federal preemption a particularly heavy one. *See Casaro v. Super Sub Associates.*
- Nothing in the excerpt of the Medicare Act suggests congressional intent to "occupy the field," of regulation of Medicare marketing materials. Thus, there is no "field" preemption.
- It is arguable that 42 U.S.C. § 1395mm(c)(3)(C) expresses congressional intent to preempt state regulation of marketing materials—that is, on the theory of "conflict" preemption.
    - But that is not a plausible theory because the excerpt from the Congressional Record makes it clear that Congress did not intend to preclude concurrent state regulation of marketing materials, as long as such state regulation does not impede the federal regulations.
- Thus, federal law does not preempt MICA § 63.1.

II. Discussion: The two headings below set forth the major parts of the discussion. The headings are *examples only* and not the prescribed headings.

- Section 63.1 contains the very specific requirement that any health care plan that includes a binding arbitration provision contain notice of that provision in at least 10-point bold red type "immediately above the signature line."
    - It is a requirement imposed by the Franklin Legislature to protect the civil and constitutional rights of plan participants by calling their attention at the last possible moment to the fact that by agreeing to submit claims to arbitration they are giving up valuable rights. *Smith v. ModernCare.*
    - It is an exercise of the State of Franklin's police powers (public health). *Cf.* Cong. Rec.
- Preferred's Elder Advantage enrollment contract fails to comply with § 63.1 and is therefore unenforceable under Franklin law.
- Preferred's counsel concedes that its Elder Advantage enrollment contract does not comply with MICA § 63.1. (*See* letter from William Caldwell.)
    - *See also Smith v. ModernCare* ("As a result, ModernCare's arbitration clause may not be enforced because of its failure to satisfy the specific requirements [i.e., that it appear "immediately above the signature line"] imposed by MICA § 63.1.")

The Federal Arbitration Act Does Not Preempt MICA § 63.1 Because § 63.1 Is a State Law That Regulates the Business of Insurance, and the McCarran-Ferguson Act Prevents Any Federal Law That Does Not Itself *Specifically* Relate to the Business of Insurance from Impairing or Superseding a State Law That Does Relate to the Business of Insurance.

- McCarran-Ferguson is an expression of congressional intent to preserve for the states the regulation of the business of insurance. *Smith v. ModernCare.*
  - It provides that "No Act of Congress shall be construed to invalidate, impair, or supersede any law enacted by any State for the purpose of regulating the business of insurance . . . unless such Act specifically relates to the business of insurance."
- Medical and health care plans, such as Preferred's Elder Advantage, are forms of "insurance."
  - HMOs such as Preferred are in the business of providing insurance; that is, the policyholder pays a fee and the HMO furnishes the services and spreads the risk among its policyholders.
    - *See Smith v. ModernCare*; *see also* Ms. Reynolds' comments in the excerpt of her interview.
    - Note also that the File is peppered with references to Elder Advantage and Medicare being health *insurance* plans.
- The question then becomes whether § 63.1 is a state law that regulates the business of insurance within the meaning of McCarran-Ferguson.
  - Section 63.1 is such a regulation. *Smith v. ModernCare* states it very clearly: "In protecting the insureds, the state has exercised its power through § 63.1 to regulate the performance of an insurance contract."
    - It regulates the language and the terms of policies HMOs can offer in Franklin. *See Smith v. ModernCare.*
  - Thus, § 63.1 is a state insurance regulation and is protected from preemption by McCarran-Ferguson unless the federal law that Preferred is asserting (the Federal Arbitration Act) *specifically* relates to the business of insurance.

- The Federal Arbitration Act is *not* a federal law that *specifically* relates to the business of insurance.
    - It is a law of general applicability that relates to contracts in general. *See Smith v. ModernCare* ("The Federal Arbitration Act is obviously not a federal law that specifically relates to the business of insurance.").
        - It makes contractual arbitration provisions enforceable "save upon such grounds as exist at law or in equity for revocation of *any contract*."
        - Caldwell's citation to *Casaro v. Super Sub Associates* is inapposite because *Casaro* dealt with the Federal Arbitration Act's preemption of a state law that did *not* relate to the business of insurance.
            - Applicants should explain why *Casaro* is not good authority for Preferred's position.
- For these reasons, the Federal Arbitration Act does not preempt MICA § 63.1.

MICA § 63.1 Is Not Preempted by the Medicare Act Because Congress Did Not Intend to Occupy the Field of Regulation of Medicare Marketing Materials and Because Application of § 63.1 to Medicare Insurance Plans Does Not Conflict with Federal Regulation in a Way That Makes Compliance with Both State and Federal Regulations Impossible.

- First, applicants should note that McCarran-Ferguson does not come into play on the question of preemption of § 63.1 by the Medicare Act.
    - That is because the Medicare Act is a federal law that relates *specifically* to the business of insurance.
        - The excerpt from the Congressional Record describes the Medicare law as providing "for the delegation of Medicare health insurance benefit administration to . . . (HMOs)."
    - Thus, whether the Medicare Act preempts MICA § 63.1 has to be analyzed under traditional "field" and "conflict" preemption doctrines. *See Casaro.*
- In order to show "field" preemption (i.e., that Congress intended to occupy the field of regulation in Medicare), Preferred carries the heavy burden of establishing that "preemption was the clear and manifest purpose of Congress." *See Casaro.*

- That is especially true here because § 63.1 falls within the police powers (regulation of public health) of the State of Franklin.

- Field preemption is ordinarily present where Congress has *expressly* or *implicitly* stated an intent to exclude all state regulation.

    - The contrary is true here. "Congress previously has stated its intent to minimize federal intrusion in the traditionally state-regulated area of medical services for the elderly." *See* CONG. REC.

    - Thus, there is no *field* preemption.

- The "conflict" preemption argument centers on § 1395mm(c)(3)(C), which Preferred cites as a provision that specifically preempts state regulation of the form and content of marketing and informational materials such as the Elder Advantage enrollment contract.

    - On the surface, this provision may appear to vest exclusive power in the Secretary of Health and Human Services (Secretary) to regulate Medicare HMO plan materials.

        - This section of the statute prohibits any HMO from distributing marketing and informational materials before they have been vetted through the Secretary for inaccurate or misleading content. If, within 45 days after submission, the Secretary has not disapproved of them, the materials are deemed to be unobjectionable.

        - Preferred's letter states that its Elder Advantage materials were submitted in compliance with § 1395mm(c)(3)(C) and that the Secretary did not disapprove. Applicants should assume this is true.

    - However, as the court notes in *Casaro*, for there to be conflict preemption, compliance with both the federal and state regulations must be "impossible." That is not so in this case.

        - First, the federal and state regulatory schemes are similar. *Id.*

            - Section 1395mm(c)(3)(C)'s requirement that the Secretary preview the materials and § 63.1's requirement that the disclosure be placed immediately above the signature line are *both* aimed at "preventing deception . . . in the area of ensuring that senior citizens are fully informed of their rights before they commit themselves to a plan of insurance upon which their very survival depends." (CONG. REC.)

- Section 63.1 actually *advances* the intent of § 1395mm(c)(3)(C) by giving vulnerable elderly participants more meaningful notice of their rights. *Id.*

- Moreover, the Congressional Conference Committee expressly acknowledges in the Congressional Record excerpt that state and federal regulation of HMO marketing and information materials can coexist without conflict.

- Thus, there is no *conflict* preemption.

Conclusion: For all the foregoing reasons, there is no federal preemption of MICA § 63.1, and Preferred's demand that Rowena Reynolds submit her case to arbitration is rejected.

In re Clarke Corporation

FILE

LIBRARY

MacKenzie, Asp & Norman LLP
Attorneys at Law
550 Enterprise Blvd., Suite 2500
Cypress, Franklin 33337

INTEROFFICE MEMORANDUM

TO:	Applicant
FROM:	Margaret MacKenzie
DATE:	July 26, 2005
SUBJECT:	*In re Clarke Corporation*

Our client, Clarke Corporation (Clarke), has been threatened with a products liability action. The specific allegations against Clarke concern an X-ray enhancing contrast dye substance known as "PureView" originally manufactured by Santoy Enterprises and then, briefly, by Clarke following Clarke's acquisition as an asset purchaser of Santoy's Drug Manufacturing Division. Mary Regan alleges her husband's death was caused by doses of PureView administered to him more than two decades ago.

As a general rule, there is no corporate successor liability in this situation. There are, however, four traditional exceptions to the general rule. I have determined that none of them applies here, so do not address them. A fifth, more recently created exception, called the product line successor rule, does give me some concern.

Please draft for my signature an opinion letter to Jasmine Clarke, Clarke's president, explaining whether the product line successor rule can be invoked to impose liability on Clarke Corporation for Mr. Regan's death. You need not be concerned with whether PureView was in fact defective because those facts have not yet been developed.

I'm attaching a memorandum regarding our firm's practice in writing opinion letters. Please follow these guidelines in preparing your letter.

MacKenzie, Asp & Norman LLP
Attorneys at Law
550 Enterprise Blvd., Suite 2500
Cypress, Franklin 33337

INTEROFFICE MEMORANDUM

TO: Associates

SUBJECT: Opinion Letters

DATE: September 8, 1995

The firm follows these guidelines in preparing opinion letters to clients:

- Begin the letter with a <u>brief</u> introductory statement of the question.

- Provide a concise one-sentence answer to the question.

- Write a brief statement of the facts relevant to the question.

- Identify and analyze all issues raised by the question. Be sure to discuss the relevant facts and authorities that support your conclusion. Because this is an opinion letter, analyze each theory or issue and all elements or factors of each issue.

Remember to write in a way that clearly addresses the legal issues but also allows the client to follow your reasoning and the logic of your conclusions.

MacKenzie, Asp & Norman LLP
Attorneys at Law
550 Enterprise Blvd., Suite 2500
Cypress, Franklin 33337

INTEROFFICE MEMORANDUM

TO: File
FROM: Margaret MacKenzie
SUBJECT: Interview of Jasmine Clarke, President of Clarke Corporation
DATE: July 25, 2005

- Clarke Corporation (Clarke) is a family-owned pharmaceutical company founded by Ms. Clarke's father, Benjamin Clarke, approximately 30 years ago. Ms. Clarke has been president of the company since her father's retirement in 2002.

- For the first 10 or so years of operation, Clarke specialized in the development and manufacture of blood-thinning medications. In approximately 1985, the company began exploring options for expanding its operations to include other product lines. To that end, it entered into discussions with several unrelated entities, including Santoy Enterprises, concerning a possible merger or acquisition. Ultimately, Clarke decided to acquire Santoy's Drug Manufacturing Division (DMD).

- Prior to the negotiations concerning DMD, Clarke and Santoy had never done any business together or, for that matter, been business competitors, since they manufactured different types of medical and pharmaceutical products.

- DMD comprised approximately 80% of Santoy's manufacturing operations. The other 20% consisted of a fledgling Industrial Chemicals Division that manufactured certain chemical solvents.

- "PureView," a contrast dye material used for enhancing medical X-rays, was one of five pharmaceutical products manufactured by DMD. PureView was DMD's least profitable product, accounting for less than 5% of DMD's total sales.

- Clarke's acquisition of DMD was accomplished through an Asset Purchase Agreement dated September 1, 1990 (copy attached), whereby Clarke purchased certain assets from and assumed certain liabilities of Santoy in exchange for cash consideration of $2.5 million. No stock of either corporation was transferred in connection with the transaction. None of Santoy's officers, directors or shareholders became affiliated with Clarke, although Clarke hired most of DMD's existing employees.

- The $2.5 million purchase price was the subject of intense arm's-length negotiations and constituted adequate consideration for the assets purchased. In retrospect, Ms. Clarke believes that Clarke paid more than it should have for DMD, since the DMD products have never been as profitable as initially projected.

- Following the sale of DMD, pursuant to the terms of the Asset Purchase Agreement, Santoy changed its corporate name to "Sentinel Enterprises."

- Sentinel invested the proceeds from the sale of DMD into its fledgling Industrial Chemical Division, which never took off. Having sold its other assets to Clarke, Sentinel was forced to shut down its operations. In 1992, two years after the DMD transaction, Sentinel filed for bankruptcy and its assets were liquidated.

- After acquiring DMD, Clarke initially continued to manufacture the five former Santoy products using identical manufacturing processes and the same product names that had been used by Santoy. Although Clarke solicited former Santoy customers for business, Clarke informed all existing and prospective customers that it, not Santoy, was now the manufacturer of those products.

- In March 1991, just six months after the DMD acquisition, Clarke discontinued production of PureView. The market just wasn't there for the product; sales had declined precipitously due to the introduction of new X-ray technology that eventually rendered contrast dye products such as PureView virtually obsolete.

- Since then, Clarke has not manufactured or sold PureView or any similar product. Clarke does, however, continue to manufacture the four other unrelated pharmaceutical products that it purchased from Santoy, which collectively account for about 15% of Clarke's total business.

- Three months ago, a report appeared in the *Journal of American Medicine* linking PureView exposure to certain forms of cancer. The report was based on a study that tracked 100 individuals who received doses of PureView more than two decades ago. The study found that within the past few years several of those individuals had developed rare, life-threatening cancerous tumors caused by their exposure to PureView.

- This is the first time that PureView has been linked to any serious medical illness. Before the study, only occasional minor complications (such as mild swelling and soreness) had been known to result from its use.

- Last week Ms. Clarke received a letter from a law firm representing the widow of a man who received doses of PureView more than two decades ago and who recently died from a malignant tumor. (See attached demand letter.)

- Ms. Clarke is very concerned about her company's potential liability for injuries that may have been caused by Santoy-manufactured PureView over the nearly 20 years that Santoy produced the substance. She wants our legal advice on whether Clarke could be held liable for these claims by virtue of its acquisition of DMD.

ASSET PURCHASE AGREEMENT
BETWEEN
SANTOY ENTERPRISES, INC. ("Seller")
AND CLARKE CORPORATION ("Purchaser")

* * * *

ARTICLE II
THE ASSET PURCHASE

2.1 Upon the terms and subject to the conditions of this Agreement, Seller sells, assigns, and transfers to Purchaser, free and clear of all encumbrances, Seller's Drug Manufacturing Division (the "Business") and all assets, licenses, permits, contracts, operations and rights owned by Seller and constituting the Business (the "Purchased Assets"), including:

(i)   All manufacturing facilities, machinery, and equipment;

(ii)   All items of inventory;

(iii)   All laboratory supplies and related research materials;

* * * *

(vi)   All customer lists and mailing lists used in the Business;

* * * *

(viii)   All trade secrets, royalty rights, work notes, market studies, consultants' reports, and similar property used in the Business;

(ix)   All goodwill associated with the Business;

(x)   All rights, title and interest in the names "Santoy," "Santoy Drugs," . . . and "PureView," and any variants thereof, and any related logos, trademarks, trade names or service marks incorporating such names;

* * * *

2.3 Purchase Price. In consideration of the transfer to Purchaser of the Purchased Assets, Purchaser agrees to deliver to Seller the sum of $2,500,000.

* * * *

2.5 Assumption of Liabilities.

(a) General Limitation on Liabilities. Seller shall transfer the Purchased Assets to Purchaser free and clear of all encumbrances, and Purchaser shall not, by virtue of its purchase of the Purchased Assets, assume or become responsible for any liabilities or obligations of Seller except liability for leases, contracts, and other agreements entered into by Seller in the ordinary course of business prior to this Agreement.

(b) Offer of Employment. Purchaser shall offer employment as of the date hereof to all of Seller's active employees in the Business ("Transferred Employees"). Purchaser shall keep on its payroll all Transferred Employees who accept Purchaser's offer of employment except for those who may resign or be terminated for cause, for at least 90 days after the date of this Agreement.

* * * *

ARTICLE V

* * * *

5.5 Change of Name. Seller will amend its Articles of Incorporation within ten (10) business days after the date of this Agreement to change its corporate name to a name dissimilar to the name by which Seller is presently known.

* * * *

5.9 Noncompetition Agreement of Seller. For a period of five (5) years, Seller shall not, directly or indirectly, (i) engage in the manufacture, sale or distribution of products similar in type or performing the same general purpose as those manufactured in the Business, or (ii) own, manage, operate or control, or participate in the ownership, management, operation or control of, any business which directly or indirectly competes with the Business.

* * * *

IN WITNESS WHEREOF, the Parties have executed this Agreement as of September 1, 1990.

SANTOY ENTERPRISES, INC.

By:

Name: Daniel Santoy
Title: President

CLARKE CORPORATION

By:

Name: Benjamin Clarke
Title: President

BENTLEY, PABLO & SUMMER LLP
ATTORNEYS AT LAW

July 21, 2005

Ms. Jasmine Clarke, President
Clarke Corporation
800 Robinson Blvd.
Cypress, Franklin 33337

Dear Ms. Clarke:

We are writing on behalf of our client, Mary Regan, concerning the death of her husband, Thomas Regan, resulting from a malignant tumor caused by his exposure to PureView, a contrast dye material used for X-ray purposes.

As you know, PureView was manufactured by Clarke Corporation's predecessor, Santoy Enterprises, from 1970 to 1990. In 1983, Mr. Regan received several doses of PureView in connection with the treatment of an injury. He developed a fatal malignant tumor as a result of his exposure to PureView and died on November 29, 2004.

In 1990, Clarke Corporation purchased Santoy Enterprises. Clarke, as the successor to the original manufacturer of PureView, is liable for all damages resulting from Mr. Regan's exposure to PureView. *Gray v. Ballard* (Franklin Supreme Court 1987).

We expect Clarke Corporation, as a respectable family-run business, to take responsibility for its liability and fully compensate Mrs. Regan for her husband's untimely demise.

Should you wish to resolve this matter without resort to litigation and thereby avoid the substantial time and expense as well as negative publicity entailed by a lengthy court action, please contact me immediately.

Please be advised that we will pursue any and all legal recourse available on behalf of our client, including the filing of a civil action for products liability against Clarke Corporation, if we do not hear from you within 10 days of the date of this letter.

Sincerely,

William H. Bentley, Esq.
Managing Partner

405 TIMBERDELL DRIVE • PURCELL, FRANKLIN • 33331
PHONE: (832) 555-7220 • FAX: (832) 555-7225

Gray v. Ballard Corporation

Franklin Supreme Court (1987)

Claiming damages for injury from a defective ladder, Michael Gray brought a products liability claim against defendant Ballard Corporation (Ballard II). Ballard II neither manufactured nor sold the ladder. However, prior to Gray's injury, Ballard II succeeded to the business of the ladder's manufacturer, the now dissolved "Ballard Corporation" (Ballard I), through a purchase of Ballard I's assets for adequate cash consideration. The trial court entered summary judgment for Ballard II and Gray appeals.

Gray alleged in his complaint that on March 24, 1979, he fell from a defective ladder while working on a construction project. It is undisputed that the ladder involved in the accident was an "old" model manufactured by Ballard I, and that Ballard II was not the manufacturer. Hence, the principal issue addressed by the parties' submissions on the motion for summary judgment was the presence or absence of any factual basis for imposing any of Ballard I's liability as manufacturer of the ladder upon Ballard II as successor to Ballard I's manufacturing business.

On July 1, 1978, Ballard I sold to Ballard II, then known as Thunderbird Corporation (Thunderbird), its "stock in trade, fixtures, equipment, trade name, inventory and goodwill," as well as its interest in the real property used for its manufacturing activities. Ballard II paid Ballard I and its principal stockholders total cash consideration of $350,000 for the assets and goodwill of Ballard I. As part of the sale transaction, Ballard I agreed "to dissolve its corporate existence as soon as practical." The possibility of Ballard II being liable for defects in products manufactured or sold by Ballard I was not specifically discussed nor was any provision expressly made therefor. Two months after the sale, Ballard I dissolved.

The tangible assets acquired by Ballard II included Ballard I's manufacturing plant, machinery, offices, office fixtures and equipment, and inventory. Ballard II used these assets to continue manufacturing operations without interruption. The factory personnel remained the same, the former general manager of Ballard I remained with the business as a paid consultant for about six months after the takeover, and identical manufacturing processes were used for producing the ladders. The "Ballard" name continued to be used for all ladders produced after the change of ownership. Ballard II also acquired Ballard I's lists of customers, whom it solicited, and it continued to employ the salespersons and representatives who had sold ladders for Ballard I. Aside from a redesign of the logo on company letterhead, there was no indication on any printed materials that a new company was manufacturing Ballard ladders, and Ballard II's representatives were instructed not to notify customers of the change in ownership.

Our discussion of the law starts with the rule ordinarily applied to determine successor liability in the context of an asset purchase transaction. The general rule is that a corporation that purchases the principal assets of another corporation in an arm's-length transaction is not liable for the debts and liabilities of the selling corporation. However, the courts have traditionally recognized four exceptions to this rule: (1) the purchaser has expressly agreed to assume liability; (2) the transaction amounts to a de facto merger of the two corporations; (3) the purchaser is a mere continuation of the seller; or (4) the transfer of assets to the purchaser is for the fraudulent purpose of escaping liability for the seller's debts.

If this approach were determinative of Ballard II's liability to Gray, we would be required to affirm the summary judgment. None of the four traditional exceptions for imposing liability on the purchasing corporation is present here. However, we have concluded that Gray's products liability claim could be pursued under a new exception to the general rule against corporate successor liability and that summary judgment must therefore be reversed.

The traditional rule against successor liability and the exceptions thereto are designed to protect commercial creditors and shareholders. They do not take into account the public policies underlying strict tort liability for defective products. The purpose of strict tort liability is to ensure that the costs of injuries resulting from defective products are not borne by the injured persons who are powerless to protect themselves. Rather, the costs should be borne by the manufacturers that put such products on the market and are able to spread throughout their customer base the cost of compensating those injured.

Under the circumstances here, imposing liability upon a successor to the original manufacturer is justified where the plaintiff can meet each of the following three conditions: (1) the virtual destruction of plaintiff's remedies against the original manufacturer caused by the successor's acquisition of the business, (2) the successor's ability to assume the original manufacturer's risk-spreading role, and (3) the fairness of requiring the successor to assume responsibility for defective products as a consequence of the successor enjoying the original manufacturer's goodwill in its continued operation of the business. We turn to an analysis of each of these conditions in the context of the present case.

Condition 1. We assume that Gray was injured as a result of defects in a ladder manufactured by Ballard I and therefore could assert liability against Ballard I. However, the practical value of this right of recovery against the original manufacturer was vitiated by the purchase of Ballard I's tangible assets, trade name, and goodwill, and the dissolution of Ballard I in accordance with the purchase agreement. The injury giving rise to Gray's claim against Ballard I did not occur until more than six months after Ballard I dissolved. Thus, even if Gray could obtain a judgment on his claim against the dissolved and assetless Ballard I, he would face formidable and probably insuperable obstacles in attempting to obtain satisfaction of the judgment from former stockholders or directors. These barriers to Gray obtaining redress from the dissolved Ballard I set him (and similarly situated victims of defective products) apart from persons entitled to recovery against a dissolved corporation for claims that were capable of being known at the time of its dissolution.

Condition 2. While depriving Gray of redress against the ladder's manufacturer, Ballard I, the transaction by which Ballard II acquired Ballard I's name and operating assets had the further effect of transferring to Ballard II the resources that had previously been available to Ballard I for meeting its responsibilities to those injured by its defective ladders. These resources included not only the physical plant, manufacturing equipment, and inventories, but also the know-how available through the records of manufacturing designs, the continued employment of the factory personnel, and the consulting services of Ballard I's general manager. With these facilities and sources of information, Ballard II had virtually the same capacity as Ballard I to estimate the risks of claims for injuries from defects in previously manufactured ladders for purposes of obtaining insurance coverage or planning self-insurance. Moreover, the acquisition of the Ballard enterprise gave Ballard II the opportunity formerly enjoyed by Ballard I of passing on to purchasers of new "Ballard" products the costs of meeting these risks. Immediately after the acquisition, it was Ballard II, not Ballard I, that was in a position to promote the

paramount policy of the strict products liability rule by spreading throughout its customer base the cost of compensating otherwise defenseless victims of manufacturing defects.

Condition 3. Imposing liability on Ballard II for injuries caused by Ballard I's defective products is fair vis-à-vis Ballard II in view of its acquisition of Ballard I's trade name, goodwill, and customer lists, its continuing production of the same line of ladders, and its holding itself out to potential and existing customers as the same enterprise. This deliberate albeit legitimate exploitation of Ballard I's established reputation as a going concern manufacturing a specific product line gave Ballard II a substantial benefit that its predecessor could not have enjoyed without the burden of potential liability for injuries from previously manufactured units.

Imposing liability upon successor manufacturers in the position of Ballard II has two consequences. First, it causes the successor taking the benefit of the original manufacturer's goodwill to also bear the burden of defective products. Second, it prevents the predecessor from reaping a windfall by selling its assets at an inflated price that does not reflect successor liability and then liquidating, thereby avoiding responsibility for subsequent injuries from its defective products. Here, by taking over and continuing the established business of producing and distributing Ballard ladders, Ballard II became an integral part of the overall manufacturing enterprise that should bear the cost of injuries resulting from defective products.

In sum, we recognize a new exception, the product line successor rule, to the traditional rule governing successor liability. Where all three of the conditions discussed above have been satisfied, a party that acquires a business and continues to manufacture the acquired product line assumes liability for defects in units of the same product line that had previously been manufactured by the entity from which the business was acquired.

Reversed.

Shatner v. Burger Company

Franklin Court of Appeal (1999)

Dennis Shatner appeals from the trial court's entry of summary judgment in favor of Burger Company, the successor to asbestos distributor Oliver Corp, in this products liability action for asbestos-related injuries.

In 1998, Shatner filed a complaint against Burger alleging that he developed mesothelioma, a latent asbestos-related disease that can manifest itself 30 to 40 years after asbestos exposure, as a result of exposure to asbestos products during his employment as a pipefitter from 1948 through 1979. Burger moved for summary judgment on the grounds that it had no liability as a "product line successor" to Oliver Corp, the corporation alleged to have distributed the asbestos to which Shatner was exposed during his career as a pipefitter.

In 1960, Burger purchased the asbestos distribution assets of Oliver Corp. As consideration for the sale, Burger agreed to pay $3.7 million in cash at closing. As part of the agreement, Oliver Corp agreed to change its name so that Burger could use the "Oliver Corp" name in connection with the asbestos distribution business. Accordingly, Oliver Corp changed its name to Laurel Products. In 1962, 15 months after the asset purchase, Laurel Products dissolved. Burger played no part in the decision to dissolve Laurel Products, nor could it have, as it had no board members in common with Laurel Products, owned no stock in the corporation, and

exercised no control over the entity. Furthermore, there was no provision in the original asset purchase agreement between Burger and Oliver Corp requiring the dissolution of the selling corporation. Three years after acquiring Oliver Corp, Burger left the asbestos business when it sold the goodwill and assets of its asbestos distribution business to an unrelated and now defunct entity.

Shatner asserts that Burger is liable under the three-condition "product line successor" test first enunciated in *Gray v. Ballard* (Franklin Supreme Court, 1987).

The first condition to be considered in deciding whether to impose product line successor liability is whether the successor's acquisition of the original manufacturer's business caused the virtual destruction of the plaintiff's remedies against that manufacturer. In *Gray*, the manufacturer/predecessor was dissolved within two months after the successor's purchase of the assets, trade name, and goodwill, in accordance with the purchase agreement. Thus, by virtue of the very terms of the agreement, that the predecessor would dissolve "as soon as practical," the predecessor ceased to exist as a business entity and the plaintiff's remedies against it were destroyed. The successor corporation, in a very real sense, caused the destruction of the remedy by its acquisition of everything the predecessor possessed, which made it an ongoing business concern answerable for its predecessor's liabilities.

Following *Gray*, the court in *Kramer v. Macintosh Inc.* (Franklin Court of Appeal 1995) held that the first condition was satisfied where the successor corporation, by purchasing nearly all of the assets of the financially strapped predecessor and obtaining financial and managerial control over the predecessor, substantially contributed to the predecessor's demise.

The same cannot be said of Burger's purchase of Oliver Corp. The corporate entity that had been Oliver Corp continued to exist as Laurel Products for 15 months, when it was dissolved and liquidated by its sole shareholder, LP International, a corporation with absolutely no affiliation to Burger. The undisputed evidence showed that Oliver Corp obtained $3.7 million in cash as adequate consideration for its asbestos business assets, that it continued as an ongoing corporate entity for 15 months after the sale, and that Burger played no role in its decision to dissolve, as the two entities had no corporate overlap. The legitimate considerations of fairness that were implicated by the circumstances in *Gray* and *Kramer* are not present here. To conclude that the first condition has been satisfied under the facts of this case would essentially eviscerate the general rule of successor *nonliability* by potentially exposing successors to liability in every case where the predecessor eventually and unilaterally dissolved after selling off its assets.

The second condition addressed by the court in *Gray* was whether the successor corporation had acquired from the predecessor those resources essential to its ability to meet its responsibility to people injured by product defects. In *Gray*, the successor corporation not only acquired its predecessor's physical plant, manufacturing equipment, and inventories, but also the know-how available through the records of manufacturing designs, the continued employment of the factory personnel, and the consulting services of the predecessor's general manager. With these resources the court concluded that the successor had essentially the same capacity as its predecessor to estimate the risks of claims against it for injuries caused by product defects and to make appropriate arrangements for insurance.

The court in *Rollins v. Hardy Systems* (Franklin Court of Appeal 1997) similarly imposed liability on the successor to a manufacturer of custom-made kelp dryers. It held that the successor, which had purchased the predecessor's ongoing business, including its name, goodwill, tools, machinery, and equipment, was in a position to protect itself from loss by expressly providing for that risk when negotiating the sale terms with the predecessor and by spreading the costs of injuries among its current customers. The court determined that, because the successor had continued in the same general business, it was liable, regardless of whether it continued to make the specific injurious product.

The Burger/Oliver Corp transaction certainly has many of the same characteristics as *Gray* and *Rollins*. Burger purchased the Oliver Corp name, physical plant facilities, and machinery, and Oliver Corp's employees became Burger's employees. The differences, however, are crucial. First, in *Gray* and *Rollins*, the defendant successor corporation was still a going concern engaged in the same business as its predecessor at the time the action against it was initiated. In this case, Burger sold Oliver Corp to an unrelated entity 31 years before Shatner brought his action to recover for his injuries. Second, the record before us indicates that Burger entered and then left the asbestos business well before the government began to regulate asbestos and long before the health risks of asbestos were well known. Thus, unlike the defendants in *Gray* and *Rollins,* who could reasonably anticipate injuries to those using their products, Burger had no way to calculate the health risks posed by asbestos and incorporate those risks into its pricing and insurance decisions.

Finally, the third condition's benefit/burden balance leads us to conclude that it would be unfair to impose product line successor liability on Burger. The passage of 35 years since Burger was engaged in the asbestos business, the short (39 months) time period it spent in the business, the impossibility at the time of envisioning the need to spread such an enormous but then unknown risk, the payment of adequate consideration for the business, and the fact that Oliver Corp continued as a corporate entity with substantial assets until dissolving without Burger's involvement, support our conclusion.

We appreciate that the product line successor rule is intended to protect the victims of manufacturing defects and to spread the cost of compensating those victims. Still, where a policy rests upon fairness, as does product line successor liability, the question of fairness must itself be applied with an even hand. The undisputed evidence presented here weighs against imposition of product line successor liability on Burger.

Affirmed.

In re Clarke Corporation
DRAFTERS' POINT SHEET

This performance test deals with the issue of corporate successor liability for defective products in the context of an asset purchase transaction. In 1990, the client, Clarke Corporation (Clarke), purchased the Drug Manufacturing Division (DMD) of Santoy Enterprises (Santoy), consisting of certain pharmaceutical products, related assets, and liabilities. Pursuant to the terms of the Asset Purchase Agreement (APA), Clarke paid Santoy $2.5 million in cash consideration. The sale was an arm's-length transaction that did not involve the transfer of any corporate stock or any overlap in officers, directors, or shareholders. One of the products purchased (and briefly manufactured) by Clarke was an X-ray enhancing contrast dye substance known as "PureView." Clarke is now being threatened with legal action stemming from the death of Thomas Regan, who was exposed to PureView more than two decades ago, when the substance was manufactured by Santoy. Mr. Regan's widow, Mary Regan, has retained counsel and is threatening to file a products liability suit against Clarke as corporate successor to Santoy. The task for applicants is to draft an opinion letter addressing Clarke's potential liability under the product line successor rule, a judicially created doctrine that applies only in the products liability arena.

The File contains the instructing memorandum from the supervising partner and the Memorandum regarding Opinion Letters, which instructs applicants on the basics of writing an opinion letter. It also contains notes from an interview with Jasmine Clarke (president of Clarke Corporation), excerpts from the 1990 APA between Clarke and Santoy, and the demand letter from Mary Regan's attorney. The Library contains the case law necessary to resolve the problem.

The following discussion covers all of the points the drafters intended to raise in the problem. Applicants need not cover them all to receive passing or even excellent grades. Grading is entirely within the discretion of the graders in the user jurisdictions.

I. Overview: Applicants' work product should resemble an opinion letter and should follow the instructions in the Memorandum regarding Opinion Letters.

- The letter should be structured as follows: A statement of the issue, followed by a one-sentence short answer, a brief statement of the facts, and an identification and in-depth analysis of the issues raised by the question, incorporating relevant facts and authorities that support the conclusions. Applicants are to discuss each applicable theory or issue and all elements or factors of each issue.

- In determining whether the product line successor rule applies, applicants must address each of the rule's three conditions and determine whether each condition has been met, analyzing the facts in the File in light of the law contained in the two cases in the Library, *Gray v. Ballard Corporation* and *Shatner v. Burger*, and the two additional cases cited in *Shatner* (*Kramer v. Macintosh* and *Rollins v. Hardy Systems*).

- Ultimately, applicants should conclude that Clarke is not liable under the product line successor rule.

II. The Law

- The court in *Gray* formulated a new exception, the product line successor rule, to the general rule against corporate successor liability.[1] This new exception applies only in the products liability context and only where all three of the following conditions are met:

  - (1) the successor's acquisition of the business caused the virtual destruction of the plaintiff's remedies against the original manufacturer;

  - (2) the successor is able to assume the original manufacturer's risk-spreading role; and

  - (3) fairness dictates that the successor should assume responsibility for defective products as a consequence of the successor enjoying the original manufacturer's goodwill in the successor's continued operation of the business.

- Determination of liability under the product line successor rule is fact-specific and turns on the particulars of each case.

III. Applying the Law to the Facts

- Is Clarke liable for injuries caused by Santoy-manufactured PureView under the product line successor rule enunciated in *Gray v. Ballard*?

- No, because two of the three conditions required for application of the product line successor rule (unavailability of remedy caused by transaction and fairness) are not

---

[1] As discussed in *Gray*, there are four "traditional" exceptions to the rule against imposing liability on a successor corporation: (1) there is an express assumption of liability; (2) the transaction amounts to a *de facto* merger of the two corporations; (3) the purchaser is a mere continuation of the seller; or (4) the transfer of assets to the purchaser is for the fraudulent purpose of escaping liability for the seller's debts. The *Gray* court noted that none of these traditional exceptions applied in that case. Applicants are told in the Instructing Memorandum not to bother with discussing these traditional exceptions to the rule against liability, as the partner has already determined that they do not apply to Clarke's situation.

satisfied, and therefore Clarke cannot be held liable for Santoy's defective product.

IV. Brief Statement of Facts

- On September 1, 1990, Clarke Corporation purchased Santoy's DMD in exchange for $2.5 million cash in an arm's-length transaction.

- Pursuant to the APA, Clarke acquired all of DMD's manufacturing facilities, machinery, inventory, customer lists, trade names, goodwill, and other assets. Clarke hired most of the existing DMD employees, but there was no management overlap or transfer of corporate stock.

- The APA contained a general limitation on liabilities clause and required Santoy to change its name to Sentinel Enterprises and not compete with Clarke for five years.

- In 1992, two years after the sale, Sentinel filed for bankruptcy.

- Using Santoy's processes and product names, Clarke made and sold five Santoy products (including PureView) but informed all customers that it was now the manufacturer.

- Pureview, an X-ray enhancing dye that represented less than 5% of DMD's total sales, was produced by Clarke for only six months; Clarke discontinued it in March 1991 when new technology rendered it obsolete. Clarke does not make any products similar to PureView, but approximately 15% of its total business comes from the other four pharmaceutical products it acquired from Santoy as part of the DMD purchase.

- Three months ago, a medical journal published a study linking PureView exposure to a rare form of cancer. Before that, Pureview had not been connected to any serious illnesses.

- Jasmine Clarke, president of Clarke Corporation, has just received a letter from an attorney representing the widow of Thomas Regan, alleging that Mr. Regan died as a result of his exposure to PureView in 1983. The letter demands that Clarke, as successor to Santoy, be held liable for damages stemming from Mr. Regan's death as a result of his exposure to Pureview.

V. Discussion

- In *Gray*, the court imposed successor liability against a ladder manufacturer that purchased and continued manufacturing the same product line that had injured the plaintiff. In so holding, the court focused on the policies underlying strict tort liability, namely protecting otherwise defenseless victims of manufacturing defects and spreading the cost of compensating them throughout society .

- The facts presented here are similar to those in *Gray* in many respects:
    - The DMD transaction involved the sale of manufacturing facilities, machinery, inventory, equipment, customer lists, trade names, goodwill, and substantially all other assets of the division (*see* APA), as did the transaction in *Gray*.
    - In both transactions, the purchasers hired on the sellers' employees, continued manufacturing operations of most or all of the same product lines using processes identical to those of the sellers, and solicited the sellers' customers.
    - The purchasers in both cases made use of the sellers' product names after the change in ownership.
    - Both in Clarke's case and in *Gray*, the offending products were manufactured by corporations that went out of business after selling their assets, and the plaintiffs' injuries arose after the sellers dissolved, thus leaving the plaintiffs in both cases without adequate remedies against the original manufacturers.
- However, key differences between the facts of this case and those of *Gray* militate against imposing successor liability on Clarke and make this case more analogous to *Shatner*, wherein the court declined to impose liability.

A. **Condition 1—Successor's Acquisition Caused Unavailability of Remedy:**

- With respect to the first condition of the product line rule, causation, Clarke's acquisition of DMD did not cause the virtual destruction of the Regans' remedies against the original manufacturer, Santoy. Here, unlike in *Gray*, the APA contained no dissolution provision. Thus, Santoy was not required to dissolve following consummation of the transaction.
    - Although the APA did contain a noncompete clause, the clause did not preclude Santoy from expanding its fledgling Industrial Chemicals Division or using the funds obtained from the DMD sale to branch out into other business avenues that could have ensured its survival as a corporation.
    - Moreover, as was the case in *Shatner*, because there was no overlap in ownership or management between Clarke and Santoy, Clarke had no way of preventing Santoy from filing for bankruptcy and dissolving. Although Clarke purchased most of Santoy's assets (DMD constituted approximately

80% of Santoy's assets), Clarke did not assume financial or managerial control over the seller (as was the situation in *Kramer v. Macintosh*, cited in *Shatner*). Thus, applicants should conclude that the facts presented here are distinguishable from those in *Kramer*.

- Santoy's (Sentinel's) bankruptcy was due to the unprofitability of its chemical division, not to any action by Clarke.

- While the APA does include a "General Limitations on Liabilities" clause, applicants who cite that provision as insulating Clarke from liability have misread the applicable law. In *Gray*, the court imposed liability on the successor corporation under the product line liability rule where the sale agreement did not "specifically discuss[] nor was any provision expressly made" for the possibility of the successor being liable for defects in products manufactured by the predecessor. Similarly, the DMD APA notes that Clarke will have continued liability for "leases, contracts, and other agreements entered into by [Santoy] in the ordinary course of business prior to this Agreement," but does not speak in particular to any liability for injuries caused by defective products.

- The fact that Santoy was required, pursuant to the APA, to change its corporate name should not affect applicants' analysis or alter the conclusion that the first condition has not been satisfied. *See Shatner*.

  - As noted in *Shatner*, "[t]o conclude that the first condition has been satisfied under the facts of this case would essentially eviscerate the general rule of successor *nonliability* by potentially exposing successors to liability in every case where the predecessor eventually and unilaterally dissolved after selling off its assets."

B. Condition 2—Purchaser's Ability to Spread Risks:

- With respect to the second product line successor rule condition, applicants should conclude that Clarke is able to assume the original manufacturer's risk-spreading role because Clarke continued to manufacture four of the five products acquired from Santoy.

- Clarke's discontinuation of PureView six months after acquiring DMD is immaterial to the analysis of this condition. Clarke need only be in the same general business as

Santoy in order to be deemed capable of absorbing and spreading the risks associated with Santoy-manufactured PureView. Applicants who conclude otherwise would be incorrect. *See Rollins v. Hardy Systems* (cited in *Shatner*) (holding that a successor that purchased its predecessor's ongoing business and continued in the same general business was in a position to protect itself from losses even though it did not continue to make the specific injurious product).

- Pursuant to the terms of the APA, Clarke acquired all the knowledge and materials (e.g., manufacturing facilities, equipment, trade secrets, consultant reports, etc.) necessary to place it in the same position that Santoy had been in with respect to having the ability to predict risks from PureView.

- Although the four remaining Santoy products account for only 15% of Clarke's business and the risks of exposure to PureView were not known until recently, there are no facts in the File to suggest that Clarke cannot spread the cost of PureView-related injuries among current customers of the continuing products.

- Even though the second condition has been met, that condition standing alone cannot support a finding of liability because all three conditions must be satisfied in order for product line successor liability to attach. *See Gray*.

C. **Condition 3—Fairness**:

- Turning to the third condition, fairness, the issue is: Would it be fair to require Clarke to assume responsibility for defective products previously manufactured by Santoy as part and parcel of purchasing Santoy's goodwill?

- Although this is a close call, on balance the facts cut against imposing liability on Clarke.

  - Clarke only briefly (for six months) manufactured PureView, which accounted for only 5% of DMD's total sales, and PureView was not profitable.

  - Like the buyer in *Shatner*, Clarke enjoyed only limited goodwill by virtue of the acquisition because (1) it was forced to discontinue production of PureView due to the product's obsolescence; and (2) unlike the purchaser/successor in *Gray,* Clarke did not hold itself out to customers as the original manufacturer of PureView.

  - Thomas Regan's exposure to PureView occurred more than two decades ago and seven years before Clarke acquired the right and ability to manufacture PureView, and PureView's defects were not capable of being known when Clarke purchased DMD in 1990. Unlike the successor in *Gray* that purchased the assets less than a year before the plaintiff's injuries arose and continued to produce the same injurious product, here the plaintiff's injuries were not discovered until 15 years after the asset purchase transaction and more than 14 years after Clarke ceased manufacturing PureView.

- Although the lapse of time between Clarke's production of PureView and Mrs. Regan's threatened lawsuit is not as great as the 35-year lapse in *Shatner* between Burger's sale of its asbestos business and Shatner's lawsuit, on balance, the equities weigh against imposing successor liability on Clarke, particularly in light of the fact that Clarke did not cause the destruction of the Regans' remedies, as it had no part in the Santoy/Sentinel liquidation.

VI. Conclusion

- Ultimately, applicants should conclude that Clarke will not be liable as a product line successor for injuries sustained by the Regans or others from Santoy-manufactured PureView because the three requisite conditions of the test set forth in *Gray* are not all met.

**February 2004 Multistate Performance Tests
and Point Sheets**

MPT 1: *Bennett v. Sands Construction Company*

FILE

LIBRARY

FILE
Bennett v. Sands

Roberts, Dinny & Stein
Attorneys At Law

MEMORANDUM

TO: Applicant
FROM: Celia Roberts
DATE: February 26, 2004
RE: *Bennett v. Sands Construction Company*

Our client, Samuel Bennett, wants us to bring an action against Sands Construction Company (SCC) to recover $45,000, which is the cost of both replacing the roof and repairing the substantial water damage to his house. The house is a custom structure, designed by an architect and built for our client by SCC, supposedly to the architect's specifications. The roof began leaking seven years ago, the first year that our client occupied the house, and continued to do so until last month, when a new contractor replaced the roof and repaired the structural damage. Bennett only learned about the extent of the problem and its cause when he brought in the new contractor.

Although there are possible contract and tort causes of action, it is apparent that there are serious statute of limitations problems with the case. Bennett has made it clear that he does not want to throw good money after bad. If the statute has run, then we need to let him know and not encourage a lost cause.

Please write a memorandum that analyzes whether the tort and contract causes of action are barred by the statutes of limitation. Be sure your analysis discusses and sets forth your conclusion as to whether we can convince a court that one or both statutes should be tolled.

Notes from Interview with Samuel Bennett
February 23, 2004

Client just paid $45,000 for new roof and structural and electrical repairs in 7-year-old house. Original roof leaked despite repeated repairs by contractor. Client claims the problem was caused by contractor who substituted a less expensive type of roof for the one specified by architect. Client didn't discover substitution until he got architect to inspect roof in September 2003.

Client contracted with Sands Construction Company (SCC) to build his house in accordance with architect's specifications. Client chose contractor after receiving proposal that was the lowest of 3 bids and after checking on reputation of SCC and its owner, Ray Sands. SCC agreed in writing to "construct house per plans and specifications" and to perform the work in a "professional and workmanlike manner." These plans and specifications called for the installation of an "EPDM rubber membrane roof." Client and Mr. Sands did not specifically discuss the substitution of a different type of roofing material from that contained in the specifications for construction of a flat roof. Client was not aware that the description of the roof contained in the "pricing sheet" attached to the contractor's proposal ("Roofing: Flat-Darbex Roof") was not a brand of rubber membrane roofing. He admits to signing the "pricing sheet" in January 1997, but did so without understanding that the substitution had been made. Says he just relied upon Mr. Sands to stick to the architect's plans and expected that any changes would be brought to his attention. Client has now gone back and compared his copies of the architect's original specifications and Sands' pricing sheet, and it is very clear that Sands substituted a "Flat-Darbex Roof" for the "EPDM rubber membrane roof" specified by the architect.

In July 1997, the building inspector issued a certificate of occupancy, and Bennett moved into the house. By October 1997, the first leaks occurred after there was a huge rainstorm. Water dripped along walls in upstairs bedrooms, damaging walls. Contractor Sands inspected after storm and said that windows were problem (see Sands letter 10/9/97 in file). Contractor convinced client that changing windows would solve problem and client agreed to pay to have work done. Client repaired damage to walls himself.

In March of 1998, the first warm day caused melting of the more than 8 inches of snow on the roof. Water poured into upstairs bedroom, and contractor said nothing could be done until snow melted completely. Lots of damage to walls. Contractor finally came a week later and admitted gutters were clogged with "construction debris that hadn't been cleaned up." Sands cleaned gutters, apologized, and repainted walls at own expense.

July 1999. Huge thunderstorm caused water to drip down face of stone wall of kitchen. Sands came next day, reported that some flashing that should have been installed wasn't and repaired it. Sent letter blaming problems on roof design (see Sands letter 7/31/99 in file).

March 2000. Small water leaks into upstairs bathroom during spring melt-off of snow. Sands inspected and blamed it on accumulations of ice in gutter system.

April 2001. Water poured down face of fireplace brick wall onto wood floor. Sands inspected after all of snow melted. Said flashing around chimney was loose and he re-cemented it at no charge. Insurance paid for sanding and refinishing living room floor.

February 2002. Water stains appeared on walls of upstairs bedroom after freezing rain and snow. Sands said, "Everyone with a flat roof is having problems right now due to unusual pattern of freezing and melting that followed the snowstorm." Advised client to re-read letter of 7/31/99. Client very angry. Repainted walls himself.

April 2003. Big storm, three days of heavy rain. Water dripped along walls of south side of house, upstairs and down, soaking carpets and ruining wallpaper and paint. Sands came and reported that seam of roof along south parapet wall had become loose due to accumulation of ice and snow from previous winter. Said, "This is a common problem with roofs of this design." Used blow-torch and special cement to reseal the seam. Charged $500 and repeated advice about redesigning the roof. Insurance paid $300 toward roof repair and additional amount for repairing walls and cleaning carpet.

September 2003. Mike Rainier, the architect who designed the house, came at client's request to assess and give advice. Inspection revealed that roofing material was not the type he specified. Said he had specified a rubber membrane roof and that the roof installed was instead a "torch-down roof." First time client knew about this. Architect said the roof design depended upon the rubber membrane to prevent leaks and that the change in materials "might account for the problem." Said that to replace roof at this stage would be "quite expensive, but may be the only effective solution." Client stunned by news, feels misled by years of dealing with Sands, whom he thought was trustworthy.

After client got written report from architect, client wrote angry letter to Sands (see Bennett letter 11/3/03 in file). Sands responded on November 18, 2003. Client called Darbex Company, roofing manufacturer, to try to get them to take responsibility. Darbex blamed it on contractor (see Darbex letter 12/3/03 in file).

Client hired Certified Roofing Contractors to replace roof for $18,000 on December 22, 2003. Job took from January 19, 2004 to February 16, 2004. When old roof was removed, substantial amount of rotted wood and wet electrical wiring was exposed. Total cost of fixing roof, wood and wiring is $45,000.

Sands Construction Company
quality builders of custom homes
4801 Industrial Park Road
Gatesville, Franklin 33415
www.Sandsbuild.com
(555)555-1133

October 9, 1997

Mr. Samuel Bennett
3216 Lauderdale Lane
Fairmont, Franklin 33417

Dear Sam:

I have inspected your home to determine the cause of the water seepage you experienced in the recent extraordinary rains. It appears that the fault is with the windows on the top floor. The window model specified by the architect, the Solara model 3000, is not well-matched to the siding on the top floor of the house. The top of the window extends past the surface of the siding and therefore collects water. It is inevitable that some of that water will get into the house and damage the interior walls.

I recommend replacing the eight model 3000 windows with the Solara model 5000. Those replacement windows will not change the appearance of the house but will be a better fit with the siding. I am confident this will solve the problem.

The charge for replacing those windows, at my cost, is $1,749. Please indicate your acceptance of this offer by signing one copy of this letter and returning it to me. We can do the work next week, weather permitting.

Very truly yours,

Ray Sands, President

Accepted:

_____

Sands Construction Company
quality builders of custom homes
4801 Industrial Park Road
Gatesville, Franklin 33415
www.Sandsbuild.com
(555)555-1133

July 31, 1999

Mr. Samuel Bennett
3216 Lauderdale Lane
Fairmont, Franklin 33417

Dear Sam:

We have completed our additional investigation of the cause of the water problem you are experiencing with your roof. We discovered that metal flashing had not been installed over some wooden banding above the upper gable walls. We have now installed that flashing and thoroughly sealed it to the wall surfaces. This will prevent the water seepage that was occurring in that area. We have done this work at no additional charge to you.

At the same time, I must share with you my misgivings about this roof. Regarding future water problems, it should be noted that the flat roof design is of high risk. As you know, the flat roof is a series of hips and valleys so designed to shed the water through the openings in the parapet walls. If the water settles or doesn't shed fast enough, you run the risk of water seeping through below. A better arrangement would be to redesign the roof and parapet to allow water to drain under the wall and into the gutter system. I would also recommend that the gutter system be built out an additional 4" to discourage dampness and water seepage through and into the side walls. Please contact me if you wish to pursue these suggestions.

Very truly yours,

Ray Sands, President

Samuel Bennett
3216 Lauderdale Lane
Fairmont, Franklin 33417

November 3, 2003

Ray Sands, President
Sands Construction Company
4801 Industrial Park Road
Gatesville, Franklin 33415

Dear Ray:

I have had nothing but trouble regarding roof leaks from the first year I moved into what was supposed to be my dream house. By my count you have been out to try to fix the problem at least 12 times in the past 6 years. Although every time you come you tell me that you have solved the problem, the fact is that each of the repairs has been only temporarily successful. The leaks always seem to return, and whatever wall or ceiling or floor that I have had fixed is again damaged by water.

I have discussed the problem with Mike Rainier, the architect who designed the house. I told him that you think that the design of the roof is the source of the problem. He said that the specifications for the roof in the original plans called for a "rubber membrane roof" but that the roof you installed is not rubber but is instead made of some other material. He says that because you substituted that material, he is not responsible for the defects in the roof. He says that I should look to you to make this right.

I was astonished and outraged to learn that the roof was not built to specifications. In our contract you guaranteed that the material described in the specifications would be used in the construction and that the work would be performed in a workmanlike manner. Nothing you have done can make up for the fact that you didn't adhere to what you promised at the time of the original construction.

Ray, I think you need to accept responsibility for this and make it right. Please assure me that you will do so before we go through another winter with the probability of more leaks.

Very truly yours,

Samuel Bennett

Sands Construction Company
quality builders of custom homes
4801 Industrial Park Road
Gatesville, Franklin 33415
www.Sandsbuild.com
(555)555-1133

November 18, 2003

Mr. Samuel Bennett
3216 Lauderdale Lane
Fairmont, Franklin 33417

Dear Sam:

I have just received your letter of November 3, 2003. Some time ago, I informed you of the potential for roof leaks at your Fairmont house. I felt that the roof as constructed would not allow for adequate drainage and runoff and that the longer this condition was allowed to exist, the worse it would get. Now after the heavy snowfall of last winter a leak has developed. The flatness of the roof and the parapet wall create a trap for snow.

According to my records, your insurance company paid approximately $1,200 to correct this situation, of which $300 was paid to me for cosmetic work, and a $200 balance remains unpaid. Surely a portion of that money should have been used to correct the problem.

As for the roofing product used on your house, the decision to use a torch-down roofing was made for pricing considerations with your full knowledge. I have reviewed our original contract, along with the specification sheet, approved and endorsed by you. The specification sheet clearly says "Flat-Darbex Roof," and your signature is on it, clear as day. Any questions regarding the selection of material should have been raised at the time of construction, not now, seven years later.

I disagree with Mike Rainier. As an architect, he should know that roofs like the one he designed are wrong for our climate and that no matter what roofing material is used, leaks will occur. While the roof that we put on your house is substantially less expensive than a rubber one, we have had very positive experiences with it in many other installations. Should you wish to replace it now, we would do so at your expense. Please let me know if you would like me to provide you with an estimate of the cost.

Very truly yours,

Ray Sands, President

The Darbex Company
2117 Maple Avenue
Nakoma, Franklin 33420
Exclusive Franklin Distributors of Darbex Roofing Supplies

December 3, 2003

Mr. Samuel Bennett
3216 Lauderdale Lane
Fairmont, Franklin 33417

Dear Mr. Bennett:

We have completed our inspection of your roof to determine whether the Darbex membrane used to construct it is defective. While we sincerely regret the problems you have had with moisture seepage, the Darbex membrane, where visible, was found to be in good condition, free from any signs of manufacturing defects, and weathering normally for its relative exposure age.

As you know, Darbex is a superior modified bitumen membrane reinforced with a high-quality nonwoven polyester mat and is one of the finest heat-weld-applied, modified bitumen membranes ever produced. However, Darbex roofing products are intended for use by professional roofers only, thoroughly trained and skilled in the use and handling of propane heat-weld equipment. It seems apparent that the installer of your roof either did not adequately prepare the sub-surface or did not sufficiently heat the material to ensure a waterproof bond. To the best of my knowledge, Sands Construction Company is not a certified installer of Darbex products.

In addition, to be eligible for a Darbex Limited Material Warranty, all exposed smooth surfaced products must be coated with an approved roof coating. Darbex particularly recommends Johns Manville TopGard® Type A aluminum emulsion roof coating. Periodic maintenance and recoating is the responsibility of the building owner. Your roof is not fully treated with this coating.

For these reasons, although the Darbex Company stands behind its product, since the problems with your roof were caused by the installer, we are unable to cover the situation under our product warranty. We recommend that you have the existing roof removed and a new Darbex membrane installed by a qualified contractor. We would be pleased to supply you with the names of such contractors on request.

Very truly yours,

Tonya Braniff
Quality Assurance Manager

Franklin Civil Code

§ 9-20. Definitions

As used in this article, the term:

* * * *

(2) "Substantial completion" means the date when construction was sufficiently completed, in accordance with the contract as modified by any change order agreed to by the parties, so that the owner could occupy the project for the use for which it was intended or a certificate of occupancy is issued or whichever comes first.

* * * *

§ 9-24. Actions on written contracts; exceptions

All actions upon written contracts shall be brought within six (6) years after the same become due and payable, or in the case of contracts for construction, upon substantial completion. However, this Code section shall not apply to actions under the Uniform Commercial Code for the breach of contracts for the sale of goods or to negotiable instruments.

* * * *

§ 9-30. Trespass or damage to realty

All actions for trespass upon or damage to realty shall be brought within four (4) years after the right of action accrues.

* * * *

§ 9-96. Tolling of limitations for fraud

If the defendant is guilty of a fraud by which the plaintiff has been debarred or deterred from bringing an action, any period of limitation established by Franklin law shall run only from the time of the plaintiff's discovery of the fraud. Tolling under this section shall apply to tort and contract actions.

* * * *

Popper v. Naybors

Franklin Court of Appeal (2000)

In this case we are asked to determine whether the four-year statute of limitations in tort actions for damage to realty[1] bars Betty Popper's claims for house damage caused by the use of synthetic stucco. First, we conclude that the six-year statute of limitations in actions for breach of written contract[2] applies to Popper's contract claim. We therefore reverse the trial court's summary judgment ruling that Popper's contract claim against the builder is barred by the four-year statute of limitations in tort actions for damage to realty. Second, we affirm the trial court's summary judgment ruling that Popper's tort claim for damage to realty is barred by the four-year statute of limitations.

The record shows that Popper contracted with Joseph Naybors to purchase a newly constructed home built by Naybors' construction company. Popper closed on her home on September 2, 1994. In 1999, Popper discovered that her home had substantial wood rot under the exterior insulation and finishing system, also known as synthetic stucco.

On March 4, 1999, Popper filed suit against Naybors, asserting claims for breach of contract and the tort of damage to realty. Naybors moved for summary judgment on all plaintiff's claims on the basis that the claims were barred by the four-year statute of limitations set forth in Franklin Civil Code § 9-30 because all claims involved damage to property. The trial court granted the motion, finding that the four-year statute of limitations was applicable because all of Popper's claims, whether framed as contract or tort, actually involved damage to realty and that the record was devoid of evidence of fraud, which would toll the limitation period.

1. Popper first contends that the trial court erred in applying the four-year statute of limitations to all her claims. We agree.

Written contracts are governed by a six-year statute of limitations. Franklin Civil Code § 9-24. The period of limitation on a construction contract commences on the date the work was substantially complete. Popper filed her action within six years of the date her home was substantially complete. Therefore, summary judgment was not warranted as to her contract claim.

We conclude that the four-year statute of limitations in § 9-30 applies only to tort actions for damage to realty. Actions arising out of contract do not fall within § 9-30's purview. The foundation for Popper's contract claim is simply the failure of Naybors to fulfill the contract for a home suitable for its intended purpose and constructed with quality workmanship and materials. That Popper has experienced consequential damages that may be described as "damage to realty" does not

---

[1] Franklin Civil Code § 9-30.

[2] Franklin Civil Code § 9-24.

change the fact that her claims are based on Naybors' contractual duty.

2. Popper also contends that the trial court erred in finding that the four-year statute of limitations applicable to actions for damage to realty had run. She claims that she timely filed her tort cause of action for damage to realty because the cause of action could not accrue until she "discovered" the damage in 1999. However, it is well established that this so-called common-law "discovery rule" does not apply to tortious damage to realty.

The common-law discovery rule, which tolls the statute of limitations until the plaintiff discovers or reasonably should have discovered the existence of a cause of action, is confined to cases of bodily injury that developed over an extended period of time.

An action under § 9-30 for damage to realty must be brought within four years of substantial completion of the work. This rule that the statute of limitations begins to run upon substantial completion of the work applies notwithstanding the fact that Popper may have had no knowledge of any alleged defects until after the substantial completion of the house. Because the home was substantially completed in mid-1994, the four-year statute of limitations expired in mid-1998, and Popper's tort claim is barred, unless the statute of limitations is tolled for some other reason.

3. Popper next contends that summary judgment on her tort cause of action was precluded by evidence of fraudulent concealment, which should have tolled the four-year statute of limitations for damage to realty until the time when the defects were discoverable. Franklin Civil Code § 9-96. This argument is based on the contention that Naybors knew about the defects in synthetic stucco systems at the time he sold the house to Popper, yet withheld this information from her and represented that the home was constructed with quality workmanship and materials. However, Popper failed to present any competent evidence rebutting Naybors' affidavit that he did not know of any problems associated with the use of synthetic stucco and did not intentionally conceal the real problem from Popper.

To establish fraudulent concealment under § 9-96 sufficient to toll the statute of limitations, Popper must prove that (1) Naybors committed actual fraud, (2) by his fraud he intentionally concealed the cause of action from Popper, and (3) she exercised reasonable diligence to discover the cause of action despite her failure to do so within the applicable statute of limitations. Moreover, to toll the statute, the concealment of a cause of action must be by positive affirmative act, not by mere silence. Some trick or artifice must be employed to prevent inquiry or elude investigation or to mislead and hinder the party who has the cause of action from obtaining the information. Here, Popper made no showing that Naybors' construction of the house or actions in selling the house to her involved fraud or that by some artifice he concealed the allegedly faulty construction.

The only evidence to support Popper's allegation of fraudulent concealment consists of (1) a 1991 article addressing moisture and wood rot problems associated with synthetic stucco, (2) deposition testimony from the president of the stucco supply company stating that he distributed installation direction brochures for buyers of his product, and (3) an expert affidavit documenting construction defects. There is no evidence rebutting Naybors' testimony that he did not know of any problems associated with the use of synthetic stucco. There is also no evidence that Naybors affirmatively concealed any allegedly defective construction or that he hindered or prevented Popper from discovering any alleged defect. Even when the damages suffered by purchaser were not the type that would be readily discernible by the purchaser without taking extraordinary action, the purchaser must show any act or artifice by the seller that was meant to deter timely discovery of the facts.

Construing the facts in a light most favorable to Popper, the record contains no evidence of fraud or fraudulent concealment that would toll the four-year statute of limitations.

Judgment affirmed in part and reversed in part.

Wolman Windows, Inc. v. JOE Industries, Inc.

Franklin Court of Appeal (1999)

Wolman Windows, Inc. (Wolman) filed a multi-count suit against JOE Industries, Inc. (JOE). The district court granted summary judgment for the defendant, holding that the claims were barred by the statute of limitations.

Wolman manufactures and sells custom-made wooden doors, windows, and other construction products. JOE makes and sells, among other things, wood preservatives. The dispute here arose from Wolman's purchase of a wood preservative called N-Rot from JOE for Wolman's use in treating its windows and doors.

Wolman purchased and used N-Rot from 1985 to 1988. On April 22, 1994, Wolman filed this suit. Wolman's central allegation is that JOE's products did not meet Wolman's expectations in preventing wood rot and deterioration in Wolman's doors and windows.

Under the Uniform Commercial Code, adopted in Franklin, contract claims must be brought within four years of their accrual. Ordinary warranty claims generally accrue upon tender of delivery. Wolman last took delivery of JOE's product in December 1988 and failed to file suit until April 1994, almost two years too late, unless the statute of limitations was tolled.

Wolman alleges that JOE fraudulently concealed the N-Rot defects forming the basis of Wolman's causes of action. Fraudulent concealment, if established, would toll the statute of limitations until Wolman discovered or had a reasonable opportunity to discover the concealed defects. *See* Franklin Civil Code § 9-96. To prevail under § 9-96, Wolman must show that JOE fraudulently concealed the very existence of the facts that establish the cause of action and that Wolman was "actually unaware" of these facts. Since these are disputes of fact, summary judgment is appropriate only where a reasonable juror could not find fraudulent concealment. The district court found that the evidence in the record did not create a genuine issue of material fact on fraudulent concealment. We agree.

The substance of Wolman's claims is that JOE warranted that N-Rot would adequately prevent wood rot, but the product failed. The first critical question therefore is whether JOE fraudulently concealed N-Rot's alleged failure to prevent rot in Wolman's wood products. Acts that can constitute fraudulent concealment include outright misrepresentations or failures to disclose information when a duty of disclosure is present, such as in a fiduciary relationship. No such disclosure duty arises from the arm's-length transactions of the parties here, notwithstanding that one of them might have possessed superior knowledge. Misleading partial disclosures, however, may constitute fraudulent concealment. If there is evidence that JOE undertook fraudulently concealing acts, the second question is whether Wolman knew or should have known of the facts that make up its cause of action. Since Wolman has not supplied any evidence of the necessary fraudulent acts, we need not reach the second inquiry.

In attempting to make out a triable case of fraudulent concealment, Wolman alleges that JOE misrepresented N-Rot's effectiveness and made misrepresentations that, while not directly vouching for N-Rot's effectiveness, tended to promote it. For example, Wolman alleges that JOE misled Wolman about long-term research supporting N-Rot's effectiveness, about N-Rot's certification by an industry standards organization, about changes in the formulation and manufacturing process for N-Rot over the years during which Wolman bought and used it, and about the similarity between the type of N-Rot sold to Wolman and the type sold to a well-known competitor. All of these misrepresentations, Wolman alleges, prevented Wolman from learning that N-Rot was failing. As we discuss below, even if JOE intentionally made such misrepresentations, those acts do not constitute fraudulent concealment.

In *Shine v. Grain Elevator Corp.* (Franklin Court of Appeal, 1981) and *Mills v. Grain Elevator Corp.* (Franklin Court of Appeal, 1985), the plaintiffs sued the manufacturer of a particular model of grain elevator that allegedly failed to protect its contents as promised. In each case, the defendant raised a statute of limitations defense.

In *Shine*, the plaintiff alleged that, while inherent and known design defects were the cause of the elevator's failure, the seller intentionally misled Shine by fooling him into believing that the problem was faulty seals, which could be fixed, and the seller attempted to repair the seals in order to deceive him. This court held that a genuine issue of material fact existed as to fraudulent concealment. In *Mills*, the plaintiff alleged that the defendant misled her by continually extolling the virtues of the elevator model in printed material, all the while knowing that the elevator did not work. This court held that this conduct did not constitute fraudulent concealment. We noted that it would have been impossible for the defendant to conceal the facts that gave rise to Mills' cause of action, because the evidence that it was defective was in Mills' yard. We distinguished *Shine*, noting that the defendant intentionally lulled the plaintiff into believing that the problems with the elevator could be, and would be, repaired.

These cases demonstrate that Wolman's allegations that JOE fraudulently misrepresented N-Rot's effectiveness do not constitute fraudulent concealment, at least where Wolman still had access to the facts that would make out its cause of action. At all times, Wolman had access to each of the very facts that establish Wolman's breach of contract action, namely N-Rot's alleged failure to prevent rot on Wolman's products. The oral and written representations that Wolman relies on to support its fraudulent concealment argument did not, and indeed could not, prevent Wolman from discovering that JOE's representations concerning the virtues of N-

Rot were false. None of JOE's alleged acts could have covered up the relevant facts.

Wolman comes closest to alleging fraudulent concealment by asserting that JOE misled Wolman about the cause of Wolman's rot problems. The record reflects that, faced with accusations by Wolman that N-Rot was failing, JOE told Wolman that JOE believed that Wolman's construction practices were to blame. At the time, JOE had information which both supported and undercut N-Rot's efficacy. For example, N-Rot's performance for several other customers had been positive, and laboratory tests of N-Rot produced many satisfactory results. On the other hand, some tests returned less favorable results, especially some water repellency tests. These facts are not evidence of fraudulent concealment. Absent some duty to disclose, not present here, JOE was not required to inform Wolman of the facts that reflected poorly on N-Rot's performance.

JOE's denial of liability alone is certainly not fraudulent concealment. At best, Wolman might be able to prove that JOE was wrong in stating that Wolman's construction practices resulted in Wolman's rot problem. But Wolman can point to no evidence that shows that JOE's representations about the cause of Wolman's rot problem were fraudulent. Thus, Wolman's fraudulent concealment claim fails.

Affirmed.

Bennett v. Sands Construction Company
DRAFTERS' POINT SHEET

The client, Samuel Bennett, has just spent $45,000 to replace the roof on his house and repair damage resulting from leaks in the original roof. He wants to sue Sands Construction Company (SCC), the contractor that built his home and installed the original roof seven years ago. The problem is that the applicable four- and six-year statutes of limitations appear to have run.

The applicants are asked to write a memorandum analyzing whether there is any way around the apparent bar of the tort and contract statutes of limitations.

SCC agreed to build the house in accordance with the architect's plans and specifications. At the time of contracting seven years ago, SCC presented Bennett with a "pricing sheet" showing that the roof to be installed was a "Flat-Darbex Roof." Bennett signed the pricing sheet without noticing that the contractor had substituted the Darbex roof for the "EPDM rubber membrane roof" specified by the architect.

Bennett moved into the house in July seven years ago and, within months, began experiencing water leaks. The problem recurred periodically until about five months ago. Each time there was a leak, Bennett would call Ray Sands, the proprietor of SCC, and Sands would attempt to diagnose and repair the leak. Sands ascribed the leaks to various problems with the types of windows, the gutters, and faulty flashing. His constant criticism, however, was of what he perceived as a faulty roof design by the architect. At one point about five years ago, Sands suggested that the roof and the gutter system be redesigned.

Five months ago, finally fed up with the abortive efforts to remedy the problem, Bennett contacted the architect who designed the house. The architect inspected the property. It was then that Bennett learned for the first time that SCC had substituted the Darbex roof. In addition, Bennett contacted the Darbex Company and learned that SCC had improperly installed the Darbex roof and that SCC was not a certified installer of Darbex products.

The File contains notes of an interview with Bennett and a series of letters chronicling the events. The Library contains the applicable statutes and two cases interpreting them.

The following discussion covers all of the points the drafters intended to raise in the problem. Applicants need not cover them all to receive passing or even excellent grades. Grading is entirely within the discretion of the graders in the user jurisdictions.

I. Overview: The task for the applicants is to write a memorandum in which they discuss whether the apparent bar of the statutes of limitations can be avoided. The work product should resemble an office memorandum from an associate to a supervising attorney.

There are two separate statutes of limitations. One, the four-year statute, applies to tort actions. The other, the six-year statute, applies to contract actions. The applicants are specifically told to explore the possibilities with respect to *both* statutes.

On the face of it, both statutes have run. The case law makes it clear that the common-law "discovery rule" (i.e., the rule that the statute of limitations does not begin to run until the discovery of the cause of action) does not apply in these circumstances. The applicants are therefore left with the possibility that SCC and Sands committed acts of fraudulent concealment, which might or might not have tolled the statutes.

On analysis of the facts and the case law, the likely outcome is that there was no fraudulent concealment that would toll the statutes and that Bennett comes too late. However, applicants will probably be tempted to construe the facts to create at least a material issue whether there was fraudulent concealment, and those whose analyses do so persuasively can receive credit.

II. The statutes of limitations: There are two separate statutes of limitations the applicants must deal with: § 9-24, the six-year statute relating to actions on written contracts, and § 9-30, the four-year statute relating to trespass or damage to realty. As the court held in *Popper v. Naybors*, the mere fact that the recovery being sought is for damage to realty does not prevent application of the longer six-year statute; i.e., if the damage results from the breach of a contractual duty, the longer, six-year statute can be applied.

The six-year contract statute: Bennett's claim for breach of contract against SCC is based on SCC's failure to construct the house in accordance with the architect's plans and specifications. The plans specified installation of an "EPDM rubber membrane roof," and SCC installed a "Flat-Darbex Roof." The installation of the substitute roof resulted in damage to the house.

There is, of course, an issue whether, in the first instance, the roof substitution constituted a breach of contract by SCC. Bennett signed the pricing sheet on which the substituted roof was clearly noted. This was arguably a modification approved by Bennett. If so, the focus shifts from a claim for failure to construct the house in accordance with the plans to a claim for breach of the promise that SCC would perform the work in a "professional and workmanlike manner." In either case, Bennett's claim arises from a breach of contract.

- Franklin Civil Code § 9-24 provides that:
  - "All actions upon written contracts shall be brought within six years after the same become due and payable, or in the case of contracts for construction, upon substantial completion."
    - The statute goes on to say that it is not applicable to contracts subject to Article 2 of the UCC. This is irrelevant, but it may be a distractor to some applicants who might try to argue that the contract in this case was for the sale of goods, i.e., a roof, which would be an incorrect analysis.
  - "Substantial completion" is defined in § 9-20 as "the date when construction was sufficiently completed . . . so that the owner could occupy the project for the use for which it was intended."
    - In this case, Bennett moved into the house in July seven years ago.
      - Accordingly, that is the apparent date on which the statute began running.[1]
      - Absent the occurrence of something to toll the statute, Bennett's contract claim is barred.

The four-year torts statute: Bennett's claim for damages, apart from the claim for breach of contract, is necessarily based on SCC's negligence in the installation of the roof; i.e., irrespective of whether, by signing the pricing sheet, Bennett authorized the substitution of the Darbex roof for the rubber membrane roof, the roof was negligently installed. That much is clear from the letter from the Darbex Company, which points out that SCC did not install the roof properly and that the damage was a result of the faulty installation.

- Franklin Civil Code § 9-30 provides that:
  - "All actions for . . . damage to realty shall be brought within four years after

---

[1] Applicants might be tempted to argue that each time SCC came to the house to make a repair there was a "new" contract to perform the repairs in a professional and workmanlike manner and that each "new" contract was breached on each occasion. Thus, the argument would go, although the repairs carried out by SCC longer ago than six years would fall outside of the statute, the repairs carried out at and after the time of the installation of the flashing in the area of the gable walls in July five years ago all fall within the six-year limitations period and that all claims for damages resulting from and after that event should not be barred.

That would be a strained argument. All claims, no matter when the damage occurred, spring from the roof installation, and, under § 9-24, all actions must be brought within six years of substantial completion. Sands installed the roof more than six years ago.

the right of action accrues."

- The first leak occurred in October seven years ago.
- That is the time at which the cause of action for damage resulting from the negligent installation of the roof accrued.[2]
- Absent the occurrence of something to toll the statute, Bennett's tort claim is barred.

III. Whether SCC engaged in fraudulent concealment that would toll the statutes: The only basis for tolling these statutes of limitations is upon a showing that SCC engaged in fraudulent concealment that prevented Bennett, in the exercise of reasonable diligence, from discovering the defect. In *Popper v. Naybors*, the court holds that Franklin does not recognize the common-law "discovery rule," i.e., the rule that would toll the statute of limitations until the plaintiff actually discovers or reasonably should have discovered the cause of action.[3]

- Franklin Civil Code § 9-96, applied and interpreted in *Popper* and *Wolman Windows*, provides that:
  - "If the defendant is guilty of a fraud by which the plaintiff has been debarred or deterred from bringing an action, any period of limitation established by Franklin law shall run only from the time of the plaintiff's discovery of the fraud."
- *Popper* and *Wolman* establish the following requirements for a showing of fraudulent concealment sufficient to toll the statutes:
  - That SCC/Sands committed *actual fraud*, either by
    - Outright misrepresentation or

---

[2] Again, applicants might try to argue that Bennett has a separate cause of action for negligence each time SCC was unsuccessful in carrying out the series of repairs over the years. Thus, they might argue that all repairs performed at and after the time of the repairs to the chimney flashing in April, three years ago, fall within the four-year torts statute and that claims for damages arising since then are not barred.

This, too, would be a strained argument. The right of action for the negligent installation of the roof, from which all claims spring, was at the latest October seven years ago when the first leaks appeared.

[3] Specifically, *Popper* holds that the common-law discovery rule does not apply to claims for *tortious damage to realty*. This leaves open the argument that the discovery rule might still be applied to claims for breach of contract.

There is nothing in the Library that would support such an argument. The best reading of the contract statute of limitations (§ 9-24) is that it is in the nature of a statute of repose. That is, the statute establishes six years as the outside limit for the assertion of contract claims, *unless* the fraud exception of § 9-96 can be brought to bear.

- Failure to disclose, or misleading partial disclosures, in the face of a duty to disclose.
- That SCC/Sands took *positive action* by artifice or trick to prevent Bennett from making inquiry or to elude investigation, i.e.,
    - That SCC/Sands "lulled" Bennett into inaction.
- That Bennett was reasonably diligent in discovering the cause of action, i.e.,
    - That Bennett knew or should have known of the defect.

The applicants are expected to apply the facts to the elements of fraudulent concealment expressed in the cases. This will require discussion and close analysis rather than a knee-jerk reaction that SCC/Sands misled Bennett because there were so many incidents that Sands *must* have been trying to cover up his own mistakes. To the contrary, close examination of the facts and their application to the law should lead to the conclusion that Bennett will probably not be able to show fraudulent concealment:

- The starting point is the inquiry of whether SCC engaged in fraud when it substituted the Darbex roof on the pricing sheet in January seven years ago.
    - Except for some vague suspicion that SCC was trying to cut corners on the contract, there is really nothing in the File to show that SCC misrepresented anything.
        - It was clearly stated in the architect's specifications that the roof was to be a rubber membrane roof, and the pricing sheet, which Sands openly presented to Bennett for signature, clearly showed that SCC intended to install a Darbex roof.
            - It might be argued that SCC/Sands, because of presumably superior knowledge, had a duty to explain the substitution, but, under a dictum in *Wolman*, that would only be the case in a fiduciary situation. Here, there was an arm's-length transaction and not a fiduciary relationship.
            - The final letter from SCC to Bennett suggests that Sands believed Bennett was aware of the substitution: ". . . the decision to use a torch-down roof was made for pricing considerations with your full knowledge."

- Unless one is prepared to ascribe to Sands a deceitful motive, which is not supported by any fact in the File, it must be concluded that Sands honestly believed Bennett was conscious of the substitution.
  - Certainly, SCC/Sands did not engage in artifice or trick to prevent Bennett from discovering the substitution.
    - All Bennett had to do was compare the architect's specifications with the pricing sheet, both of which were presumably in his possession, and the difference would have put him on notice.
    - Thus, at all times he had the means of discovering the facts. *Wolman*.
- There is nothing to suggest that there was any attempt to defraud or conceal when Sands suggested that the first leak, in October seven years ago, could be cured by replacing the top floor windows. Likewise, it does not appear that Sands undertook the subsequent repairs pretextually just to cover up the initial substitution or faulty installation.
  - The subsequent repairs appear to have been undertaken in good faith by SCC without any effort to hide anything from Bennett and without any knowledge that there was any problem with the way SCC had installed the roof.
    - Indeed, in Sands' final letter to Bennett, he points out that he has had trouble-free experience using the Darbex product in other installations. *Cf. Wolman*, where the efficacy of a product in some applications was a factor considered by the court in determining that no duty arose to disclose problems in other applications.
  - Even Bennett concedes that each repair seemed at first to fix the problem (see Bennett's letter to Sands).
  - The fact, subsequently revealed by the letter from the Darbex Company, that SCC was not a "certified" Darbex installer might be evidence of SCC's negligence, but there is nothing about that to suggest fraud.
- The most persuasive evidence of the absence of fraudulent concealment is the fact

that, as early as July five years ago, SCC/Sands expressed "misgivings" to Bennett about the roof design (see Sands' second letter to Bennett).

- That was tantamount to telling Bennett that, notwithstanding interim repairs, the leaks were likely to recur.

- It was also tantamount to telling Bennett that his architect had screwed up and should be consulted.

- Had Bennett heeded those "misgivings," he would have done sooner rather than later what he ended up ultimately doing, i.e., consulting his architect, learning of the substitution, and pursuing an action.

- Thus, even if the initial roof substitution and the subsequent events can be construed to create an inference of fraudulent concealment, the means of discovering the cause of action were at all times readily available to Bennett.

  - SCC/Sands did nothing to prevent Bennett "from timely obtaining the true facts," *Popper*; and, "At all times [Bennett] had access to each of the very facts that establish [SCC's] breach of contract . . . ." *Wolman.*

    - Bennett knew he was experiencing recurring damage over a period of years;

    - He knew the successive repairs were ineffectual;

    - He could have ascertained the substitution by merely looking at documents in his possession, and, even if he was incapable of comprehending the impact of the substitution, it would have put him on notice; and

    - Had Bennett heeded Sands' misgivings about the design, he would have brought the architect in sooner and discovered the cause of action.

- Accordingly, it is not likely that we can overcome the bar of the statutes of limitations.

MPT 3: *Rivera v. Baldisari Amusement Parks, Inc.*

FILE

LIBRARY

Smith, Taylor & Isely
Attorneys at Law

MEMORANDUM

To: Applicant
From: Thomas Isely
Subject: *Rivera v. Baldisari Amusement Parks, Inc.*
Date: February 24, 2004

We represent Cara Rivera, who was injured when she fell from the Ferris wheel at Wild Wonder World ("WWW"), an amusement park owned and operated by Baldisari Amusement Parks, Inc. ("Baldisari") here in Great Bend. The trial is set to begin in 60 days, and I need your help in getting the trial exhibits ready for use at trial.

Counsel for Baldisari has said that she will not stipulate to the authenticity of several items of evidence we intend to introduce at trial. She may end up waiving her objections once we get to court, but because she might not, we need to be prepared.

I have prepared a list entitled "Items of Evidence" which describes the only items I'm concerned about and identifies individuals connected with the evidence we want to authenticate. Assume that all the evidence is admissible if properly authenticated and do not concern yourself with potential hearsay issues. All I am concerned about at this stage is that we satisfy the procedural steps necessary for producing the items in court and can establish that they are authentic. We want to do this *by the most direct and efficient method,* so if there is a way of shortcutting the procedures to avoid wasting courtroom time with the live testimony of a parade of record custodians and sponsoring witnesses, we should opt for the shortcut.

Please draft a memorandum in which you answer the following questions for each item of evidence:
- What steps must we take to ensure that the evidence is available in court?
- What must we do to establish the authenticity of each item of evidence?

In answering these questions, in addition to citing the applicable rules and code sections, be sure to discuss narratively how the governing section(s) of the Franklin Rules of Evidence and/or the Franklin Code of Civil Procedure enable us to produce each of the items of evidence in court and establish its authenticity.

Organize your memorandum along the following lines, as to each item of evidence:

A heading specifying the item of evidence, and under each heading:

a. the steps necessary for getting the item to court, and

b. what needs to be done to authenticate the item.

Items of Evidence

Opposing counsel will not stipulate to the authenticity of the following items of evidence:

1.   Frank Electronics, Inc.'s personnel file on Cara Rivera: Ms. Rivera is employed by Frank Electronics, Inc. She has been off work for the past 18 months as a result of the accident. Just before she was injured, she had been promoted to the position of Vice President of Manufacturing at a substantially higher salary than her previous position. Because of her extended absence, Frank filled the position with another person. Frank's personnel file on Ms. Rivera contains the documentation that shows the details of the promotion and its subsequent rescission. Nancy Sanders, Frank's Director of Human Resources, is the custodian of those records.

2.   WWW's personnel file on Brady Spitz: Spitz, the employee who was operating the Ferris wheel at the time of the accident, quit his job at WWW after the incident. We have been unable to find and depose him, so we must assume he will be unavailable to testify at the trial. In pretrial discovery, we learned that WWW maintained a personnel file on Spitz and that the file contains his last known address and shows he was repeatedly disciplined for drinking on the job.

3.   State safety inspection report: About a year before the accident, the Franklin Department of Public Safety conducted an inspection and cited Baldisari for a number of deficiencies in the maintenance and operation of the WWW Ferris wheel, including a defect that caused the wheel to surge forward at times. In its report, the Department required Baldisari to repair the defect and recommended that Baldisari install automatic seat-guard locks. Baldisari did not retain a copy of the report in its files.

4.   Baldisari's maintenance records: Baldisari has a maintenance department, which retains records of all maintenance performed on its equipment, including the Ferris wheel. Among those records is correspondence showing that Baldisari declined to purchase automatic seat-guard locks for the Ferris wheel.

5.   Hospital and medical records: Ms. Rivera was taken from the scene of the accident to Franklin General Hospital. The hospital's records include bills, charts, x-rays, test results, etc., relating to her emergency room treatment, surgery, and hospitalization until she was released one month later to return home.

Ripka Investigations
1216 Meade Street
Redding, Franklin 33754
(555) 554-7108
ripka@srch.com

June 23, 2003

Thomas Isely, Esq.
Smith, Taylor & Isely
One Court Center, Suite 1805
Great Bend, FR 33706

Re: *Rivera v. Baldisari Amusement Parks, Inc.*

Dear Tom:

I have completed the investigation you asked me to make in connection with the *Rivera* case, and here is what I have found:

1. <u>Police Officer</u>: I spoke with Officer Arnold Hurlbet of the Great Bend PD, who responded to the scene. He interviewed Brady Spitz, the Ferris wheel operator. Spitz admitted to Officer Hurlbet that he drank "a lot" of muscatel wine in the hours before the accident and that he (Spitz) "guesses" he had neglected to engage Ms. Rivera's seat lock so that she was ejected from her seat on the Ferris wheel when it for some reason surged violently.

2. <u>U.C.C. Filings</u>: In the office of the Secretary of State, I found a recent U.C.C. 1 showing Upland Bank as the secured party and Baldisari Amusement Parks, Inc., as the debtor on the Ferris wheel located at Baldisari's Wild Wonder World facility in Great Bend. The U.C.C. 1 indicates that Baldisari is the owner.

3. <u>Department of Public Safety</u>: The Department's records show that Baldisari has a long record of citations for safety violations relating to the operation of Wild Wonder World park. Specifically, with respect to the Ferris wheel, there is an inspection report dated January 29, 2003, showing that the Department issued a safety violation citation to Wild Wonder World relating to a mechanical defect that caused the Ferris wheel to surge at odd times. The Department also recommended installation of automatic seat-guard locks. A copy of the record is enclosed. The inspector who made the report is David Steele. The head of the Department's Bureau of Records is Marta Jones.

4. <u>Television Reporter</u>: I also interviewed Jake Meerstein, a news reporter from WGVP. He told me he covered the accident and interviewed a woman who was waiting in line to ride the Ferris wheel. She told him that she had told the operator that Ms. Rivera's seat-locking device was not locked. The woman said that she could smell alcohol on the operator's breath and that he told her to mind her own business. Mr. Meerstein told me that he would make sure the tape was preserved and that he would check his notes to find out her name.

5. <u>Brady Spitz</u>: I have been unable to locate Mr. Spitz. The night manager at the Bay View Residence Hotel at 423 Carlton Street, Great Bend, FR 33706, which was Spitz's last known address, says he "checked out a long time ago and didn't leave a forwarding address." None of the other hotel residents I spoke to had any idea where Spitz is.

Please let me know if there is anything further you need.

Very truly yours,

John Paul Ripka

WALKER ON EVIDENCE IN THE FRANKLIN COURTS (3d ed. 2004)

The Requirement of Authentication[1]

Franklin Rule of Evidence (FRE) 901(a) provides the standard for authenticating exhibits and other forms of nontestimonial evidence. It establishes an across-the-board rule that something is properly authenticated by "evidence sufficient to support a finding" that it is "what the proponent claims." Unless an exhibit is self-authenticating, formal proof of authenticity must be offered before the evidence can be admitted or even shown to the jury. Frequently, authentication is a formality to which the parties agree before trial, but, if counsel do not agree on authenticity, then authentication will have to be done at trial.

Authentication is a separate and distinct issue from *production* of the evidence. Before evidence can be authenticated, it must be brought to court either voluntarily or by compulsion of process, such as subpoena or other authorized statutory method. The provisions by which production at trial can be compelled are found in the Franklin Code of Civil Procedure (FCCP).

The preliminary showing of authenticity required by FRE 901(a) necessarily depends on the nature of the thing in question, and often a single exhibit can be authenticated in several different ways. The traditional steps to authenticate an exhibit are the following: (1) having the exhibit physically in court; (2) having the exhibit marked for identification; and (3) authenticating the exhibit by the testimony of a witness (called a "sponsoring witness") unless the exhibit is self-authenticating.

By far, the most common method of authenticating documents and other physical evidence is to have the sponsoring witness, either a custodian of the evidence or other possessor of it, appear in court and testify that the evidence is what the proponent claims it to be. However, certain types of evidence, such as those specified in FRE 902, are "self-authenticating" so that extrinsic evidence of authenticity is not necessary. The Franklin Code of Civil Procedure sets forth additional procedures for production and authentication of certain business records. These types of records can be submitted under seal with a supporting affidavit, thus avoiding the need for live testimony about authenticity. These shortcuts save judicial and trial time, and the principle is that the materials are unlikely to be anything other than what they appear to be and that, for the convenience of the parties and the court, they should be admitted without the requirement of extrinsic authenticating evidence.

---

[1] This section contains excerpts and paraphrasing from Mueller & Kirkpatrick, *Evidence* (1995).

Franklin Rules of Evidence

Rule 901. Requirement for Authentication or Identification

(a) General Provisions

The requirement for authentication or identification as a condition precedent to admissibility is satisfied by evidence sufficient to support a finding that the matter in question is what its proponent claims.

(b) Illustrations

By way of illustration only, and not by way of limitation, the following are examples of authentication or identification conforming to the requirements of this rule:

(1) *Testimony of witness with knowledge.* Testimony that the matter is what it is claimed to be.

(2) *Nonexpert opinion on handwriting.* Nonexpert opinion as to the genuineness of handwriting, based upon familiarity not acquired for purposes of the litigation.

(3) *Comparison by trier or expert witness.* Comparison by the trier of fact or expert witnesses with specimens which have been authenticated.

(4) *Distinctive characteristics and the like.* Appearance, contents, substance, internal patterns, or other distinctive characteristics, taken in conjunction with circumstances.

(5) *Voice identification.* Identification of a voice, whether heard firsthand or through mechanical or electronic transmission or recording, by opinion based upon hearing the voice at any time under circumstances connecting it with the alleged speaker.

(6) *Telephone conversations.* Telephone conversations, by evidence that a call was made to the number assigned at the time by the telephone company to a particular person or business, if (A) in the case of a person, circumstances, including self-identification, show the person answering to be the one called, or (B) in the case of a business, the call was made to a place of business and the conversation related to business reasonably transacted over the telephone.

(7) *Public records or reports.* Evidence that a writing authorized by law to be recorded or filed and in fact recorded or filed in a public office, or a purported public record, report, statement, or data compilation, in any form, is from the public office where items of this nature are kept.

(8) *Ancient documents or data compilation.* Evidence that a document or data compilation,

in any form, (A) is in such condition as to create no suspicion concerning its authenticity, (B) was in a place where it, if authentic, would likely be, and (C) has been in existence 20 years or more at the time it is offered.

(9) *Process or system.* Evidence describing a process or system used to produce a result and showing that the process or system produces an accurate result.

(10) *Methods provided by statute or rule.* Any method of authentication or identification provided by the laws of the State of Franklin or by other rules prescribed by the Franklin Supreme Court pursuant to statutory authority.

Rule 902. Self-authentication

Extrinsic evidence of authenticity as a condition precedent to admissibility is not required with respect to the following:

(1) *Domestic public documents under seal.* A document bearing a seal purporting to be that of the United States or of any state, district, commonwealth, territory, or insular possession thereof, or the Trust Territory of the Pacific Islands, or of a political subdivision, department, office, or agency thereof, and a signature purporting to be an attestation or execution.

(2) *Domestic public documents not under seal.* A document purporting to bear the signature in the official capacity of an officer or employee of any entity included in paragraph (1) hereof, having no seal, if a public officer having a seal and having official duties in the district or political subdivision of the officer or employee certifies under seal that the signer has the official capacity and that the signature is genuine.

(3) *Foreign public documents.* * * *

(4) *Certified copies of public documents.* A copy of an official record or report or entry therein, or of a document authorized by law to be recorded or filed or actually recorded or filed in a public office, including data compilations in any form, certified as correct by the custodian or other person authorized to make the certification, by a certificate complying with paragraph (1), (2), or (3) of this rule or complying with any law of the State of Franklin or rule prescribed by the Franklin Supreme Court.

(5) *Official publications.* Books, pamphlets, or other publications purporting to be issued by public authority.

(6) *Newspapers and periodicals.* Printed materials purporting to be newspapers or periodicals.

(7) *Trade inscriptions and the like.* * * *

(8) *Acknowledged documents.* * * *

(9) *Commercial paper and related documents.* * * *

(10) *Presumptions under the laws of the State of Franklin.* * * *

(11) *Domestic records of regularly conducted activity accompanied by affidavit.* The original or duplicate of a record of a regularly conducted activity that would be admissible under Franklin Code of Civil Procedure § 1991.

(12) *Certified foreign records of regularly conducted activity.* * * *

* * * *

Rule 1003. Admissibility of Duplicates

A duplicate is admissible to the same extent as an original unless (1) a genuine question is raised as to the authenticity of the original, or (2) in the circumstances it would be unfair to admit the duplicate.

* * * *

Franklin Code of Civil Procedure

§ 1984. Subpoena; notice to produce party or agent; method of service; production of books and documents

(a)   In the case of the production of a party to any civil action or of a person for whose immediate benefit an action is prosecuted or defended or of anyone who is an officer, director, or managing agent of any such party or person, the service of a subpoena upon any such party or person as a witness is not required if written notice requesting the party or person to attend at a trial of an issue therein, with the time and place thereof, is served upon the attorney of that party or person.

(b)   The notice specified in subsection (a) may include a request that the party or person bring with him or her books, documents, or other things. The notice shall state the exact materials or things desired and that the party or person has them in his or her possession or under his or her control. The procedure provided in this subsection is an alternative to the procedures specified in § 1985 but not to those specified in § 1986.

§ 1985. Subpoena defined; affidavit for *subpoena duces tecum*; issuance of subpoena in blank

(a)   The process by which the attendance of a custodian is required is the subpoena. It is a writ or order directed to a person requiring the person's attendance at a particular time and place to testify as a custodian. It may also be a *subpoena duces tecum* and require a custodian to bring any books, documents or other things under the custodian's control that the custodian is bound by law to produce.

(b)   An affidavit shall be served with a *subpoena duces tecum* issued before trial specifying the exact matters and things desired to be produced and stating that the custodian has the desired matters or things in his or her possession or under his or her control.

(c)   The clerk, or a judge, shall issue a subpoena or *subpoena duces tecum* signed and sealed but otherwise in blank to a party requesting it, who shall fill it in before service. Alternatively, an attorney at law who is the attorney of record in an action or proceeding may sign and issue a subpoena or *subpoena duces tecum* to require attendance or to produce matters or things described in the subpoena, before the court in which the action or proceeding is pending or at the trial of an issue therein. The subpoena in such a case need not be sealed.

§ 1986. Employment records; notice to employee of subpoena; motion to quash or modify subpoena

(a)   Not less than 15 days prior to the date called for in a *subpoena duces tecum* for the production of employment records, the subpoenaing party shall either (1) obtain a written authorization signed by the employee to release the records, or (2) serve or cause to be served on the employee whose records are being sought a copy of the *subpoena duces tecum*, the affidavit supporting the issuance of the subpoena, and the notice described in subsection (c). This service shall be made to the employee personally or at his or her last known address.

(b)   Prior to the production of the records, the subpoenaing party shall serve or cause to be served upon the custodian an attestation of compliance with subsection (a).

(c)   Every copy of the *subpoena duces tecum* and affidavit served upon an employee in accordance with subsection (a)(2) shall be accompanied by a notice, in a typeface designed to call attention to the notice, indicating that (1) employment records about the employee are being sought from the custodian named on the subpoena; (2) the employment records may be protected by a right of privacy; (3) if the employee objects to the custodian furnishing the records to the party seeking the records, the employee shall file papers with the court prior to the date specified for production on the subpoena; and (4) if the subpoenaing party does not agree in writing to cancel or limit the subpoena, an attorney should be consulted about the employee's interest in protecting his or her rights of privacy, including the right to bring a motion to quash or limit the subpoena.

* * * *

§ 1990. Compliance with *subpoena duces tecum* for business records of non-parties

(a)   When a *subpoena duces tecum* is served upon a custodian of records of a business in an action in which the business is neither a party nor the place where any cause of action is alleged to have arisen, and the subpoena requires the production of all or any part of the records of the business, it is sufficient compliance therewith if the custodian, within 15 days after the receipt of the subpoena in any civil action, delivers by mail or otherwise a true, legible, and durable copy of all the records described in the subpoena to the clerk of the court together with the affidavit of the custodian stating in substance each of the following:

(1)   The affiant is the duly authorized custodian of the records and has authority to certify the records.

(2)   The copy is a true copy of all the records described in the *subpoena duces tecum.*

(3)   The identity of the records.

(b)   The copy of the records shall be separately enclosed in an inner envelope, sealed, with the title and number of the action and date of the subpoena clearly inscribed thereon; the sealed envelope shall then be enclosed in an outer envelope, sealed, showing the number and title of the action, and directed to the clerk of the court.

(c)   The copy of the records shall remain sealed and shall be opened only at the time of trial, upon the direction of the judge in the presence of all parties who have appeared in person or by counsel at the trial.

§ 1991. Affidavit laying the foundation for admission of business records of non-parties

If the affidavit specified in § 1990(a) contains statements that (1) the records were prepared by the personnel of the business in the ordinary course of business at or near the time of the action, condition, or event, (2) it was the regular practice of that business activity to make the record, (3) describe the mode of preparation of the records, and (4) the original business records would be admissible in evidence if the custodian had been present and testified to the matters stated in the affidavit, then the copy of the records is admissible in evidence. The affidavit is admissible as evidence of the matters stated in the affidavit and is sufficient to meet the requirements of Rule 902(11) of the Franklin Rules of Evidence.

Rivera v. Baldisari Amusement Parks, Inc.
DRAFTERS' POINT SHEET

The applicant works for a firm that represents Cara Rivera, a plaintiff in a personal injury action that is about to go to trial. The supervising partner is concerned that the opposing counsel is going to object on authenticity grounds to the documents and other exhibits he intends to introduce in Ms. Rivera's case in chief. The task assigned to the applicant is to assist the partner in getting the exhibits ready for introduction at the trial.

Specifically, the applicant is asked to write a memorandum spelling out exactly what has to be done to compel production of the documents and exhibits in court for use at trial and to lay the foundation for (i.e., authenticate) them for introduction in evidence. The partner's memo prescribes the format the applicant is expected to use. Applicants are told to assume that all the evidence is relevant and admissible if properly authenticated.

The File consists of the partner's instructing memo, a list of the exhibits in question and a letter-report from an investigator. The Library contains an excerpt from *Walker on Evidence in the Franklin Courts* and sections of the Franklin Rules of Evidence (FRE) and the Franklin Code of Civil Procedure (FCCP) that bear on the task. The *Walker* excerpt is intended to give the applicants a thumbnail sketch of the meaning and intent of the requirement for authenticating trial exhibits, as well as some hints as to the alternative means of producing them in court.

The following discussion covers all of the points the drafters intended to raise in the problem. Applicants need not cover them all to receive passing or even excellent grades. Grading is entirely within the discretion of the graders in the user jurisdictions.

Overview: The applicants' work product should resemble an office memo and should address both questions posed by the partner for each of the items of evidence.

- The items of evidence with which the applicants must deal are described briefly in the Items of Evidence list prepared by the partner, and additional information about some of them is given in the report from John Ripka, the investigator.
  - The applicants will have to pull information from both sources to perform the task.
- As to each item of evidence, the applicants must do the following:
  - Identify the item of evidence they are dealing with;

- State what steps must be taken to compel production of that particular item in court;
- State what needs to be done to establish the authenticity of each item.
    - In connection with these last two steps, the partner's instructions tell them to use the "most direct and efficient" method.
    - As is suggested in *Walker* and as some of the Rules and Code sections provide, there are some time-saving shortcuts available that obviate the need for requiring the attendance of live witnesses and in-court testimony (e.g., alternative means of requiring production of business records).
        - Wherever possible, the applicants are expected to bring those shortcuts to bear.
- Cite to the appropriate sections of the Rules and Code.
    - They can cite these separately at the end of each section or, as is done in this point sheet, include them in the discussion as they go through the foregoing steps.
        - The important thing is that they cite the Rules and the Code discriminatingly, not just randomly throw in a string of citations covering all the possible sections.
- Somewhere in their answers, applicants should refer to FRE 1003 for the proposition that duplicates of documents are admissible to the same extent as originals, barring any question of authenticity.

I. **Frank Electronics' personnel file on Cara Rivera:** According to the partner's Items of Evidence list, this file contains important information relating to the wage and promotion loss Ms. Rivera suffered as a result of her injuries at WWW. The documents are therefore "material" to the issues in the case.

- The situation regarding Ms. Rivera's personnel file is different from that relating to Mr. Spitz's file (*infra*).
    - There are no privacy concerns because Ms. Rivera has put her employment status in issue and she, herself, is requesting production of the file.

- Therefore, the elaborate cross-notice provisions of FCCP § 1986 are inapplicable.
  - In the unlikely event that her employer, Frank Electronics, balks at producing the file, Ms. Rivera's counsel could furnish Frank with a "written authorization signed by the employee to release the records." (FCCP § 1986(b)(2).)
- The personnel file is clearly a "business record" and can be subpoenaed under FCCP § 1990, *et seq.*
  - In this case, counsel can take advantage of the shortcut procedure of having Frank lodge the documents with the court in a sealed envelope; i.e., Frank is neither a party nor a place where the injury occurred.
  - Accordingly, Ms. Rivera's attorney should issue and serve on Frank's custodian a *subpoena duces tecum* with the appropriate supporting affidavit.
    - That would most likely be Nancy Sanders, Frank's Director of Human Resources.
  - There is no need to state in the subpoena that the witness is required to appear in court.
    - Accordingly, Frank can seal and lodge the records as provided in FCCP § 1990 and execute an affidavit that complies with § 1991.
    - The affidavit will serve to authenticate the records. FCCP § 1991.

II. **WWW's personnel file on Brady Spitz:** From the partner's Items of Evidence list and Ripka's report, it is known that the personnel file will show prior incidents of discipline for drinking on the job. Spitz is nowhere to be found. His last known address, however, is available. The information is sufficiently "material" to support a *subpoena duces tecum* (*infra*).

- Because of privacy considerations, the personnel file involves special statutory considerations that must be complied with.

- First, Ms. Rivera's counsel must obtain or issue a *subpoena duces tecum* requiring Baldisari to bring the personnel file to court at the time of trial.
  - The subpoena may be obtained from the court clerk or be issued directly by the requesting attorney. FCCP § 1985(c).
  - Since it is a *subpoena duces tecum*, it must be accompanied by an affidavit specifying the exact matters being sought, the materiality of the matter to the issues in the case, and that the matters are in Baldisari's possession or control. FCCP § 1985(b).
- The fact that it is a personnel file that is being sought has other ramifications:
  - Production in court cannot be compelled by the summary procedure requesting a party to the action to bring the documents to court under FCCP § 1984(b).
  - The affidavit supporting the subpoena must contain specified statements advising the employee whose records are being sought of the fact of the subpoena and his or her rights to object, including the right to bring a motion to limit or quash the subpoena. FCCP § 1986(a) and (c).
  - The subpoena and the affidavit must then be served on the employee either personally or at his or her last known address, observing certain time limits. FCCP § 1986(a).
    - Although it will probably be futile to send the subpoena to Spitz's last known address, Rivera's counsel will have to do it to avoid a challenge to the subpoena by Baldisari.
  - Then, it must be served on Baldisari's "custodian of records" with a proof of service attesting to compliance with all of the foregoing.
- Finally, the *subpoena duces tecum* must require Baldisari's "custodian" to appear in court and bring the personnel file with him/her.
  - This is so even though the personnel file would no doubt qualify as a "business record," which would ordinarily be susceptible to compelling production by the summary procedure set forth in FCCP § 1990, *et seq.*, i.e.,

- Compliance with a *subpoena duces tecum* for business records by submitting copies and an affidavit to the court in a sealed envelope.
- However, this summary procedure is not available here because FCCP § 1990 limits it to a *subpoena duces tecum* served on a custodian where the business is "neither a party nor the place where any cause of action is alleged to have arisen."
  - Here, Baldisari is *both* a party and Baldisari's Amusement Park (WWW) is the place.
- Thus, although it is unlikely that Baldisari will challenge the authenticity of a personnel file from its own records once it has been produced in court, Rivera's counsel will have to go through the motions and elicit the testimony of Baldisari's custodian regarding the business nature of the documents, i.e.,
  - That they were made at or near the time of the occurrence of the matters set forth therein;
  - That they were kept in the course of regularly conducted activity; and
  - That they were made as a regular practice.
  - See FRE 902(11).

III. **State safety inspection report:** The partner's Items of Evidence list and the investigator's report show that this report contains evidence of citations for violations related to the operation and maintenance of the Ferris wheel and evidence of the Department of Public Safety's recommendation for installation of automatic seat-guard locks. The inspection and report were made by Inspector David Steele, and the head of the Department's Bureau of Records is Marta Jones.

- This document is a "public record" and can be authenticated either by calling a sponsoring witness (Steele or Jones) or by getting a certified copy.
  - Again, FRE 902(4) provides that a certified copy suffices to prove the contents of the document.
  - Since getting a certified copy that complies with FRE 902(11) will avoid the necessity of issuing and serving a *subpoena duces tecum*, calling a witness, and examining the witness on the stand, this is the

procedure for which the applicants should opt.

IV. **Baldisari's maintenance records:** It is known from the partner's Items of Evidence list that these records exist and are kept in Baldisari's maintenance department files. They contain correspondence showing that Baldisari declined to purchase the automatic seat-guard locks. They are clearly "material" for purposes of a *subpoena duces tecum*.

- In this case, Ms. Rivera's counsel should issue and serve upon Baldisari's "custodian" of the maintenance records a *subpoena duces tecum* with a supporting affidavit.

- To satisfy the requirement that the affidavit should specify exactly what it seeks production of (FCCP § 1985(b)), it should ask for records that relate to the Ferris wheel "surge" problem experienced by Ms. Rivera and the correspondence relating to the seat-guard locks.

- The subpoena should require the in-court appearance of the custodian.

  - This is axiomatic because, even though the maintenance records are clearly business records (*supra*), the summary procedure of lodging the documents with the court in a sealed envelope is not available under FCCP § 1990 because Baldisari is a party as well as the place (WWW) where the cause of action arose.

  - The custodian would then be examined on the stand as to the bona fides and means of preparation and retention of the records in the ordinary course of business.

V. **Hospital and medical records:** These are the records from the various health care and service providers that rendered services to Ms. Rivera. The expenses are obviously recoverable as damages, and for that reason, the records are material to the issues of the case. They are all business records of the entities that furnished the services. Since the records relate to Ms. Rivera's treatment, there are no privacy concerns such as those that accompany requests for production of third-party medical records.

- Thus, Ms. Rivera's attorney should issue business records *subpoenas duces tecum* and the required supporting affidavits and serve them on the record custodian at Franklin General Hospital, requiring them to lodge with the court the records and affidavit in a sealed envelope. FCCP § 1990 *et seq.*

- The affidavit will serve to authenticate the records from the hospital. FCCP § 1991.

MPT 2: *State v. Miller*

FILE

LIBRARY

State of Franklin
State's Attorney, Williamson County
Courthouse Square
Fairfield City, Franklin 33001

MEMORANDUM

TO: Applicant   February 24, 2004
FROM: Karla Lee, Assistant State's Attorney
RE: *State v. Miller*

Defendant, Tom Miller, is charged with two counts of aggravated assault, which involve domestic violence against Jan Adams. The charges result from actions he took on October 29, 2003, and November 5, 2003. He pleaded not guilty to the charges and the case is set for jury trial.

At a pretrial conference we gave him timely notice, as required by Franklin Rule of Evidence 418E, of our intention to introduce at trial evidence of his three prior acts of violence. He has been convicted of a prior assault upon Jan Adams on February 12, 2003, and one assault upon a minor, Sara Kelly, in the presence of her mother, Jan Adams, on September 21, 2002. We also know of an earlier assault upon Jan Adams on or about July 4, 2001. No charges were ever filed on the July 4, 2001, incident.

Defense counsel objected to the admission of this evidence, claiming that:

- None of the prior incidents constitutes domestic violence under Franklin Penal Code § 501, and therefore, Franklin Rule of Evidence 418 does not apply;
- Each prior incident constitutes inadmissible character evidence under Franklin Rule of Evidence 404A; and
- Even if the evidence is admissible under Franklin Rule of Evidence 404B or 418, the court should exercise its discretion under Franklin Rule of Evidence 403 to exclude the evidence.

Judge Gebippe has ordered both parties to submit concurrent briefs in support of our positions on each objection raised by defense counsel. Please prepare ours. Because of the concurrent filing, we will not have an opportunity to submit a rebuttal brief, so be sure to set forth all our arguments.

State of Franklin
State's Attorney, Williamson County
Courthouse Square
Fairfield City, Franklin 33001

MEMORANDUM　　　　　　　　　　　　　　　　　　　　　　July 1, 2000

TO:　　　Assistant State's Attorneys
FROM:　John Copper, State's Attorney
RE:　　　Persuasive Briefs and Memoranda

To clarify the expectations of the office and to provide guidance to all attorneys, all persuasive briefs or memoranda, such as Memoranda of Points and Authorities, to be filed in state court shall conform to the following guidelines.

All of these documents shall contain a Statement of Facts. Select carefully the facts that are pertinent to the legal arguments. The facts must be stated accurately, although emphasis is not improper. The aim of the Statement of Facts is to persuade the tribunal that the facts support our position.

Following the Statement of Facts, the Argument should begin. This office follows the practice of writing carefully crafted subject headings that illustrate the arguments they cover. The argument heading should succinctly summarize the reasons the tribunal should take the position you are advocating. A heading should be a specific application of a rule of law to the facts of the case and not a bare legal or factual conclusion or statement of an abstract principle. For example, improper: THE WITNESS IS COMPETENT TO TESTIFY. Proper: A FIVE-YEAR-OLD WHO ADMITTED HER MOTHER WOULD NOT PUNISH HER FOR LYING, BUT STILL TESTIFIED SHE KNEW THAT LYING WAS WRONG, IS COMPETENT TO TESTIFY.

The body of each argument should analyze applicable legal authority and persuasively argue how the facts and law support our position. Authority supportive of our position should be emphasized, but contrary authority should generally be cited, addressed in the argument, and explained or distinguished. Do not reserve arguments for reply or supplemental briefs.

Assistants need not prepare a table of contents, a table of cases, or the index. These will be prepared after the draft is approved.

TRANSCRIPT OF INTERVIEW WITH JAN ADAMS
BY DETECTIVE TINA RUIZ

November 15, 2003

Det. Ruiz: Good Afternoon, Ms. Adams. I am Tina Ruiz, the detective assigned to this case. I know you have already talked to the police about this, so I ask your patience as we go through it again.

Ms. Adams: That's okay. I understand.

Q: You've said it's okay for me to tape record this, right?

A: Yeah, that's okay.

Q: Let's start with some background information. Where do you live?

A: Fairfield City, here in Franklin.

Q: Tell me about Tom Miller.

A: He and I met in June 2001.

Q: How would you describe your relationship?

A: It was a close, personal relationship. I guess you would call it intimate. We lived together. I even added Tom to the lease and we shared expenses for almost a year. That was until the end of September 2002.

Q: In September 2002, what happened?

R: I moved out of the apartment with my daughter, Sara. She was six years old at the time. Anyway, on October 1, 2002, we moved into a different apartment in Fairfield City.

Q: Did Mr. Miller move with you and Sara?

A: No, but Tom and I had planned to move together. In fact, he helped choose the new apartment and we split the cost of the security deposit. We also had keys made for both of us. Then we had a fight and split up. Sara and I moved without Tom, but I never got the key back from him.

Q: So, Mr. Miller didn't live with you after you moved on October 1, 2002, right?

A: That's right.

Q: And, how about a year later in October 2003? He wasn't living with you then either, was he?

A: No, he wasn't.

Q: Now I know this may be difficult, but we need to review what happened a few weeks ago. Can you tell me what happened on October 29, 2003?

A: Tom came to the apartment and let himself in. My daughter, Sara, was at school and after lunch, I decided to take a nap so I went to bed. Then, around 2:30 in the afternoon, I heard someone come into the apartment. It was Tom.

Q: Then what happened?

A: He came into my bedroom and swore at me, and yelled at me to get up off the bed. He was real mad.

Q: Did he say why he was angry?

A: He said he found out that I'd been talking to my ex-husband, Charles Kelly, Sara's dad.

Q: What happened after Mr. Miller yelled at you?

A: He ordered me to get Charles on the phone. Tom grabbed the phone from me and started yelling at Charles and cursing him over the phone. He told Charles to stay away from me or else he'd regret it. He kept saying, "There'll be trouble." Tom has always been jealous of my relationship with Charles. I've always felt that Tom's hatred of Charles makes him resent Sara. He knows it hurts me when he takes it out on Sara.

Q: Getting back to October 29, 2003, what else happened?

A: I told him I had had enough and I didn't want to see him anymore. Then, he slapped me so hard I hit my head against the wall. He warned me that if I reported him to the police and he went to jail, "When I get out, I'm going to kill you and your precious little Sara." Then he left.

Q: What did you do?

A: Well, about then Sara came home from school. I called Mr. Liang—that's the apartment manager—and asked him to change the locks.

Q: Did you see Mr. Miller again?

A: Yes, about a week later. He came back around 1:00 A.M. on November 5, 2003, pounding on my door and window, making noises, yelling for me to let him in.

Q: Did you let him in?

A: No way. Mr. Liang apparently told Tom to leave the property. I guess he heard all the commotion. Anyway, Tom left, but about two hours later, Tom called the apartment, telling me to open the door. He must have called three or four times over a couple of hours.

Q: Did you talk with him?

A: No, I let the answering machine take the messages. I knew it was Tom, though. I have caller ID and it was his phone number and it was his voice on the machine. No doubt about that.

Q: Did he say anything else?

A: Yeah, he told me that I would regret sending him away, and that I had better let him in or else, and that I would find out what he could do to me and Sara if I called the police again. In the last call, he told me he would never allow me to leave him, and said, "You're my woman until I say so." Those were his exact words on the answering machine.

Q: After the phone calls, what happened?

A: About two hours after his last telephone call, I heard a crash in Sara's room. I went in there and saw a great big rock and glass all over the floor. I looked out and saw Tom standing there. The next day I went to a women's crisis center for help in getting a restraining order, and I gave a statement to a police officer. By the way, have you spoken to Tom?

Ruiz: Very briefly. He pretty quickly asked for a lawyer.

Adams: I assume he denies everything.

Ruiz: Absolutely, denies he did it, says it was probably Charles who threw the rock. Was October 29, 2003, the first time you had trouble like this with Mr. Miller?

A: No. He had caused trouble for me before, that was why we broke up when we were moving.

Q: Tell me about that.

A: On September 21, 2002, I remember the date. That's when I asked him to pack his stuff and leave because he had yelled at Sara and pushed her against a wall.

Q: What happened?

A: Sara had been sick and when she is sick, she gets whiny and tired and cranky and Tom can't stand her then. So he got mad at her and told her to quit whining. She said she wasn't whining, and he told her to shut up and listen to him and then he pushed her into the wall. Then he left the apartment.

Q: What did you do?

A: I called the police. I thought that it would teach him a lesson. That's when I told him he was not moving with us.

Q: On this date in September when he pushed Sara, did Mr. Miller hurt you?

A: No, but I could not stand to see Sara get hurt. That was when I drew the line. I told him to get out.

Q: Was there another time when he hurt you?

A: On February 12, 2003, he came over. He was about to go to court for the incident where he pushed Sara. He wanted me to change my story and drop the charges.

Q: What happened?

A: I said there was nothing I could do about it because the prosecuting attorney told me that it was in the state's hands now. Tom got real mad and pushed me against the wall and stuck his finger in my eye and hit me in the face and choked me. He said that I would live to wish I had never called the police. Finally, he left and I called the police. About an hour after the police left, a rock broke my living room window. I was in the bedroom at the time and I heard this crashing noise. I went into the living room and saw that the window was broken. Then I saw Tom's car leaving the driveway immediately afterwards.

Q: Were you hurt when the rock came in the house?

A: No. I was in the bedroom and there is no way he could have hit me from outside when I was in the bedroom.

Q: Was there any other time when he hurt you?

A: Wait a minute! I just remembered! Right after we started dating—we'd been going out a few weeks—we'd been at a bar with a lot of friends. This was July 4—three years ago. As we were leaving, we were in the parking lot, everyone started talking and arguing. Someone asked Tom what it was like to date Charles' woman and Tom got really mad and pushed me, pushed me hard. I fell.

Q: What happened after that?

A: Nothing, really. Mike, one of my friends, took me home. I didn't call the police or anything like that.

Q: Tom was convicted for both the September 2002 assault on Sara and the February 2003 assault on you, right?

A: Yes.

Q: But he wasn't charged or convicted for what happened on July 4, 2001, in the parking lot?

A: That's right.

Q: Can you add anything else to what you have told me?

A: No, except that this has been so horrible. I'm scared for Sara and I guess, I'm scared for me, too.

Franklin Penal Code

§ 211. Aggravated Assault

A person is guilty of aggravated assault if the person:

(a) attempts to cause serious bodily injury to another, or causes such injury purposely, knowingly or recklessly under circumstances manifesting extreme indifference to the value of human life; or

(b) attempts to cause or purposely or knowingly causes bodily injury to another with a deadly weapon.

* * * *

§ 501. Domestic Violence—Definitions

As used in this title:

(a) "Abuse" means intentionally or recklessly causing or attempting to cause a person bodily injury, or placing a person in reasonable apprehension of imminent serious bodily injury.

(b) "Domestic violence" means abuse committed by an individual against an adult or a fully emancipated minor who is a spouse, former spouse, cohabitant, former cohabitant, or person with whom the individual has had a child or is having or has had a dating or engagement relationship. For purposes of this subsection, "cohabitant" means two unrelated adult persons living together for a substantial period of time, resulting in some permanency of the relationship. Factors that may determine whether persons are cohabiting include a combination of circumstances, such as (1) sexual relations between the parties while sharing the same living quarters, (2) sharing of income or expenses, (3) joint use or ownership of property, (4) the parties' holding themselves out as husband and wife, (5) the continuity of the relationship, and (6) the length of the relationship.

Franklin Rules of Evidence

Rule 403. Discretion of court to exclude evidence

The court in its discretion may exclude evidence if its probative value is substantially outweighed by the probability that its admission will (a) necessitate undue consumption of time or (b) create substantial danger of undue prejudice, of confusing the issues, or of misleading the jury.

Rule 404. Evidence of character to prove conduct

A. Evidence of a person's character or a trait of his or her character (whether in the form of an opinion, evidence of reputation, or evidence of specific instances of his or her conduct) is inadmissible when offered to prove his or her conduct on a specified occasion.

B. Evidence of past crimes, civil wrongs, or other acts is not admissible to prove the character of a person in order to show action in conformity therewith. It may, however, be admissible for other purposes such as proof of motive, opportunity, intent, preparation, common plan, identity, or absence of mistake or accident.

* * * *

Rule 418. Evidence of past instances of specified offenses

A. Subject to subsections D and E, in a criminal action in which the defendant is accused of a sexual offense, evidence of the defendant's commission of another sexual offense or offenses is not made inadmissible by Rule 404.

B. Subject to subsections D and E, in a criminal action in which the defendant is accused of an offense involving domestic violence, evidence of the defendant's commission of other domestic violence is not made inadmissible by Rule 404.

C. As used in this section, "domestic violence" has the meaning set forth in § 501 of the Franklin Penal Code.

D. Nothing in this section shall be admissible if a court pursuant to Rule 403 deems it inadmissible.

E. When a party in a criminal action intends to introduce evidence pursuant to subsection A or B above, the party intending to introduce the evidence must give the defendant notice of its intent thirty (30) days prior to the trial of the criminal action.

State v. Grubb

Franklin Supreme Court (1990)

The defendant, Brian K. Grubb, was charged with assault and battery on his wife, Kelly Grubb. The defendant denied assaulting his wife and testified at trial that she assaulted him. On rebuttal, Deidra Hoskins, defendant's ex-wife, testified over defendant's objection that she had been assaulted by the defendant on two occasions. Defendant was convicted of assault and battery and now appeals, claiming that the court erred in allowing his ex-wife to testify.

Franklin Rule of Evidence 404A codifies the general rule that evidence of a person's character is not admissible for the purpose of proving that the person acted in conformity with his character on a particular occasion. Offering evidence of a person's character poses an inherent risk that the trier of fact will be distracted from the central issues in the case and decide the case based upon the defendant's character rather than upon the operative facts. Character evidence is generally excluded not because it lacks relevancy, but because its probative value is substantially outweighed by the danger of unfair prejudice.

Franklin Rule of Evidence 404B, however, allows other prior acts to be admissible for other purposes, such as proof of motive, opportunity, intent, preparation, plan, knowledge, identity, or absence of mistake or accident.

Defendant claimed self-defense. He also testified to an alternative, albeit somewhat inconsistent, defense of lack of intent to cause harm or accident. Specifically, Grubb testified that it was his wife who jumped on him (not vice versa) and that he simply grabbed her and pulled her off. He said that he did not assault her nor did he cause her any injury. He further testified that if she did sustain injuries, they occurred when he tried to pull her off him or when she jumped on him and they fell down the stairs.

When an accused asserts self-defense, he does not seek to negate any of the elements of the offense that the state is required to prove. Self-defense is not a denial or contradiction of evidence offered by the state to prove the essential elements of the charged crime. Rather, an accused admits the prohibited conduct, but claims that the surrounding facts or circumstances justified the conduct, therefore excusing the accused from criminal liability. In cases where the accused asserts only self-defense and accordingly does not deny or contradict the essential elements of the charged crime, the state cannot properly utilize prior crimes, wrongs, or acts by the accused to establish his intent, or demonstrate that the injuries suffered by his victim were not the result of accident, as such matters are uncontested and simply not in issue.

However, in this case Grubb not only asserted a claim of self-defense, but also alleged that his wife's injuries were accidental and not the result of any intentional (or knowing) conduct on his part. To that extent, intent and absence of accident, two matters specifically identified in Rule 404B, were at issue in this case. Accordingly, the state was entitled to utilize the evidence regarding defendant's assaults on his former wife to meet its burden of proving that Grubb intended to injure his wife and that her injuries were not accidental.

Judgment affirmed.

State v. Beck

Franklin Court of Appeal (2002)

Defendant Bill Beck appeals from his conviction for aggravated assault. He claims that, at his trial, prior acts of domestic violence were admitted over his objection. He concedes that Franklin Rule of Evidence 418B permits the admission of prior instances of domestic violence as relevant evidence, but he claims that the probative value of their admission was substantially outweighed by the prejudice to him.

On December 3, 1999, Sue Beck was leaving a grocery store when Bill Beck met her at her car and demanded that she give him a ride. The Becks were married for three years as of December 3, 1999, but were living apart on that date. Sue Beck took Bill Beck to her home so he could call a cab. Once there, Bill Beck began slapping Sue Beck on the face and upper body and yelling at her. He accused her of cheating on him. Finally, he struck several hard blows to her face and walked out. She called the police.

At trial, Sue Beck testified to prior instances of domestic violence. Specifically, she testified that on May 31, 1998, while they were living together, Bill Beck was arrested after he slapped Sue on her face and hit her on her upper body at their home earlier that day. Sue also testified that on November 25, 1998, they were again living together. On that date, Bill came home from work and accused her of seeing other men. He then struck her on the face and upper body with his fist. She fell

down due to the blows. He walked out. After a few minutes, Sue called the police. She testified that they have been separated since November 25, 1998.

On January 17, 1999, Bill Beck pleaded guilty to the assaults of May 31 and November 25, 1998, and was sentenced to time served and placed on probation for six months. At the trial for the December 3, 1999 incident, Bill Beck admitted pleading guilty to the prior charges but said his lawyer told him it was the only way to stay out of jail.

Defendant asserts, correctly, that Rule of Evidence 418D makes the admissibility of evidence of prior domestic violence under Rule 418B contingent on whether the evidence is more probative than prejudicial under Rule 403. Rule 403 requires a weighing of certain specific factors: (1) an examination of the nature, relevance and possible remoteness of each such offense; (2) the degree of certainty of its commission; (3) the burden on the defendant of defending against the uncharged offense; (4) the likelihood of confusing, misleading or distracting the jurors from their main inquiry; and (5) its likely prejudicial impact on the jurors.

The weighing process under Rule of Evidence 403 depends upon the trial court's consideration of the unique facts and issues of each case. We will not overturn or disturb a trial court's exercise of its discretion under Rule

403 in the absence of manifest abuse or unless we find that its decision was arbitrary and capricious.

The prior incidents of domestic abuse introduced in this case were of the same nature and displayed a pattern of abuse, all within the eighteen months prior to the crime for which Bill Beck was charged. The past instances, to which he pleaded guilty, were very similar to and were no more egregious than the charged offense. There is no question about their commission, nor must Bill Beck defend against them, having already admitted them. Thus, there is little reason to believe that the jury will be confused, misled, distracted, or unduly prejudiced by this evidence.

The judgment of the trial court is affirmed.

13

State v. Miller
DRAFTERS' POINT SHEET

In this performance test item, the applicant is employed by the State's Attorney and is assisting in the prosecution of the defendant, Tom Miller. Mr. Miller is charged with two domestic violence offenses against Jan Adams, the woman with whom he had previously cohabited, and her grade-school-age daughter, Sara Kelly. Miller was previously convicted of separate assaults against Jan Adams and Sara. According to Adams, in another incident very early in their relationship, Miller had assaulted her, but was never charged for that incident.

The State's Attorney, in compliance with Franklin Rule of Evidence (FRE) 418E, served notice on Miller's attorney that it intended to introduce evidence of the three prior acts of violence at defendant's trial. Defense counsel raised three objections, and the judge ordered the parties to submit concurrent briefs on the issues raised in defense counsel's objections.

Applicants' task is to write the brief. The File contains the instructional memo from the supervising State's Attorney, which sets forth defense counsel's three objections, an office memo prescribing the format and contents of briefs and memoranda, and a transcript of a police detective's interview with Jan Adams. The Library contains various sections of the Franklin Rules of Evidence and the Franklin Penal Code as well as two appellate cases bearing on the subject.

The following discussion covers all of the points the drafters intended to raise in the problem. Applicants need not cover them all to receive passing or even excellent grades. Grading is entirely within the discretion of the graders in the user jurisdictions.

I.   Overview: The task is to write a persuasive brief arguing that evidence of Miller's prior acts of violence is admissible against him under the appropriate statutes. The work product should resemble a brief that follows the instructions in the office memo Re: Persuasive Briefs and Memoranda, including a statement of facts and arguments preceded by expositive section headings.

The applicants should address each of the objections:

- That none of the prior incidents constitutes domestic violence under Franklin Penal Code § 501, and therefore, FRE 418B does not apply;

- That each prior incident constitutes inadmissible character evidence under FRE 404A; and

- That, even if the evidence is admissible under FRE 404B or 418B, the court should exercise its discretion under FRE 403 to exclude the evidence.

II. **Statement of Facts:** Some applicants may wish to set forth the facts at length. Others may wish to state only enough facts to set the scene and import other facts as necessary into their arguments. Either way is acceptable as long as the Statement of Facts adequately informs the court of the nature of the case and the issues.

The following chronology of facts might be included in the Statement:

- Tom Miller and Jan Adams met in June 2001.

- Jan Adams has a grade-school-age daughter, Sara Kelly, whose father is Charles Kelly.

- After they met, Miller and Adams lived together in an "intimate" relationship for almost a year. They were cotenants on the lease of their apartment and shared expenses.

- As early as July 4, 2001, in an incident outside a bar, Miller became angry about a remark someone made about Adams' being "Charles' woman" and shoved Adams to the ground. Adams' friend, Mike, took her home after the incident.

- This incident was not reported to the police, and Miller was not charged.

- On September 21, 2002, Miller became angry with Sara because she was "whining," and he yelled at her and pushed her against the wall. Adams told Miller to pack up and get out. Adams reported this incident to the police.

- Adams and Sara moved to another apartment that she and Miller had been planning to move to; Miller had a key to the new apartment.

- On February 12, 2003, when Miller was getting ready to go to court regarding the September 21 incident, he went to Adams' apartment and tried to convince her to change her story and drop the charges. When she refused, Miller pushed her against the wall, stuck his finger in her eye, hit her in the face and choked her. Miller left and Adams called the police.

- About an hour after the police left, Adams heard a crash in her living room. She found a rock and a broken window. She saw Miller's car leaving the driveway immediately afterwards.

- On October 29, 2003, Miller let himself into the apartment, found Adams in the bedroom, and began yelling in a jealous rage because he heard she had been "talking with Charles Kelly."

- When Adams told Miller she did not want to see him anymore, he slapped her so hard that she hit her head on the wall.

- As he was leaving, Miller warned Adams he would "kill you and your precious little Sara" if she reported the incident to the police.

- Adams believes that Miller's hatred of Charles Kelly makes him resent Sara and that, "He knows it hurts me when he takes it out on Sara."

- On November 5, 2003, Miller showed up at Adams' apartment at about 1:00 A.M. and began yelling and pounding on the door until the landlord commanded him to leave.

- In the next couple of hours, Miller phoned and left messages on Adams' answering machine threatening dire consequences if she called the police again. Miller said, "You're my woman until I say so."

- About two hours after Miller's last phone call, Adams heard a crash in Sara's room. There, she found a large rock and glass on the floor. She looked out of the window and saw Miller standing there. Adams reported this incident to the police.

III.   Argument: Applicants' arguments should address each of defense counsel's objections. One format is for each *objection* to be the subject of a separate heading followed by argument relating to that heading. Alternatively, applicants can organize their briefs by each *incident* and then respond to defense counsel's objections as they relate to the particular incident. The applicants are expected to merge the facts and the law to make a persuasive argument. The headings appearing below are exemplars only and are not intended as the *only* acceptable headings.

- THE FEBRUARY 12, 2003, INCIDENT IS ADMISSIBLE AS AN INCIDENT OF DOMESTIC VIOLENCE UNDER FRE 418B.[1]

    - The February 12, 2003, incident: This is the incident in which Miller beat Adams because she refused to "drop the charges," threatened her for having called the police, and threw a rock through her living room window. He was

---

[1]Somewhere in their briefs, applicants should recognize that the other two incidents (especially the incident involving Sara) probably do *not* qualify as "domestic violence" under § 501 and FRE 418. For these two incidents, applicants should argue that they are admissible under FRE 404B. This discussion follows below.

convicted for this offense.

- This incident satisfies all the definitional requisites for domestic violence under Penal Code § 501(b):
  - It is unclear exactly when Miller and Adams began living together. She says they had lived together "for almost a year" and that they separated in September 2002. Thus, they had probably lived together from September 2001 to September 2002, which by any measure was a sufficiently long relationship under § 501(b). By February 2003, they had been living apart for five months, but they were nonetheless "former cohabitants."
  - They lived in an "intimate" relationship (which means they probably had sexual relations) while living in the same apartment; they shared expenses; both were "on the lease," thus satisfying the joint use of property factor; and, apparently, the relationship was a continuous one.
  - The passage of a mere five months from the time of their separation does not render the incident so remote in time as to divorce it from their former cohabitational relationship.
  - Accordingly, it is admissible under FRE 418B as domestic violence, irrespective of FRE 404.
    - To be sure, it is still subject to the court's discretion under FRE 403. (See *infra*.)
- The September 21, 2002, incident is admissible under FRE 404B: This is the incident in which Miller became angry with Sara and shoved her against the wall. He was convicted for this offense.
  - This, too, occurred after Miller and Adams had been living together for a year and all the cohabitation factors recited in § 501(b) were present.
  - The difficulty with trying to cast it as "domestic violence" is that it does not meet the definitions.

- Section 501(b) requires that the "abuse" be committed against an adult or fully emancipated minor. Sara was then six years old.
- Notwithstanding that Adams says Miller took things out on Sara only as a way of hurting Adams (i.e., emotionally injuring Adams), it does not meet the definition of "abuse" under § 501(a), which requires "bodily injury."
- Thus, this incident is probably not admissible under FRE 418B, but would be under FRE 404B. (See *infra*.)

- The July 4, 2001, incident: This is the incident in which Miller became angry over the "Charles' woman" remark and shoved Adams to the ground in the parking lot. It was not reported to the police, and he was not charged with an offense.
  - This is probably not an incident of domestic violence.
    - Miller and Adams had not yet begun cohabiting.
    - According to Adams, it happened "right after we started dating." Although this fact *might* bring it within the § 501(b) rubric of abuse against one with whom "the suspect . . . has had a dating . . . relationship," the relationship was incipient at the time, and none of the § 501(b) factors is present.
    - However, applicants could make a persuasive argument here that a "dating relationship" existed and argue that the dating relationship alone is a basis for classifying this incident as one of domestic violence under § 501, therefore making the evidence admissible under FRE 418B.
    - The better course of action is to argue admissibility under FRE 418B, but in the alternative under FRE 404B.

- THE INCIDENT OF FEBRUARY 12, 2003, IS ADMISSIBLE IRRESPECTIVE OF WHETHER IT IS CHARACTER EVIDENCE, AND THE SEPTEMBER 21, 2002, AND THE JULY 4, 2001, INCIDENTS ARE ADMISSIBLE UNDER FRE 404B TO SHOW MOTIVE, INTENT, OR COMMON PLAN.

- As shown above, the February 12 incident is clearly an incident of domestic violence and is admissible irrespective of FRE 404.[2]
  - And, in any event, it is a past crime (Miller was convicted of it) that can be used to show motive, opportunity, intent, and common plan under 404B: "Evidence of past crimes, civil wrongs, or other acts . . . may, however, be admissible for other purposes such as proof of motive, opportunity, intent, preparation, common plan, identity, or absence of mistake or accident."
  - In either case, it remains subject to the court's discretion under FRE 403. (See *infra*.)
- Even if it is determined that the September 21 incident does not qualify as an incident of domestic violence (*supra*), it is a past crime (Miller was convicted of it) that can be admitted to show motive, opportunity, intent, and common plan.
- Applicants could argue any of the following or any of the alternative purposes listed in 404B, provided they support their arguments:
  - Motive: Miller knows it hurts Adams when he takes his anger out on Sara. He is also deeply distrustful of Adams' relationship with Charles Kelly, Sara's dad, and because of this, he resents Sara and his violent outburst reflects that hostility. Miller also wants to exert power and control over Adams by being violent with her and Sara.
  - Common plan: Miller has repeatedly sought to control and intimidate Adams by threats and violence against her and Sara.
  - Intent: Miller has denied all allegations against him. Therefore, the State has to prove all the elements of the assault charges, including that he intended to cause injury in the 10/29/03 and 11/4/03 incidents. His violent "pushing" is relevant to proving his intent to cause injury.
  - Again, admission of this evidence is subject to the court's discretion under FRE 403.

---

[2]FRE 404A prohibits admission of character evidence to prove propensity. FRE 404B's first sentence prohibits the admission of other acts to prove propensity.

- The July 4 incident is also admissible under FRE 404B.

  - The difference is that Miller was not convicted of this incident and has denied it.

  - However, it is still a past *wrong* or *act* and should be admitted to show any of the listed acceptable purposes under FRE 404B. FRE 404B does not limit other acts to those resulting in convictions.

- Applicants could argue any of the following or any of the alternative purposes listed in FRE 404B, provided they support their arguments:

  - Motive: Defendant's jealousy over Adams' relationship with Charles Kelly fueled his violence against Adams. He also tried to assert power and control over Adams using violence with her and threats of violence.

  - Common plan: This was the first of several violent outbursts directed at Adams (and Sara) that Miller used to intimidate and control Adams.

  - Intent: Such violent outbursts were intended to cause harm—they were not done in self-defense or as a result of an accident.

    - Admission of this evidence is subject to the court's discretion under FRE 403. (See *infra*.)

- IN EXERCISING ITS DISCRETION UNDER FRE 403 AND 418, THE COURT SHOULD CONCLUDE THAT ADMISSION OF THE EVIDENCE WILL NOT UNDULY CONSUME TIME OR CREATE A SUBSTANTIAL DANGER OF UNDUE PREJUDICE.

  - Applicants should remind the court that it has very broad discretion in these matters and that it will be reversed only in cases of "manifest abuse." *State v. Beck.*

  - Here, applicants should address the *Beck* factors in light of each of the three incidents:

    - The February 12, 2003, incident (beating Adams because she would not drop the charges) falls under FRE 418 and is a prior conviction.

    - The September 21, 2002, incident (assaulting Sara) probably doesn't fall under FRE 418 but is also a prior conviction.

- The July 4, 2001, incident (shoving Adams to the ground in the parking lot) might be, but is probably not, a domestic violence violation and is not a prior conviction.

- The test the court is required to apply to protect a defendant's due process right to a fair trial is discussed best in *State v. Beck*. Applicants should apply these factors based on the available facts.

  - The nature, relevance, and remoteness of the event.
  - The degree of certainty that the defendant committed the offense.
  - The burden placed on the defendant of defending against uncharged offenses.
  - The risk of confusing or misleading the jurors.
  - The prejudicial impact on the jurors.

- The February 12, 2003, incident: This is the incident in which Miller beat Adams severely because she refused to drop the charges and he threw a rock through her living room window.

  - In its nature, it is very similar to the October 29 and November 5, 2003, incidents with which he is currently being charged.
    - It is similar to the abuse he engaged in on October 29.
    - It involves the same threats about what he would do if she called the police.
    - At that time, he also threw a rock through a window (then it was through the living room window; on November 5, it was through Sara's bedroom window, a difference without a distinction).
  - Its relevance is that it shows Miller's propensity and a pattern of domestic violence.
  - It is not remote either in time or in place. It occurred at the same apartment just seven months or so before the current October 29 offense.
  - There is no doubt that Miller committed the act. He was convicted,

so it will not unduly consume time at the trial in proving it.

- Miller has denied the current charges; admission of the evidence of the prior conviction will *help* rather than hinder the jury in confirming that it is Miller's modus operandi. Moreover, it is a prior conviction, as to which there cannot be any confusion.

- It will not create a substantial risk of prejudice on the jurors because it is a crime of the same kind (certainly no worse) than that with which he is currently charged.

- The September 21, 2002, incident: This is the one in which Miller shoved Sara against the wall.

  - In its nature and relevance are that it is similar to the November 5 rock-throwing incident in that it illustrates his animus toward Sara. Moreover, this is the incident that led to the February 12 beating of Adams, i.e., he beat her because she refused to drop the charges for the assault on Sara.

  - It is not remote either in time or in place because it occurred a little over a year ago in the apartment where Adams and Miller were living together.

  - There is no question of certainty that Miller committed the earlier assault against Sara because he was convicted. It will not unduly consume time at the trial to prove it using Adams' testimony, nor will it confuse the jury.

  - Admission of the incident will not create a substantial risk of undue prejudice because it is not significantly worse than the pending offense (throwing a rock through the child's bedroom window, a place he knew would be occupied by the child late at night because he knew the layout of the apartment).

- The July 4, 2001, incident: This is the one in which Miller shoved Adams to the ground over the "Charles' woman" remark.

  - In its nature and relevance, it is similar to the October 29 incident with which Miller is now charged. On October 29, he raged against

Adams and slapped her so hard that she hit her head against the wall because he was jealous that Adams had been talking with Charles Kelly. That same rage and jealousy precipitated the earlier July incident in the parking lot.

- Although he was never charged or convicted for the parking lot incident, it is a past act that can come in under FRE 404B to show any of the purposes listed.

- The fact that it is an uncharged offense will necessarily involve some consumption of time at trial. However, putting forth evidence of this incident is not qualitatively different from putting forth evidence of the incident for which Miller was convicted. Here, in addition to Adams' testimony, Adams' friend, Mike, could also testify that he saw the incident. Mike took her home after Miller pushed her.

- It will not confuse the jurors to hear this evidence. Rather, it will help them understand the impact that Miller's jealousy had on his behavior toward Adams.

  - Moreover, Miller has denied the current charges, so it is appropriate that evidence of past similar acts be admitted under FRE 404B provided that the court can do so within the strictures of FRE 403. *State v. Grubb.*

- Admission of this evidence will not unduly prejudice the jurors because the July 4 incident is not nearly as egregious as the charges Miller currently faces. *State v. Beck.*

- Therefore, the court should admit the evidence of all three past incidents.

Graham Realty, Inc. v. Brenda Chapin

FILE

LIBRARY

The Legal Aid Society
Briggs Neighborhood Office
Civil Division
Avon, Franklin 33210

To: Applicant
From: Joseph Murray, Supervising Attorney
Date: July 27, 2004
Re: *Graham Realty, Inc. v. Brenda Chapin*

Our client, Brenda Chapin, is a tenant living in an apartment owned by Graham Realty, Inc. (GRI). She has withheld her monthly rent of $1,000 for seven months because of the poor condition of her apartment. GRI is suing her for eviction and recovery of back rent. We have tried to settle the matter, but negotiations have broken off because of GRI's refusal to make any concessions regarding much-needed repairs in our client's apartment and the common areas of the building. The matter is set to be heard next week before the Housing Division Court.

To successfully defend against GRI's suit for eviction and recovery of back rent, we will have to prove that GRI breached the implied warranty of habitability. Assuming that we can prove such a breach, we also intend to seek damages available to Ms. Chapin as a result of GRI's breach.

Please draft a case planning memo for the summary eviction proceeding before the Housing Division Court. Citing the relevant legal authority, your memo should identify:

1) the elements we must establish to prove that GRI breached the implied warranty of habitability and the evidence available to establish these elements; and

2) the remedies available to Ms. Chapin, the elements of those remedies, and the evidence available to us to establish those elements. (You need not concern yourself with admissibility issues.)

You should also discuss whether there is any relief that Ms. Chapin might be entitled to pursue that *cannot* be obtained in this summary proceeding. If there is, state what it is and explain why.

Follow our office's "Case Planning Memorandum Guidelines" in drafting your memo. These guidelines include an excerpt of a case planning memorandum used in an unrelated case. As the guidelines instruct, do not include a separate statement of facts because here at the Legal Aid Society, these memos are strictly internal documents used to prepare for court.

The Legal Aid Society March 4, 2003

Case Planning Memorandum Guidelines

Our office follows the practice of using a case planning memorandum (CPM) to prepare for court. A CPM is an internal document that identifies and evaluates, as applicable, the client's claims, counterclaims, defenses, and/or remedies. For each of these, cite the **Legal Authority**, including statutory and case law as applicable; the **Elements** that must be proven in order to establish the client's right to prevail; and the **Supporting Evidence** available to establish each element, including testimonial evidence, documentary evidence, and physical evidence.

A CPM should not include a separate statement of facts, as it is intended as a reference tool for attorneys already familiar with the case. Attached as an example is an excerpt from a CPM drafted for _Jimenez v. Brown Apartments_, a case we litigated in January 2002.

Excerpt from *Jimenez* Case Planning Memorandum

Claim: Breach of Franklin Fair Housing Law/Unlawful Housing Discrimination

Legal Authority: Section 530 of the Franklin Fair Housing Law prohibits a landlord from rejecting a prospective tenant's rental application solely because the application does not meet a particular income-to-rent ratio. A landlord's rejection of an application, notwithstanding the tenant's proof of actual ability to pay, is prima facie evidence of a violation of this section. *(Mooney v. Lutz Management Co.)*

Element #1: The landlord refused to lease residential premises to a prospective tenant because the tenant did not meet the minimum income-to-rent ratio.

Evidence available to show Brown Apartments refused to rent to David Jimenez based on his income level:
- Testimony of Jimenez that he completed Brown's standard rental application form, including providing information about his income.
- Copy of the application Jimenez submitted to Brown.
- Copy of Brown's standard rental application form, stating (in very fine print) that all tenants must have monthly income equal to four times monthly rent.
- Letter from Brown rejecting Jimenez's rental application.

Element #2: The prospective tenant established actual ability to pay rental amount.

Evidence available to show Jimenez's actual ability to pay rent charged by Brown:
- Jimenez's bank statement showing $5,000 in savings account.
- Written financial reference from previous landlord.

Remedy: Punitive Damages

Legal Authority: A court will award punitive damages to a tenant for a violation of § 530 when such conduct is a pervasive practice by a landlord. *(Chong v. Riverside Apartments, LLC*—punitive damages upheld where landlord exhibited repeated disregard for the rights accorded tenants under § 530)

Element: The landlord's pervasive practice is to reject applicants based on income level without considering actual ability to pay rent.

Evidence available to prove that Brown's pervasive practice violates § 530:
- Copy of Brown's standard rental application form.
- Testimony of Brown's rental agent that the standard rental application form is used for *all* prospective tenants in Brown's five high-rise complexes in Avon.
- Copy of Brown's rental agent manual, which states that "rental agents must screen each prospective tenant for compliance with minimum income requirements using payroll statements only. . . ."

The Legal Aid Society
Briggs Neighborhood Office
Civil Division
Avon, Franklin 33210

To: File
From: Virginia Eilson, Intake Officer
Date: July 26, 2004
Re: Intake Notes: *Graham Realty, Inc. v. Brenda Chapin*

I interviewed Brenda Chapin, who has retained us to represent her in the summary eviction proceeding that is pending against her, *Graham Realty, Inc. v. Brenda Chapin.*

Client resides at Graham Towers, on the seventh floor in apartment 7B. Graham Towers is owned by Graham Realty, Inc. (GRI). When client moved into the apartment a year ago, some repairs were needed. She doesn't want to move if the apartment is repaired. "The housing market is so tight that I don't think I can find anything that would be better than this place at the price, but I want it to be fixed up." Client says her block is becoming "fancier." Herb London, GRI's building manager, told Ms. Albert, the owner of the grocery store at the corner and a friend of Ms. Chapin, that GRI wants to cash in on these apartments.

Client has about two years left on a 3-year lease at $1,000 per month. Utilities are not included in the rent. Graham Towers is a large and very old apartment building in the Briggs section of Avon. The apartment consists of two bedrooms, a living room, bathroom, and kitchen.

Client lives in the apartment with her two daughters, Harriett, age 3, and Mary, age 14. Her husband passed away two years ago. She was initially shown the apartment by Herb London. At that time, she noticed some of the repairs that were needed. Mr. London assured her that the repairs would be made, and she signed the lease. She paid rent for five months, but repairs weren't made and things got worse. Beginning in January 2004, client stopped paying her rent to try and force the owner to make the needed repairs.

Now GRI is suing to evict her and to collect the $7,000 in back rent.

Client complains that the bathroom ceiling leaks. A few chunks of plaster have fallen, injuring her daughter Mary; see copy of letter in file. Client wants to be reimbursed for daughter's medical bills as well as her (client's) lost wages. The ceiling looks like it is about to fall. One wall in the bathroom is discolored by a smelly, slimy green fungus that is spreading. She says the smell is overpowering.

Herb London promised to repair numerous cracks and holes in walls in the apartment and to paint. Nothing has been done to date. More plaster is falling from ceilings and walls. The entire apartment needs painting and plastering. "Why should I have to keep my promise to pay rent if he didn't keep his promise to fix the place?"

Heat and hot water sometimes don't work. Client has had to use her electric stove to heat apartment sometimes and has had to buy and use electric space heater. She has had to heat water on the stove to use for washing dishes and bathing. The space heater cost $79. Her electric bills have skyrocketed because of her additional use of the heater and the stove.

Client is very angry about rats. There are rat holes in the bedrooms and kitchen. She regularly sets traps and has killed four rats. GRI's building superintendent (Victor) came up and killed a rat once. She has had to throw away food in boxes (cereal, rice, etc.) after rats got into them. Rat droppings are everywhere, but there is no extermination service. Her daughters complain that they are afraid that the rats will come out as soon as the lights are turned off at night. She wants GRI punished for ignoring her situation.

In addition, the elevator has been unreliable, sometimes out of service for three to four days at a time. All of neighbors get angry when elevator is broken.

Client says she has constantly complained. Speaks to Victor often and has called London many times. She doesn't usually get through but leaves messages on London's answering machine and with secretary. Sent a letter to Herb London listing complaints; see copy of letter in file. She has taken pictures of some of the conditions (will bring them in if we need them) and reported her problems to the Avon Department of Buildings. Inspector came several times and gave her a copy of report. See copy of report in file. During the inspections, the hot water was working.

Client believes that the repairs should be made immediately. She is willing to pay some of rent but "not much" from time she moved in until the repairs are completed. "Why should I pay good money for an apartment that is in bad condition and not worth nearly what GRI is charging? Some of my neighbors have moved out. Mr. London isn't renting those vacant units. Victor told me he's holding on to them, waiting for the rest of us to give up and leave in disgust. I really don't want to be forced out, but I refuse to pay $1,000 a month to live in a dump."

804 7th Avenue, Apt. 7B,
Avon, Franklin 33210
May 21, 2004
Re: Problems in Graham Towers Apt. 7B

Mr. Herb London
Graham Realty, Inc.
222 French St.
Avon, Franklin 33210

Dear Mr. London,

Over the past months, I have repeatedly called your office in an effort to get you to make repairs in my apartment. Usually when I call and give your secretary my name, I am told that you are not in. Other times I have left a message on your answering machine. On the few occasions when you have actually taken my calls, I have explained that there are a number of problems in the apartment. In all, my notes indicate that I have called eight times to complain.

In addition to my phone calls to you, I have spoken with Victor, the building superintendent, on many occasions about the problems in my apartment. I have even shown him the conditions that need to be fixed. Each time we talk, he tells me that he needs your permission before he can do anything. In spite of all my attempts, no repairs have been made in my apartment.

I am now upset about three particularly disturbing developments. First, two weeks ago, while my 14-year-old daughter, Mary, was using the bathroom, a large chunk of plaster fell from the ceiling, knocking her to the floor and causing a gash in her scalp, which required 10 stitches to close. This was very painful and we are both quite upset. My daughter missed a day of school and I missed a day of work. We also had to pay the hospital, and when I asked you to reimburse me, you refused. All of this could have been prevented if you had fixed the leaks in the ceiling that I have been complaining about for months.

Second, as you well know, we frequently do not have any heat in the building. When this happens, we are forced to make do by operating our electric stove, as well as the space heater we were forced to buy. It still isn't warm enough in the bedrooms. Furthermore, it is not safe to run the stove all night long. While we do not want to do anything that creates a fire hazard, we also do not want to freeze on cold nights.

Finally, late last night, Mary woke me up screaming because she was awakened by a rat that ran across her bed. We have complained about the rats before, but the problem is getting worse. My daughters are afraid to go to sleep for fear that a rat will bite them.

This situation is intolerable. You must do something to repair our apartment immediately, pay my daughter's medical bills, and compensate us for the pain you have caused. Thank you.

Very truly,

Brenda Chapin

City of Avon Department of Buildings, Office of the Building Inspector

Violation Report

Address: **804 7th Avenue, Apt. 7B**, Avon, Franklin 33210 Date: July 6, 2004

HPD#	Range	Block	Lot	CD	Census	Stories	A Units	B Units	Owner
3394	801-807	90210	2141	10	**Tract** 21800	8	100	0	Graham Realty Inc.

There are 5 violations listed below for Apartment 7B. Arranged by category-
A class: 0   B class: 2   C class: 3

Class Definitions

A: "Non-hazardous," such as minor leaks, chipping or peeling paint when no children under the age of six live in the home, or lack of signs designating floor numbers. An owner has 90 days to correct an A violation before fines will be assessed.

B: "Hazardous," such as public doors not self-closing, inadequate lighting in public areas or lack of posted Certificate of Occupancy. An owner has 30 days to correct a B violation before fines will be assessed.

C: "Immediately hazardous," such as inadequate fire exits, the presence of rodents or lead-based paint, or lack of heat, hot water, electricity, or gas. An owner has 24 hours to correct a C violation before fines will be assessed.

Apt.	Date Reported	Hazard Class	Violation ID #	Description
7B	February 2004	B	270421	repair broken or defective plastered surfaces and paint walls and ceilings in the entire apartment.
7B	February 2004	C	270422	abate the nuisance consisting of rodents in entire apartment.
7B	March 2004	B	321123	abate the nuisance consisting of evidence of a water leak on the bathroom ceiling.
7B	March 2004	C	321124	abate the nuisance consisting of mold-like substance existing along the south wall of the bathroom from ceiling to floor.
All	April 2004	C	398927	restore elevator service.

# *Avon Gazette*	
Section C: Real Estate	July 20, 2004

Uptown Boomtown

By Emily Saylor

Marianne Conrad moved to Graham Towers fourteen years ago, when more than half the apartments were vacant and neighborhood drug dealers preyed on residents. Now the courtyard mailboxes carry the names of lawyers and doctors alongside those of pensioners, and rumors of co-op conversion swirl.

"A year ago, I could have bought a house in the Briggs section of Avon, but not now," Ms. Conrad says. "I can't afford it. And I'm basically middle-class. Unless you're upper management and making close to $300,000, I don't think anyone else can afford it, either. Today, a shell of a building in this area goes for $250,000. And I'm talking about no roof, no windows."

She's determined, however, not to let this boom pass her by completely. "I'm a social character, and I know lots of folks in Briggs, so I hear about things," Ms. Conrad says. "I'm always looking for my little niche, so I went

three months ago and got a real estate license. Now if I hear about a house, I need to sell it."

Reaction to these changes is mixed at Graham Towers. Most tenants are pleased to see recent renovations to the building's exterior. However, longtime residents are apprehensive about the gentrification of the towers. According to Ms. Conrad, they are also concerned that "management is trying to force existing tenants out by ignoring necessary repairs so they can bring in well-heeled tenants and charge substantially higher rents."

In 1994, movie producer Dan Jackson used Graham Towers as the all-too-believable setting for a crack factory in "Broken Dreams." Ten years later, a company Jackson co-founded with his sister, Nicki, is just as keenly capturing the moment: Urban Box Office Network is the first major media outlet to move its headquarters to Briggs. Given the trend at Graham Towers and in the neighborhood, it won't be the last.

Franklin Real Property Law

§ 500. Warranty of habitability

1.   In every written or oral lease or rental agreement for residential premises, the landlord shall
        be deemed to warrant that

           (a) the premises so leased or rented and all areas used in connection therewith in
           common with other tenants or residents are fit for human habitation and for the uses
           reasonably intended by the parties; and

           (b) the occupants of such premises shall not be subjected to any conditions that would be
           dangerous, hazardous, or detrimental to their life, health, or safety.

2.   Any agreement by a lessee or tenant of a dwelling waiving or modifying the rights as set
        forth in this section shall be void as contrary to public policy.

3.   In determining the amount of damages sustained by a tenant, the court shall not require
        expert testimony.

Franklin District Court Act

§ 240. Housing Division of the Franklin District Court

A division of the court shall be devoted to actions and proceedings involving the enforcement of state and local laws for the establishment and maintenance of housing standards.

All summary proceedings to recover possession of residential premises or to remove tenants therefrom and to render judgment for rent due, including those cases in which a tenant alleges a defense relating to a stay of eviction proceedings or any action for rent abatement upon failure to make repairs, shall be brought in the Housing Division of the Franklin District Court.

Regardless of the relief originally sought by a party, the court may employ any remedy, program, procedure, or sanction authorized by law for the enforcement of housing standards that are effective to accomplish compliance or to protect and promote the public interest. This shall include, but not be limited to, the reduction of rent through abatement as well as the imposition of remedial and punitive damages.

Virgil v. Landy

Franklin Court of Appeal (1997)

Defendant appeals from a judgment rendered by the Housing Division of the Franklin District Court. The court ordered defendant landlord to pay plaintiff damages in the amount of $4,945 as reimbursement of all rent paid and additional compensatory damages. The award covered a 14-month period during which plaintiff rented a residential apartment in defendant's apartment building. On appeal, defendant raises two issues: first, whether the court correctly calculated the amount of damages; and second, whether the court's award to plaintiff of the entire amount of rent paid to defendant was proper since plaintiff remained in possession of the apartment for the entire 14-month period.

In October 1995, plaintiff began occupying an apartment in defendant's apartment building. Plaintiff has paid all rent due under her tenancy. Upon moving into the apartment, plaintiff discovered a broken kitchen window. Defendant promised to repair it, but, after waiting a week and fearing that her two-year-old grandchild might cut himself on the shards of glass, plaintiff repaired the window at her own expense. After moving in, plaintiff discovered that the toilet would flush only by dumping pails of water into it. The toilet remained mechanically inoperable throughout the period of plaintiff's tenancy. In addition, the bathroom light and wall outlet were inoperable. Plaintiff also discovered that the water pipes leaked down the walls of her back bedroom. As a result of this leakage, a large section of plaster fell from the back bedroom ceiling onto her bed and her grandson's crib. These conditions were brought to the attention of the defendant, but he never corrected them. Plaintiff moved her and her grandson's bedroom furniture into the living room and ceased using the back bedroom.

The court held that the state of disrepair of plaintiff's apartment, which was known to the defendant, substantially reduced the value of the leasehold from the agreed rental value and constituted a breach of the implied warranty of habitability. The district court based its award of damages on the breach of this warranty and on breach of an express contract. Defendant argues that, because plaintiff never abandoned the demised premises, it was error to award her the full amount of rent paid.

A lease is a contract between the landlord and the tenant wherein the landlord promises to deliver and maintain the demised premises in habitable condition and the tenant promises to pay rent for such habitable premises.

In the rental of any residential dwelling unit an implied warranty exists in the lease, whether oral or written, that the landlord will deliver over and maintain, throughout the period of the tenancy, premises that are safe, clean, and fit for human habitation. *See* Franklin Real Property Law § 500. The implied warranty of habitability covers all defects in the essential facilities of the residence. This implied warranty of

A substantial violation of an applicable housing code shall constitute prima facie evidence that there has been a breach of the warranty of habitability. One or two minor violations standing alone that do not affect the health or safety of the tenant shall be considered *de minimis* and not a breach of the warranty.

Regardless of whether there are Housing Code violations, in determining whether there has been a breach of the implied warranty of habitability, courts should inquire whether the claimed defect has an impact on the safety or health of the tenant.

In order to bring a cause of action for breach of the implied warranty of habitability, the tenant must first show that he or she notified the landlord of the deficiency or defect not known to the landlord and allowed a reasonable time for its correction.1

The statute, Franklin Real Property Law § 500, and its companion provision, § 240 of Franklin District Court Act, give the court wide latitude in assessing damages. The measure of rent abatement damages shall be the difference between the value of the dwelling as warranted and the value of the dwelling as it exists in its defective condition. In

---

1 As we held in *Rosenbaum v. Chavkin* (1990), a tenant may, where there has been a breach of the implied warranty of habitability, withhold the payment of rent. That permits the tenant to shift the burden and expense of bringing suit to the landlord, who can better afford to bring the action, and to then raise the breach of the implied warranty of habitability as a counterclaim.

habitability cannot be waived.

determining the fair rental value of the dwelling as warranted, the court may look to the agreed-upon rent as something the two parties have agreed to as proper for the premises as impliedly warranted. Then the court should consider testimony and other evidence to determine the percentage reduction of habitability or usability by the tenant attributable to the defects.

In determining the percentage reduction of habitability, the trial court should consider the area affected, the amount of time the tenant is exposed to the defect, the degree of discomfort and annoyance the defect imposes, the quality of the defect as health-threatening or just intermittently annoying, and the extent to which such a defect causes the tenant to find the premises uninhabitable. For example, damages are recoverable when the tenant cannot bathe comfortably because there is inadequate hot water, or must worry about insect infestation spreading disease, or must avoid certain rooms if there is inadequate weather protection.

The tenant's damages are calculated by reducing the agreed rent by this percentage reduction of habitability, and multiplying the difference by the number of months of occupancy. The tenant will be liable only for the reasonable rental value, if any, of the property in its imperfect condition during the tenant's period of occupancy.

Damages for discomfort and annoyance are not susceptible to precise calculation. For that reason, the damages awarded for rent abatement, including discomfort and annoyance, may not exceed the total rent otherwise due. Accordingly, because we hold that a 100 percent rent abatement is the maximum that may be awarded to a tenant in an ordinary breach of implied warranty case, we reverse the trial court's decision awarding $1,500 in additional compensatory damages.

Separate damages, however, are available for remedial measures taken by the tenant when the landlord is notified of the defect but fails to remedy it within a reasonable time, and the tenant has incurred out-of-pocket expenses to remedy the defect. In this case, the tenant paid for the repair of a window. Accordingly, the trial court's award of $225 for remedial measures was proper.

Punitive damages may also be awarded in the proper circumstances to punish conduct that is morally culpable. cSuch an award serves to deter a wrongdoer from repetitions of the same or similar actions. And it tends to encourage prosecution of a claim by a victim who might not otherwise incur the expense or inconvenience of private action.

As we have repeatedly held, when a landlord, after receiving notice of a defect, persistently fails to make repairs that are essential to the health and safety of the tenant, the landlord is morally culpable and an award of punitive damages is proper. *See Main v. Stocker Realty* (Franklin Court of Appeal, 1996). When such behavior points to the bad spirit and wrong

intention of the defendant, and would support a finding of willful and wanton or fraudulent conduct, punitive damages may be increased.

The trial court denied an award to plaintiff of punitive damages without explaining why. The record evinces a pattern of intentional conduct on the part of defendant for which the term "slumlord" surely was coined. Defendant's conduct was culpable and demeaning to plaintiff and clearly expressive of a wanton disregard of plaintiff's rights.

The trial court found that defendant was aware of defects in the essential facilities of plain- tiff's apartment and promised plaintiff that repairs would be made, but never fulfilled those promises. These findings point to the bad spirit and wrong intention of the defendant, and would support a finding of willful and wanton or fraudulent conduct. We remand to give the trial court the opportunity to reconsider or explain its refusal to award punitive damages.

Affirmed in part, reversed in part, and remanded.

Bashford v. Schwartz

Franklin Court of Appeal (2001)

This appeal is from an order of the Housing Division of the District Court, which denied a motion by petitioner landlord to sever respondent tenant's counterclaims. The issue presented is whether the aggrieved tenant may raise in this summary eviction proceeding a counterclaim seeking damages for the loss of property that allegedly occurred as a result of the landlord's failure to provide adequate security.

The tenant stated that for a number of months she had complained to the landlord that the front door to her apartment was insecure and required replacement. This was never done. She stated that following her complaints an intruder forced open her front door and burglarized her apartment. Respondent asserts that she is entitled to damages for loss of property based on the landlord's failure to replace the front door.

While tenants may, in this nonpayment proceeding, counterclaim for damages sustained by reason of landlord's breach of the implied warranty of habitability as embodied in § 500 of the Franklin Real Property Law, the proper measure of those contract damages is the difference between the fair market value of the premises if they had been as warranted, as measured by the rent reserved under the lease, and the value of the premises during the period of the breach. *See Virgil v. Landy* (Franklin Court of Appeal, 1997).

Where questions of negligence, proximate cause, and damages are contested and require discovery and proof that would delay the summary proceedings, those claims are more appropriately tried outside the limited sphere of the landlord-tenant proceeding. While § 240 contains language giving the Housing Division Court authority to "employ any remedy," the point is that these are *summary* proceedings intended to allow quick and effective resolution of traditional landlord-tenant disputes and enforcement of the Housing Code. The Housing Division of the District Court, according to the legislation that created it, is "devoted to actions and proceedings involving the enforcement of state and local laws for the establishment and maintenance of housing standards." (Franklin District Court Act § 240).

Reversed.

Graham Realty, Inc. v. Brenda Chapin
DRAFTERS' POINT SHEET

The Avon, Franklin, Legal Aid Society represents Brenda Chapin, a tenant in Graham Towers, an apartment building owned by Graham Realty, Inc. ("GRI"). GRI has sued Ms. Chapin in a summary proceeding to evict her and collect the rent she has withheld for the past seven months. The suit is brought in the Housing Division of the Franklin District Court. The procedures are governed by § 240 of the Franklin District Court Act, which is contained in the Library.

Ms. Chapin has two years left to go on her lease and has been withholding her $1,000 monthly rent payments for seven months because of the deplorable condition of her apartment. She has repeatedly given notice to GRI of the very severe defects but GRI has failed to make any repairs.

Section 500 of the Franklin Real Property Law creates an implied warranty of habitability, and one of the cases in the Library, *Virgil v. Landy*, holds that a tenant may defend against eviction by asserting her claims for breach of this implied warranty.

The supervising attorney has asked applicants to draft a case planning memorandum to prepare for the upcoming hearing before the Housing Division Court. The memorandum should, citing the relevant law, identify the elements necessary to prove that GRI breached the implied warranty of habitability and the evidence available to establish those elements. Applicants must also identify the remedies available to Ms. Chapin, the legal bases and elements thereof, and the evidence supporting her right to recover them. Finally, applicants are to identify any relief that Ms. Chapin may be entitled to but that is not attainable in this summary proceeding and explain why.

The format and purpose of a case planning memorandum are explained in the File's Case Planning Memorandum Guidelines. The Guidelines also include an example of an unrelated case planning memorandum for applicants to refer to in drafting theirs. They are specifically told not to include a separate statement of facts and not to concern themselves with issues of admissibility of the evidence.

The following discussion covers the points the drafters intended to raise in the problem. Applicants need not cover them all to receive passing or even excellent grades. Grading is entirely within the discretion of the graders in the user jurisdictions.

I.   **Breach of the Implied Warranty of Habitability:** As a predicate to her defense against GRI's action for eviction and recovery of back rent, Ms. Chapin will have to prove that GRI has breached the implied warranty of habitability.

- <u>The Legal Authority</u>: Section 500 of the Real Property Law and *Virgil v. Landy* are the relevant authorities on this point:

    - Section 500 implies in every lease of residential premises a warranty that

        - the premises are fit for human habitation and the uses reasonably intended, and

        - the occupants will not be subjected to conditions that would be dangerous, hazardous, or detrimental to their life, health, or safety.

    - *Virgil* requires that the tenant notify the landlord of the defects.

- <u>The Elements to Be Proved and the Available Evidence</u>:

    - <u>Element</u>: The claimant is a lessee and a tenant of the apartment.

        - <u>Evidence</u>:

            - Ms. Chapin signed a written lease, which she can presumably produce.

            - She can testify that she and her daughters have occupied the apartment for the past year.

            - The court could presume the existence of a landlord-tenant relationship because Graham must have alleged that relationship in order to maintain its claim for eviction.

    - <u>Element</u>: The premises are not fit for human habitation or the uses reasonably intended by the parties.

        - <u>Evidence</u>:

            - Ms. Chapin and, presumably her older daughter, Mary, can testify that since they moved in, there have been water leaks, falling plaster, a spreading "smelly, slimy green fungus," cracks and holes in the walls, rat infestation, and erratic hot water, heat, and elevator service.

            - She can produce the Violation Report from the City of Avon Department of Buildings.

            - This evidence should satisfy the dictum in *Virgil v. Landy* that "A substantial violation of an applicable housing code shall constitute prima facie evidence that there has been a breach of the warranty of habitability."

- Element: The premises subject the tenant to conditions that are dangerous, hazardous, or detrimental to life, health, and safety.

  - Evidence:

    - The Violation Report shows five violations that have persisted for three to five months (since February 2004) that are classified as "hazardous" and "immediately hazardous." The rodent infestation, the mold-like substance, and erratic elevator service are classified as "immediately hazardous."

    - Ms. Chapin and Mary can testify as to these conditions.

    - They can also testify to the lack of hot water, which certainly adversely affects their ability to maintain personal hygiene (not being able to bathe regularly) and health (not having hot water to wash their dishes).

- Element: The tenant gave notice to the landlord.

  - Evidence:

    - Ms. Chapin can testify that when Herb London, GRI's building manager, first showed her the apartment, she pointed out certain defects to him.

    - She can testify that she spoke to Mr. London by phone and left numerous messages reporting the defects.

    - She can produce the notes of her attempted telephone contacts referred to in her letter to Mr. London.

    - Presumably, GRI has a copy of the Violation Report.

    - She reported the rats and other defects to Victor, GRI's building superintendent, who killed a rat in the apartment.

- Thus, there is ample evidence that GRI breached the implied warranty of habitability and that GRI had notice of its breach.

II.   **Available Remedies:** Applicants should glean from § 240 and *Virgil* that Ms. Chapin can obtain the following remedies:

- rent abatement, specified in § 240 and explained in *Virgil;*

- damages for remedial measures (i.e., out-of-pocket losses), also in § 240 and *Virgil*;

- punitive damages, the bases for which are explained in *Virgil*.

III. Rent Abatement:

- The Legal Authority: Section 240 of the District Court Act and *Virgil*:
  - Section 240 provides for rent abatement as a remedy for breach of the warranty of habitability.
  - *Virgil* articulates the measure of and the components for this remedy.
    - The measure of rent abatement damages is "the difference between the value of the dwelling as warranted and the value of the dwelling as it exists in its defective condition."
    - The percent of rent abatement is a matter for the court, and, in figuring the amount, the court considers the following factors:
      - the area affected;
      - the amount of time the occupant has been exposed to the defects;
      - the degree of discomfort the defects impose;
      - the quality of the defects as health-threatening as opposed to merely intermittently annoying;
      - the extent to which the defects cause the tenant to find the premises uninhabitable.
    - *Virgil* holds that the tenant remains liable for only "the reasonable rental value, if any, of the property in its imperfect condition during the tenant's period of occupancy," and that the court may make a reasonable estimate of the percent of rent abatement.
    - In further support of the notion that damages need not be precisely ascertainable, § 500 provides that in determining the amount of the tenant's damages, no expert testimony shall be required.
- The Elements to be Proved and the Available Evidence: To establish her right to recover rent abatement, Ms. Chapin will have to prove the following:
  - Element: The fair rental value of the apartment in its warranted condition.
    - Evidence:
      - The lease document will show the rent at $1,000 per month, which is presumed to be the reasonable value of the

apartment in its warranted condition. *See Virgil.*

- Element: The factors the court will use to estimate the percent rent abatement:

  - Evidence regarding the area affected:

    - Ms. Chapin can testify that the apartment consists of two bedrooms, a living room, bathroom, and kitchen.

    - She can testify that the bathroom has a ceiling leak, falling plaster, and a spreading mold-like substance.

    - She can testify that there are cracks and holes in the walls throughout the apartment.

    - She can testify that the entire apartment needs painting.

    - She can testify that the bedrooms and kitchen have rat holes.

    - She can testify as to the presence of rats and probably produce the corroborating testimony of Victor, GRI's building superintendent, who killed a rat in her apartment.

    - She can produce the photos she has taken of these conditions.

    - She can testify and produce neighbors' testimony as to the erratic elevator service, which would be considered a breach under § 500 because it occurs in the common area of the building.

    - She can produce the Building Department's Violation Report, which shows the areas affected and states that, as to the paint and plaster defects and the rat infestation, it is the "entire apartment."

    - She can testify about the sporadic availability of heat and hot water and presumably produce her electricity bills to corroborate it.

  - Evidence regarding amount of time she has been exposed to the conditions:

    - She can testify that she has been exposed to some of the conditions from the first day of occupancy (when Herb London first showed her the apartment and promised to fix the defects).

- The Violation Report will show how long the violations listed in the report have persisted.
- She can testify and produce the testimony of neighbors as to the frequency, duration, and total time that the elevator was inoperable and heat and hot water weren't available.
- She can testify as to how long she has seen signs of rats.
- Her electricity bills will corroborate the stretches of time during which she has been without hot water and heat.

- <u>Evidence regarding the degree of discomfort</u>:
  - This will be established by the testimony of Ms. Chapin and Mary (e.g., fear of rats, inability to sleep, repeated calls to landlord, call to the inspector, the photos, etc.).
  - Perhaps it can be corroborated by testimony from neighbors.
  - Ms. Chapin's letter to Herb London corroborates the discomfort endured ("It isn't warm enough in the bedrooms").
  - Her testimony and that of the neighbors about the erratic elevator service is evidence of extreme discomfort, given that the apartment is on the 7th floor.

- <u>Evidence regarding the quality of the defects as health-threatening versus merely annoying</u>:
  - The Violation Report is evidence that *all* of the violations for which GRI was cited fall into the "hazardous" and "immediately hazardous" categories.
  - Ms. Chapin's testimony about the rats and their droppings will show a health-threatening condition.
  - Her testimony and corroborating evidence about the lack of hot water and heat will show the same.
  - Her testimony about the "smelly, slimy green fungus" will show a health threat.
  - Likewise, her testimony about the erratic elevator service will establish evidence of a health threat, given that is it a 7th floor

apartment.

- Evidence regarding the extent to which Ms. Chapin found the premises uninhabitable:
  - This is fairly subjective and can be established from the testimony of Ms. Chapin and her daughter.
  - Testimony about having to heat water for bathing and doing dishes and keeping the kitchen stove lit and buying an electric heater to provide heat will show the extremes to which she had to go to make it barely liveable.

- Although applicants are not asked to argue what *amount* the rent abatement should be, it would not be out of order for them to argue that, as in *Virgil,* the circumstances here justify the court abating the entire amount, especially in light of GRI's reprehensible lack of responsiveness to the conditions.
  - The recommendation would include requiring GRI to refund $5,000 for the five months Ms. Chapin paid and denying GRI recovery of the $7,000 she has withheld.
  - This recommendation would be based on the evidence of the serious, pervasive, and hazardous conditions in the apartment.
  - Under § 240, the court has broad powers to fashion the remedies.

IV. **Damages for Remedial Measures (Out-of-Pocket):**

- The Legal Authority: Section 240 and the *Virgil* holding that damages for remedial measures are recoverable "when the landlord is notified of the defect but fails to remedy it within a reasonable time."
  - The items at issue here are the space heater and the exorbitant electric bills.
  - Applicants may try to include Mary's hospital bills and Ms. Chapin's loss of a day's pay. However, the *Bashford v. Schwartz* case should provide a strong enough hint that these expenses are not recoverable in a summary proceeding.

- The Elements to be Proved and the Available Evidence: To establish her right to recover out-of-pocket losses, Ms. Chapin will have to prove the following:
  - Element: The tenant notified the landlord of the defects.
    - Evidence:

- Ms. Chapin can testify that she repeatedly called and left messages for Herb London regarding the various defects, including the lack of heat in the apartment.

- She can produce the letter she wrote to Mr. London, which mentions specifically that, as a result of his failure to restore heat in the building, she had to buy a space heater.

- Notice to London/GRI as to the lack of hot water (which is partly the reason why her electric bills ran up) may be problematic because there is no mention of it in her letter or in the Violation Report. Presumably, however, she can testify that she told GRI about it in one or more of her many telephone messages to Mr. London and her discussions with Victor.

  - Since the court has "wide latitude in assessing damages" *under Virgil*, it may be enough for her to show that her skyrocketing electric bills attributable to the space heater, of which she *did* give notice, are sufficient to encompass the bulk of the amount.

- Element: The landlord failed to remedy the defects in a reasonable time.
  - Evidence:
    - Ms. Chapin can testify that, notwithstanding notice and repeated requests, the defects have *never* been remedied.
    - The Violation Report.

- Element: The tenant incurred out-of-pocket expenses specifically in order to remedy the defects she had reported to the landlord.
  - Evidence:
    - She can testify that she had to buy a space heater because there were extended periods when the building had no heat.
    - Presumably she can produce the heater and its receipt.
    - She can testify that she had to use electricity to heat water for bathing and doing dishes when there was no hot water.
    - She can presumably produce her skyrocketing electric bills to

contrast what she normally would have used with what she had to use under the conditions caused by the lack of heat and hot water.

- Ms. Chapin might also be able to recover the cost of the food she had to throw away because of the rat droppings; the evidence would consist of her testimony, and, perhaps the testimony of Victor, the building superintendent.

V. Punitive Damages:

- The Legal Authority: Section 240 specifically authorizes an award of punitive damages and *Virgil* articulates the requisite bases.
  - *Virgil* states that punitive damages are appropriate "when a landlord, after receiving notice of a defect, persistently fails to make repairs that are essential to the health and safety of the tenant."
    - There must be "willful and wanton or fraudulent conduct."
- The Elements to be Proved and Available Evidence: To establish her right to recover punitive damages, Ms. Chapin will have to prove the following.
  - Element: The landlord received notice of the defects that are detrimental to the tenant's health and safety.
    - Evidence:
      - See above discussion under "Remedial Measures" regarding the notice issue as to the lack of hot water and heat, which are health and safety issues.
      - Ms. Chapin can testify about having given oral notice to Victor, GRI's building superintendent, regarding the rat infestation.
      - She can also produce the letter and the Violation Report to establish notice of the rat infestation.
        - According to the Violation Report, GRI had 24 hours in which to abate this "immediately hazardous" violation and did not do so.
      - She can testify about the lapses in elevator service and produce the Violation Report to show the same thing.

- Again, this is classified as an "immediately hazardous" violation, which GRI had 24 hours to correct but did not do so.
- With respect to the mold-like substance, the broken plaster, and need for paint, she can testify and produce the Violation Report, which classifies these defects as "hazardous."
  - The Violation Report gives GRI 30 days to correct these defects, and the Report is only 21 days old. Thus, GRI still has a few days.
  - However, Ms. Chapin can probably testify that she gave notice more than 30 days ago (her letter of complaint to Herb London is dated 60 days ago).
- Element: The landlord failed to repair these defects affecting health and safety.
  - Evidence:
    - Again, Ms. Chapin can testify that, notwithstanding notice and repeated requests, the defects have *never* been remedied.
- Element: The landlord's conduct was willful and wanton or fraudulent.
  - Evidence:
    - Ms. Chapin can testify as evidence of fraudulent conduct that when Herb London first showed her the apartment, she pointed out several defects and he "assured" her that the repairs would be made.
      - She signed the lease in reliance on those assurances, and it now appears that London/GRI never intended to make the repairs.
    - Ms. Chapin's testimony, her notes, her letter, and the Violation Report show frequent and repeated complaints, which GRI has ignored for a whole year. Since there is no doubt that GRI had ample notice of the serious and pervasive defects, its failure/refusal to act is willful and wanton as applied by the court in *Virgil.*

- Further evidence of a "bad spirit and wrong intention" (*See Virgil*) is found in the *Avon Gazette* article in the File. The irresistible inference is that GRI's *real* intention is to make living in Graham Towers so intolerable that the tenants will move out so that GRI can take advantage of the neighborhood's gentrification.
  - GRI's studied indifference to the defects in Graham Towers, coupled with evidence of gentrification, will be clear and convincing evidence of willful and wanton conduct supporting an award of punitive damages.

VI.   Remedy Not Obtainable in This Summary Proceeding:

- Ms. Chapin has said she wants to be reimbursed for her daughter's medical costs as a result of the wound caused by the falling plaster and for one day's lost wages.
- Applicants should draw on *Bashford v. Schwartz* for the proposition that "Where questions of negligence, proximate cause, and damages are contested and often require discovery and proof that would delay the summary proceedings, those claims are more appropriately tried outside the limited sphere of the landlord-tenant proceeding," which is "intended to allow quick and effective resolution of traditional landlord-tenant disputes."
- These damages are beyond "remedial measures," for which recovery is allowed.
- GRI probably would contest these claims, and the delays suggested by the *Bashford* court would occur.
- Accordingly, Ms. Chapin will probably not be able to recover these damages as part of her counterclaims in this case.

Wells v. Wells

FILE

LIBRARY

Broyles and Lemansky
Attorneys at Law
2398 S. 25th Street
Franklin City, Franklin 33173-3209

MEMORANDUM

To: Applicant
From: Pamela Broyles, Senior Partner
Re: *Wells v. Wells*
Date: July 29, 2004

We have just finished the evidentiary hearing in a family court proceeding in which our client, Joan Wells, petitioned the court for permission to remove her minor son, Sammy, from the State of Franklin to the State of Columbia. We ordered an expedited hearing transcript, and it is in the file.

Joan's petition is based on the assertion that she intends to relocate to Columbia to accept a new job. Sammy's father, Fred Wells, opposes the petition.

The judge has given us two days to submit concurrent briefs. This is where I need your help.

Please draft our brief in support of Joan's petition following the instructions in the Firm's memorandum on persuasive briefs. You should use all the relevant evidence as appropriate to support the arguments in the brief. Since we will not have the opportunity to present a rebuttal brief, be sure to anticipate and refute Fred's arguments.

Broyles and Lemansky
Attorneys at Law
2398 S. 25th Street
Franklin City, Franklin 33173-3209

MEMORANDUM   September 8, 1999

To: All Lawyers
From: Litigation Supervisor
Subject: Persuasive Briefs

All persuasive briefs shall conform to the following guidelines:

All briefs shall include a Statement of Facts. The aim of the Statement of Facts is to persuade the tribunal that the facts support our client's position. The facts must be stated accurately, although emphasis is not improper. Select carefully the facts that are pertinent to the legal arguments. However, in a brief to a trial court, when the evidentiary hearing has just been completed, the Statement of Facts section of the brief may be abbreviated because it can be assumed that the court has the facts in mind.

The firm follows the practice of breaking the argument into its major components and writing carefully crafted subject headings that illustrate the arguments they cover. Avoid writing briefs that contain only a single broad argument heading. The argument heading should succinctly summarize the reasons the tribunal should take the position you are advocating. A heading should be a specific application of a rule of law to the facts of the case and not a bare legal or factual conclusion or a statement of an abstract principle. For example, improper: IT IS NOT IN THE CHILD'S BEST INTERESTS TO BE PLACED IN THE MOTHER'S CUSTODY. Proper: EVIDENCE THAT THE MOTHER HAS BEEN CONVICTED OF CHILD ABUSE IS SUFFICIENT TO ESTABLISH THAT IT IS NOT IN THE CHILD'S BEST INTERESTS TO BE PLACED IN THE MOTHER'S CUSTODY.

The body of each argument should analyze applicable legal authority and persuasively argue how the facts and law support our client's position. Authority supportive of our client's position should be emphasized, but contrary authority also should generally be cited, addressed in the argument, and explained or distinguished. Do not reserve arguments for reply or supplemental briefing.

The lawyer need not prepare a table of contents, a table of cases, a summary of argument, or an index. These will be prepared, when required, after the draft is approved.

TRANSCRIPT OF HEARING

July 28, 2004

THE COURT: This matter is here on the petition of Joan Wells for permission to remove the minor child, Sammy, from the state, specifically to Columbia. In 2002, when Joan and Fred Wells were divorced, this court awarded joint custody to the parents and designated Joan Wells primary physical custodian. Because Joan Wells indicated her intention to remove Sammy from Franklin and Fred Wells has opposed that move, this court must now decide if the custody arrangement ordered in 2002 should be modified. Present are Joan Wells, her attorney, Ms. Broyles, and Fred Wells, and his counsel, Mr. Simpson. We are ready to proceed with evidence. Ms. Broyles, call your first witness.

THE PETITIONER, Joan Wells, WAS SWORN AND IDENTIFIED.

PAMELA BROYLES: What are you asking the court to do, Ms. Wells?

JOAN WELLS: I am asking the court to permit me to take my six-year-old son, Sammy, to Columbia City so that I can take a position as an associate professor of Irish Literature and Studies in the Irish Studies Department at Columbia State University in Columbia City, Columbia, and can better care for Sammy.

Q: Why do you wish to relocate?

A: I have just completed my doctoral degree in Irish literature. Now I can obtain a position in my field at a higher salary. This will better my life and my ability to provide for Sammy.

Q: How will Sammy be cared for if you relocate?

A: Sammy will live with me. I have found a home near campus that is a bit larger than our present home. Sammy will attend elementary school at the McAuliff Elementary School, near campus. It is a wonderful school, being staffed with so many graduates of CSU. It has an after-school program for days when I must teach late. The quality of life for children in Columbia City is great—the parks, recreational programs, youth center, great cultural opportunities in music and the other arts—Sammy will have a great life.

Q: Can you tell us anything else about the educational opportunities for Sammy?

A: CSU offers a tuition discount to children of its professors so Sammy will be able to attend college at half the cost of tuition. That will save me and Fred a lot of money.

Q: What do you propose regarding Sammy's relationship with his father?

A: I want to be sure Sammy stays in touch with his father. I would never come between him and his father. Ever since we separated, I made sure that Sammy has a photo of himself and his father by his bed. Fred can send new photos from time to time. I also have a digital camera and can send Fred photos of Sammy via e-mail. Sammy still likes to be read to. Fred can tape books and Sammy can listen to the tapes before he goes to bed. I will have Sammy send Fred a packet of school papers and art projects every week so Fred can see how Sammy is doing. I know Fred is very interested in Sammy's music and other activities so we can even record events like Sammy's school plays, concerts, and sports activities, and send a videotape to Fred.

Q: Anything else regarding Sammy and his father?

A: Fred can call him whenever he wants, and when Sammy is older, he can e-mail his father as well. Whenever Sammy wants to call Fred, I will let him, of course. If Fred wants to purchase a computer camera for himself and Sammy, I will see that it gets hooked up at home and Sammy and Fred can see and talk with each other every day.

Q: What about visits with his father?

A: While Sammy is so young, he can fly with me to Franklin, for a week at Thanksgiving, a week in December, and a week during spring break. I would like Sammy to see my family then too, but he can spend most of the time with Fred. Of course, I will see that Sammy gets to Fred's for several weeks in the summer, preferably two weeks with Fred in June and another two weeks in July. And if Fred wants to go on vacation with Sammy for a week or two, he can do that. When Sammy is older, he can fly to see Fred. Fred is also welcome to come visit in Columbia.

Q: Tell the court what brought about this relocation.

A: Well, teaching at the university level in Irish studies has always been my dream. When Fred and I had just started dating, I told him that my goal was to get a doctoral degree in Irish literature and teach at the best university possible.

Q: Fred has suggested that you are moving to get away from him and his new wife and that you refuse to talk to Kathleen, his new wife. Can you address that?

A: I never said that I refused to talk to her. What I said was this: Kathleen and I have a past history. When Fred married her, I suggested that it would be best if Fred and I limit our discussions about Sammy to just ourselves.

Q: Are you concerned that Sammy will have trouble adjusting if you move?

A: I am concerned that we make the move as easy on Sammy as possible. That is why I want to be settled before the school year starts. But Sammy is a very resilient child. He has just finished kindergarten, so this is an ideal time for the move—before he gets really settled into school.

BROYLES: I have nothing further for this witness.

THE COURT: Cross-examination, Mr. Simpson?

THOMAS SIMPSON: Thank you, Your Honor.

Q: Right now, Fred is with Sammy almost 40 percent of the time.

A: Yes, it comes to about that.

Q: If Sammy goes with you to Columbia, Fred will have less time with Sammy, isn't that right?

A: That depends on how frequently Fred comes to Columbia.

Q: Isn't it true that Sammy has been very active in the Franklin City Children's Choir here in Franklin City, Franklin?

A: Yes.

Q: Isn't it true that Fred has been an assistant director for the choir and has been able to encourage Sammy to develop his musical talent?

A: Yes. But let's not forget—Sammy is only six years old.

Q: Isn't it true that there is no comparable children's choir in Columbia City?

A: So far, I have not found one, but I will encourage Sammy's musical talents.

Q: Fred cares more about Sammy's musical talent than you do, doesn't he?

A: I think it's important to develop all of Sammy's talents.

Q: Isn't it true that Fred has been a loving father who has cared for Sammy and been very involved in his life?

A: Yes. I have never said that Fred is anything but a caring parent.

Q: Fred also goes to teacher's conferences and to doctor's visits, and generally is very involved in all aspects of Sammy's life. Is that right?

A: All true.

Q: And isn't it true that Fred has participated in every important decision about Sammy's life?

A: Yes.

Q: Haven't there been times when the two of you have disagreed about Sammy's upbringing?

A: Occasionally.

Q: On those occasions, haven't the two of you been able to resolve your differences?

A: Sure. We've talked about the issues. I respect his opinion. In fact, because he teaches children, I usually go along with him on issues involving Sammy's schooling.

SIMPSON: No further questions, Your Honor.

COURT: Call the next witness.

THE WITNESS, Michael McBryan, WAS SWORN AND IDENTIFIED.

BROYLES: How do you know Joan Wells?

McBRYAN: I am the department chair for English and Irish Literature at Franklin State University and was the committee chair for Joan's doctoral dissertation. Joan was an excellent student and shows much promise in scholarship and teaching Irish literature.

Q: Is it possible that Franklin State University will offer her a position on the faculty?

A: No. We have a policy against hiring our own graduates. Even if we did not, the position she has been offered at CSU is a very prestigious one. We cannot meet the salary. Further, they have a whole department devoted to Irish studies so she will have colleagues who will encourage her in ways that we could not. Plus, she will be eligible for raises that will make her more financially secure.

BROYLES: I have no more questions for this witness Your Honor.

THE COURT: Mr. Simpson, any cross?

SIMPSON: Yes, Your Honor. Thank you.

SIMPSON: Isn't it true that Joan Wells has tenure at the community college?

A: True.

Q: Having tenure—in essence, doesn't that mean she is ensured employment at the community college for the rest of her life?

A: In general, yes, that is what it means.

SIMPSON: That is all I have for this witness, Your Honor.

THE COURT: Ms. Broyles, any other witnesses?

BROYLES: We call the court's attention to the stipulations previously presented to the court. Sammy's physician reports that Sammy, age six, is healthy and developing normally. His teacher indicates that he did well in school during his kindergarten year and is well prepared to move into first grade. He is progressing well in school and seems emotionally and socially well adjusted. Finally, the parties have stipulated that there are four nonstop flights a day

between Franklin City, Franklin, and Columbia City, Columbia, and that the airlines offer

unaccompanied minor service for children flying without an adult. Petitioner rests.

THE COURT: Very well. Mr. Simpson, call your first witness.

RESPONDENT, Fred Wells, WAS SWORN AND IDENTIFIED.

SIMPSON: Tell the court about your relationship with your son, Sammy.

FRED WELLS: Ever since Joan and I separated, I have made sure that Sammy is number one in my

life. I talk to him on the phone several times a week. As the court ordered in the decree,

Sammy is with me every weekend and one week in the summer, and on half the major

holidays. In addition to what the court ordered, at least once during the week, year round, we

have dinner together, and he and I go to movies and children's plays at least once a month.

He has not yet shown much interest in sports but if he does, I will be at his games. We play

T-ball in the yard when he is with me.

Q: What else do you and Sammy do when he is with you?

A: He and I play card games and board games and play trucks together. Normal father-son stuff.

I put him to bed and work with him on his school projects, and help him get dressed in the

morning, and prepare meals for him. When Joan and I were married, I was very involved in

his day-to-day care. When he is with me on weekends, I read him several stories every night

before he goes to bed.

Q: How is Sammy involved in the Franklin City Children's Choir?

A: Sammy is very musically talented. I am a music teacher and I could tell early on that he was

talented. So we enrolled him in the Franklin City Children's Choir. The director loves

Sammy's voice and has already given him several solos. At his age, they have practices three

times a week for six weeks each fall and spring and put on two major concerts a year. In a

few years, he will tour with the choir. The choir goes all over the United States and to

Europe every other year. If he stays in the choir until he is 18, he will have outstanding

experiences and be well prepared for a college audition, if that is what he wants. There is no

children's choir like this in Columbia City.

Q: Do you think Sammy has the talent to have a career in music?

A: It is very, very possible. Talent like his is rare and needs to be cultivated if he is to have a

chance at a career. Joan will not develop it like I would. Taking him to choir is just too much hassle for her. Plus, I help him with singing practice and can really be his singing mentor.

Q: Where are Sammy's grandparents, cousins, and other family located?

A: My parents live about 80 miles south of Franklin City. Joan's parents are 40 miles away in the other direction. On Joan's side of the family, Sammy has two cousins his age and on my side there are also two cousins his age, all in Franklin City. They are his most frequent playmates. Plus, he has three older cousins and one younger one, all in the area.

Q: What concerns do you have if Joan moves away with Sammy?

A: Sammy had a lot of trouble adjusting after the divorce. He was almost four at the time. He regressed to baby talk for a while and went through a period of not wanting to play with other kids or go to anyone's home. In fact, Joan and I arranged for the daycare counselor to work with him. He has gotten over all that and seems fine now. I am afraid he will regress again if he moves. I am concerned that he will lose me as a father. A child needs a mother and a father. I would never take Sammy from his mother, but it seems she wants to take him from me. As far as I know, Joan knows no one in Columbia City. Sammy knows no one there—no school pals, no cousins, no playmates. He will be lonely. He could be here with me.

Q: You have remarried. How does Sammy relate to Kathleen, your new wife?

A: Sammy gets along with my new wife. I was very careful to introduce Kathleen to Sammy early in our relationship to be sure he could get along with her. The only problem since I remarried has been Joan. Joan used to work with Kathleen at the community college, and they did not get along. Joan will not even talk to her. If Kathleen answers the phone when Joan calls for Sammy at my house, Joan immediately asks for me and will not even say hello to Kathleen. I am afraid that Joan is moving in order to avoid dealing with Kathleen. Or else she is jealous that I have moved on with my?? life and she has to make a bigger splash by getting a new job and moving to a new city.

Q: If Joan did move away with Sammy, how would you be able to spend time with him?

A: There is no way I could see Sammy on a regular basis if he moves to Columbia. I cannot afford to fly out there and the drive is too much for a weekend. It's more than 10 hours one way. Even if I could get there, where would I stay with Sammy? I would have no way to be with him in a home environment. He is too young to fly to Franklin by himself. Joan's proposal means that I will see Sammy about eight weeks a year—eight out of 52! Now, if you add up all the time, he currently spends about 20 weeks a year with me. I am afraid he will forget me. I won't be there for school plays and concerts and his Little League games and whatever else he does. I cannot be a father to him and children need a father.

Q: Fred, how will you be able to make decisions about Sammy's education, health, and the like if Joan moves?

A: I won't be able to. Because I will be hundreds of miles away, I won't go to school conferences, doctor appointments, etc.

Q: Then, how would you have input into these decisions?

A: I would have to rely on Joan to fill me in. I would never feel that I had firsthand information or that I was involved in the decisions.

SIMPSON: Thank you, Mr. Wells. Your Honor, I have no more questions for this witness.

THE COURT: Ms. Broyles, do you wish to cross-examine?

BROYLES: Yes. Thank you, Your Honor.

BROYLES: Isn't it true that Joan has been a good mother?

A: Yes.

Q: Isn't it true that the choir was your idea, not Sammy's?

A: I believe it was a joint decision—mine, Joan's and Sammy's.

Q: Isn't it true that Joan has never gotten in the way of your time with Sammy?

A: True.

Q: In fact, she has voluntarily agreed that you can spend significantly more time with Sammy than even what the court ordered in the divorce decree, isn't that right?

A: Yes. I guess so.

Q: You can always telephone or e-mail doctors and teachers to get information about Sammy, can't you?

A: Yes.

Q: Except for this proposed move, you and Joan have resolved disagreements about Sammy's welfare, haven't you?

A: Yes.

BROYLES: That is all I have for this witness, Your Honor.

THE COURT: Mr. Simpson, call the next witness.

     THE WITNESS, Maria Niro, WAS SWORN AND IDENTIFIED.

SIMPSON: How do you know Sammy Wells?

A: I am a counselor at the day care center Sammy attended. At the time of the divorce, his parents asked me to help Sammy through the adjustment period. I am trained to work with children going through losses, like death or divorce. I do play therapy to help them express their feelings. So I worked with Sammy for about eight weeks.

Q: Was Sammy having adjustment problems?

A: Yes, the normal ones. Like any child whose parents are divorcing, Sammy directly and indirectly expressed fears about where his bed and his clothes and toys would be, who would feed him and put him to bed and take him to day care.

SIMPSON: Thank you, Ms. Niro. I have no more questions, Your Honor.

THE COURT: Ms. Broyles?

Q: You are not a licensed social worker or counselor, are you?

A: No, no, but I have been trained to work with kids experiencing divorce and death. Had I thought Sammy needed professional counseling, I would have told the Wells family to take him to a professional. But all he needed was some help through some difficult months.

Q: So, Sammy didn't exhibit an unusual level of stress as a result of his parents' divorce?

A: No. It was a relatively mild case, as these matters go.

Q: And while you were working with him, Sammy got over these fears?

A: Yes. Like most children, he adapted to the new routine.

Q: So, he has adjusted well to living separately with his mother and father?

A: Yes.

Q: And you haven't worked with Sammy in the last year?

A: That's right.

BROYLES: No further questions, Your Honor.

SIMPSON: The respondent rests, Your Honor.

THE COURT: All right. We have concluded the evidence. It's clear that, constitutionally, the court does not have the authority to prohibit Ms. Wells from moving. The sole issue, therefore, before the court is whether Joan can take Sammy with her. I want to make a decision very soon. I want both counsel to submit a post-trial brief within 48 hours. There will be no rebuttal briefs, so address all the issues in this post-trial brief. We are adjourned.

FRANKLIN DISSOLUTION OF MARRIAGE ACT

Section 30. Definitions.

For purposes of this article, the following words shall have the following meanings:

    (1) JOINT CUSTODY. Joint legal custody and joint physical custody.

    (2) JOINT LEGAL CUSTODY. Both parents have equal rights and responsibilities for major decisions concerning the child, including the child's education, health care, and religious training. The court may designate one parent to have sole power to make certain decisions while both parents retain equal rights and responsibilities for other decisions.

    (3) JOINT PHYSICAL CUSTODY. Physical custody is shared by the parents in a way that assures the child frequent and substantial contact with each parent. Joint physical custody does not necessarily mean physical custody of equal durations of time. The court may designate one parent as the primary physical custodian.

    (4) SOLE LEGAL CUSTODY. One parent has sole right and responsibility to make major decisions concerning the child, including the child's education, health care, and religious training.

    (5) SOLE PHYSICAL CUSTODY. One parent has sole physical custody and the other parent has rights of visitation except as otherwise provided by the court.

Section 109. Removal of child.

The court may grant leave, before or after judgment, to any party having sole legal custody or sole or primary physical custody of any minor child or children to remove such child or children from Franklin whenever such approval is in the best interests of such child or children.

Section 402. Best interests of child.

The court shall determine custody in accordance with the best interests of the child. The court shall consider all relevant factors including:

    (1) the mental and physical health of all individuals involved;

    (2) the child's adjustment to the child's home, school, and community;

    (3) the interaction and interrelationship of the child with the child's parent or parents, the child's siblings, and any other person who may significantly affect the child's best interests;

    (4) the wishes of the child's parent or parents as to the child's custody.

Marshall v. Marshall

Franklin Supreme Court (2001)

Sue Ellen Marshall petitioned the court for leave to remove the parties' son, Michael, from the state of Franklin to the state of Columbia. As a result of their divorce in 1998, Sue Ellen and Forest were awarded joint custody of Michael, then three years old. The court designated Sue Ellen the primary physical custodian.

The record in this case reveals on Sue Ellen's side that Sue Ellen has been offered a job in her field of nursing administration in Phillips, Columbia, at a salary significantly higher than she is currently earning and with greater career potential; and Michael has an asthma condition that will be controlled more effectively in Columbia, although it is being adequately controlled in Franklin City.

The evidence on Forest's side shows that he has been a loving and involved parent; since the divorce, he has taken full advantage of all the time he has physical custody to be with Michael; he telephones Michael twice a week, although Sue Ellen requires advance notice of the calls and limits them to five minutes each; Forest coaches Michael to develop his swimming skills and, although Sue Ellen has lodged objections with Michael's school, Forest has chaperoned school-related field trips; both sets of grandparents, whom Michael visits frequently and who are an important part of Michael's life, live within 20 miles of Franklin City; Sue Ellen has steadfastly refused to allow Forest any flexibility in the physical custody arrangements or the telephone communications. Forest has been actively involved in decisions about Michael's medical care, education, and religious upbringing through direct contact with the pediatrician, teachers, coaches, and ministers.

The only evidence presented by Sue Ellen concerning her plans for visits between Forest and Michael after the move was that Michael would spend three weeks in the summer and one week during winter break with Forest, with flights to be at Forest's expense. She also agreed to permit the twice-weekly telephone calls of five minutes' duration, also at Forest's expense.

The trial court denied the petition because it was not in Michael's best interests to be separated from his father. The appellate court reversed, holding that the trial court had failed to properly apply the judicially created presumption that a parent with sole legal custody or sole or primary physical custody may move the child from Franklin. The appellate court noted that Sue Ellen had provided a valid reason for the move. The appellate court did not address Sue Ellen's motivation or the effects of the move on Michael.

On this appeal, Forest asserts that the appellate court's interpretation of Section 109 of the Franklin Dissolution of Marriage Act failed to account for the objecting parent's relationship with the child by not requiring findings concerning the effect of Michael's separation from his father in determining the best interests of the child.

In interpreting Section 109 in the context of joint custodial situations, the court must balance the benefits derived from the parent's move, the need for finality in custody decrees, the rights of both custodial parents to make decisions for the child, the interest of the child in having a loving relationship with both parents, and the rights of both parents.

We interpret Section 109 to require the parent with primary physical custody who wishes to move with the child from this state to present a legitimate reason for the move. Once a legitimate reason has been established, a presumption is created in favor of the parent petitioning to move. The other parent can rebut the presumption by showing that the move is not in good faith or it is not in the best interests of the child. The parent seeking to rebut the presumption has the burden of persuading the court that the move is in bad faith or is not in the best interests of the child. This standard, although fact-based, recognizes the realities of a mobile society, while also seeking to prevent the primary custodial parent from undermining a child's relationship with the other parent.

Improved employment, educational opportunities, or health of the custodial parent, the new spouse, or the child are examples of legitimate reasons for a move. A move designed primarily to interfere with the relationship between the other parent and the child does not constitute a legitimate reason.

Sue Ellen has established a legitimate reason for the move—better employment for herself and improved health for Michael. There is a question, however, as to whether Forest carried his burden of persuading the court that the move is not in the best interests of Michael. Unquestionably, the move will affect the time Forest spends with Michael. The amount of time alone is not sufficient to harm the parent-child relationship, where there is a strong relationship and where the parents take other steps to encourage the relationship.

More troubling was the evidence that in the past Sue Ellen may have sought to interfere with Forest's relationship with Michael through limiting telephone calls and other measures. Based on the record, this court cannot determine whether Forest demonstrated that the move is not in the best interests of Michael. Because we cannot determine whether the trial court understood the proper test or whether the court properly considered the factors concerning best interests, we must remand to the trial court to determine whether Forest has rebutted the presumption and carried his burden of persuasion.

Feldman v. Feldman

Franklin Court of Appeal (2002)

Howard and Ruth Feldman were granted joint custody of their daughters at the time of their divorce in 1998. Ruth, who is the primary physical custodian, now petitions for removal of the daughters from Franklin to Columbia.

The daughters lived with Howard between August of 2000 and December of 2001, while Ruth completed a master's degree in speech therapy, and thereafter, lived primarily with Ruth.

Ruth's new husband has recently been promoted and transferred by his company to Columbia. The daughters, who are now 13 and 15, are in good health, do well in school, and are active in tennis. Ruth has testified that the school district in Columbia has an active tennis team as well as a solid academic program.

Howard opposes the move because of its effect on his relationship with the girls. At a minimum, Howard sees the girls every weekend and has dinner with them once during the week. He regularly attends parent-teacher conferences and the girls' sports competitions, even when their mother does not. Because of the distance, if the girls move, the girls will not see their father on a regular basis. Further, Howard cannot afford to fly to Columbia to participate in their activities.

Howard concedes that, until now, he and Ruth have been able to jointly reach decisions about the girls and resolve disagreements about their care. However, he believes that Ruth is moving so far away so that the girls will develop a closer relationship with their new father that will drive a wedge between him and the girls.

Ruth proposes that the girls can fly, at her cost, to Franklin for one three-day weekend each month, September through February. She will bring the girls to Franklin for Thanksgiving, the winter break, and an extended summer break so they can spend time with their father, his family, and Ruth's family who remain in Franklin. Further, the girls have cell phones so that they can call their father regularly. She also suggests that Howard and the girls can e-mail every day to maintain contact. Finally, Ruth will arrange with the schools to send duplicate report cards to Howard.

In *Marshall v. Marshall*, our Supreme Court created a presumption that the primary custodial parent may remove the children from the state provided the parent seeking to relocate shows a legitimate reason for the move. Ruth has shown a legitimate reason for the move—improved employment of a parent or the spouse. Howard attempts to establish bad faith by presenting evidence that the move is designed to ruin his relationship with his daughters.

Howard relies on the case of *Davis v. Davis*, in which this court prohibited Mr. Davis from removing the children because he himself conceded that his reason for removing the children was to stop the mother's "bad influence." The court determined, however, that the mother was a loving parent whose influence was one of a concerned parent. Additionally, Ms. Davis presented evidence that Mr. Davis had a long history of trying to alienate the children from their mother. No such evidence was presented here, where Ruth has supported a close relationship between the girls and their father. Howard failed in his effort to show bad faith.

Howard's second contention is that the move is not in the best interests of the children. In determining "best interests," the court is guided by the factors listed in Section 402 of the Franklin Dissolution of Marriage Act. Section 402 directs the court to consider the child's health, adjustment to home, school, and community, and the interaction of the child with parents and siblings.

Howard cites the case of *Lewis v. Lewis*, in which this court denied a petition for removal because of the negative effect the move would have on the health and adjustment of the child. The child was developmentally disabled and deaf. Expert testimony established that she needed very specialized care that was available in Franklin but not in Columbia, and that any change in routine, especially a relocation, would set back her progress by a year or more.

Unlike the *Lewis* case, the Feldman girls are healthy, well adjusted in their present home, and capable of adjusting to a new environment. They have visited the school they will attend if the move is permitted. Whether they remain in Franklin or move to Columbia, they will have promising careers, educationally and socially.

The children have a strong and healthy relationship with each parent. Both parents have been closely involved in the upbringing of the girls. Certainly, if the move is permitted, it will affect the time the girls spend with their father. The issue, however, is whether the move is in their best interests. It is, of course, in their best interests to have a good relationship with their father, as well as with their mother. While their relationship with Howard will be changed, we do not believe it will be destroyed. Ruth's plans for continuing contact provide Howard meaningful involvement in the children's lives.

Ruth has proposed reasonable means by which the girls can communicate with Howard on a regular, indeed daily, basis. Further, they will see Howard face-to-face at least once every month, during all but spring tennis season.

The trial court's order permitting the removal is affirmed.

Wells v. Wells
DRAFTERS' POINT SHEET

In this performance test item, applicants are asked by the senior partner who represents Joan Wells to prepare a brief in support of Joan Wells' petition to remove her child from the state in order to take new employment in a neighboring state. Under the Franklin Dissolution of Marriage Act Section 109, Joan is required to submit the petition to the court because she has joint custody of the child with Fred Wells.

When Joan and Fred Wells were divorced in 2002, they were granted joint custody of their son, Sammy. Joint custody is defined as joint legal custody and joint physical custody. In Franklin, joint physical custody does not mean equal durations of time with each parent. Now Joan has the opportunity for a new position in her field, requiring her to relocate from Franklin to Columbia.

Joan wishes to move in order to accept a position as associate professor of Irish Literature and Studies at Columbia State University in Columbia City, Columbia. She wishes to take the couple's son, Sammy, with her. In anticipation of the move, Joan has arranged for Sammy's care and upbringing and for various means of maintaining a relationship with his father, Fred. Fred opposes the petition to remove the child from the state on several grounds. He argues that Sammy's development in general and especially in music will be adversely affected. Fred also claims that it will be hard for him to carry out his responsibilities as a legal custodian if Sammy is separated from him. He believes that the move is motivated by a desire to separate him from his son or by Joan's jealousy toward his new wife.

Both parties presented testimony to the court during a hearing and the senior partner ordered an expedited transcript of the testimony. At the conclusion of the testimony, the court ordered the parties to file concurrent briefs, with no rebuttal. The task for applicants is to prepare the persuasive brief that Joan will file.

The File contains the instructing memorandum from the senior partner, an office memorandum regarding persuasive briefs, and the transcript of the hearing, which includes the stipulations entered by the parties. The Library contains excerpts from the Franklin Dissolution of Marriage Act, a Franklin Supreme Court opinion, and a Franklin Court of Appeals opinion. The File does not contain evidence concerning the effect of separation of a six-year-old from his father. Nor does the Library contain any law that makes the child's wishes a factor to be considered. Applicants who discuss those issues are acting outside the materials given.

The following discussion covers all of the points the drafters intended to raise in the problem. Applicants need not cover them all to receive passing or even excellent grades. Grading is entirely within the discretion of the graders in the user jurisdictions.

I. **Overview:** The office memorandum regarding persuasive briefs gives applicants the template for writing their answers in the form of a brief. Thus, it is expected that the work product will resemble a brief such as a lawyer would file with a court. Graders will have to decide how to weight the subjective components of "persuasiveness."

- There should be a statement of facts that explains the nature and essential features of the case, although, as the office memo explains, it should be abbreviated.

- The argument section should be broken down into carefully crafted headings that summarize the ensuing arguments. The arguments themselves should weave the law and the facts together into persuasive (as opposed to objective) statements of the case for the client.

Applicants are told that both sides are to file the briefs within 48 hours and that there will be no rebuttal briefs; therefore, applicants should anticipate the arguments of the opposite side and address them here.

II. **Statement of Facts:** This should include a brief recitation of the operative facts. Inasmuch as the trial judge already knows the facts, applicants should include only the key facts in the Statement of Facts and expand on them when they incorporate them into the legal argument part of the brief, but the Statement of Facts should at least describe the essence of the dispute.

- Essentially, applicants should explain that:
  - Joan and Fred Wells were divorced in 2002, and they were awarded joint custody of Sammy, now 6. Joan has primary physical custody of Sammy.
  - Joan Wells has completed her doctoral studies and has been offered a position as an associate professor in Irish Literature and Studies, her chosen field, at Columbia State University in Columbia City, Columbia.
  - She wishes to move to Columbia and take Sammy to live with her in Columbia.
  - Fred Wells, Sammy's father, opposes the move.

III. **Argument:** The argument section should reflect the steps in the legal analysis. Applicants should argue that the Franklin Supreme Court has interpreted Section 109 of the Franklin

Dissolution of Marriage Act to require that the parent who has sole or primary physical custody and who seeks to remove the child from the state establish a legitimate reason for the move. *Marshall v. Marshall*. Once that parent has done so, there is a presumption that the parent may remove the child. The presumption may be rebutted by evidence from the objecting parent that the move is not being made in good faith or that it is not in the best interests of the child. *Marshall v. Marshall*.

The following headings are suggestions only and should not be taken by the graders to be the only acceptable ones.

- <u>Moving to Take a Position as Associate Professor Which Will Improve Her Employment Opportunities and Her Financial Security Constitutes a Legitimate Reason for the Move and Entitles Joan Wells to a Presumption That the Petition Should Be Granted.</u>

The first issue is whether Joan Wells has met her burden of offering a legitimate reason for the move. Franklin Dissolution of Marriage Act Section 109; *Marshall v. Marshall*. Legitimate reasons include improvements in the education, employment, or health of the parent or child. *Marshall v. Marshall*. Joan Wells has presented evidence of a legitimate reason for the move:

- The predicate for Joan's entitlement to the judicially created presumption is that she is a parent with "primary physical custody." She meets that requirement. *See* the court's introductory statement in the transcript.
- She has been offered a position as an associate professor in Irish Literature and Studies at Columbia State University, Columbia City, Columbia.
- The position is in her field of study and offers a better career path for her than her present position at the community college, and at Columbia State University, she will have colleagues to encourage her work.
- She is not likely to be hired by the Franklin State University, which has a policy against hiring its own graduates.
- The new position offers a higher salary, the promise of raises, and the potential for reduced tuition for Sammy, the child.

Thus, Joan has met her burden. She is entitled to a presumption in favor of granting her petition. *Marshall v. Marshall*.

Because the court instructed the parties that there will be no rebuttal briefs, applicants must anticipate the arguments that Fred Wells is likely to make and must address them as well.

- <u>Sammy's Ability to Maintain a Father-Son Relationship with Fred Wells and Sammy's</u>

Health and Normal Development Rebut Any Speculation About Sammy's Possible
Regression, the Lack of Opportunity to Join a Children's Choir, or the Possible Harm to the
Father-Son Relationship.

A parent who objects to the petition to remove a child from the state may try to show that it
is not in the best interests of the child. *Marshall v. Marshall*. To determine the best interests of the
child, the court must consider the factors specified in Section 402 of the Franklin Dissolution of
Marriage Act. *Feldman v. Feldman*. These factors include:

- The mental and physical health of all involved;
- The child's adjustment to the child's home, school, and community;
- The interaction and interrelationship of the child with the child's parents, siblings, and any other person who significantly affects the child's best interests; and
- The wishes of the child's parents as to custody.

The applicants should distinguish the *Lewis* case in which the court denied the petition to
move where the *Lewis* child was deaf and developmentally disabled and in need of a routine. There,
expert testimony supported the belief that the move would cause the *Lewis* child to regress by at
least a year. Unlike the *Lewis* child, Sammy is developing normally and has demonstrated his ability
to adjust to past changes. There is no expert testimony in this case predicting his likely regression,
simply some speculation by a day care center counselor who also allowed that he is as likely to
adjust well.

Fred may claim that the move is not in the best interests of Sammy. To prove that the move is
not in the best interests of Sammy, Fred may assert:

- At the time of the divorce, Sammy regressed and needed assistance in dealing with the divorce;
- Sammy has no friends or family in Columbia;
- Sammy will not have the unique opportunities for developing his talent that he has with the Franklin City Children's Choir because Columbia does not have a comparable children's choir;
- Joan will not develop the talent as would Fred, who is a music teacher;
- Sammy will see his father only eight weeks a year instead of weekly as at present;
- Unlike the children in *Feldman*, Sammy is young;
- Fred will not be able to participate in Sammy's activities.

Applicants should argue, however, that Joan has effectively rebutted this evidence by showing:

- Sammy did adjust after the divorce with some limited assistance, and the counselor who worked with him at that time, a witness called by Fred, cannot predict that he will regress. The counselor had not worked with Sammy for over a year;
- Sammy is resilient as evidenced by his past ability to adapt, and the move is being made in advance of the start of the school year in order to give him a chance to adjust;
- Sammy is developing normally and is well adjusted and ready to advance in school;
- It is too early to realistically assess Sammy's musical talents but Joan will encourage the development of those talents along with others;
- As described above, Joan has a history of supporting Sammy's relationship with Fred.

Applicants should argue that the evidence taken as a whole fails to show that the move is not in the best interests of the child. In fact, the evidence shows that this move is much like that in the *Feldman* case where the court approved the petition to remove the children.

- <u>Fred Will Be Able to Carry Out His Responsibilities after the Move as a Joint Parent Through Telephone and E-mail Contact with Schools, Doctors, and Others.</u>

Fred may argue that he will be unable to carry out his responsibilities as a parent with joint legal custody (i.e., his decision-making responsibilities and his ability to maintain a loving relationship), if the move is permitted. He may suggest that the move is a ruse to set aside the court's original custody order because it will completely deprive him of joint *physical* custody. A parent, such as Fred, with joint legal custody has equal rights and responsibilities for major decisions concerning the child, including but not limited to the education of the child, health care, and religious training. *See* Section 30 of the Franklin Dissolution of Marriage Act. Fred may claim that he cannot effectively participate in decisions about Sammy because:

- He cannot effectively obtain firsthand information about Sammy and will have to rely on Joan for information about Sammy;
- He will not be able to be present for teacher-parent conferences or for doctor visits.

However, Joan has countered this evidence by testimony that:

- Fred can obtain this information through telephone or e-mail contact with the teachers and doctors;
- Joan will arrange for Sammy to regularly send packets of his schoolwork to Fred.

- Joan and Fred have a history of discussing issues that arise concerning Sammy and have been able to work out their differences in the past.

Based on this evidence, applicants should persuade the court that Fred will be able to continue to be a joint legal custodian for Sammy, even though his physical custody will be diminished.

- <u>Evidence That Teaching Irish Literature Is a Lifelong Dream and That Joan Will Support the Father-Son Relationship through Telephone, E-mail, and Computer Conferencing as Well as In-Person Visits Rebuts Any Suggestion of Bad Faith.</u>

A parent objecting to the removal of the child from the state may rebut the presumption by showing that the move is in bad faith. A move is in bad faith if it is designed to interfere with the parent-child relationship. *Marshall v. Marshall; Davis v. Davis.* Applicants should distinguish *Davis*, in which the father admitted that the reason for the move was to eliminate the "bad influence" of the mother. The court determined that the mother was a loving parent and denied the father's petition.

The facts in this case are much closer to those in *Feldman* where the court permitted the move. In *Feldman*, the mother had encouraged the close relationship between the children and their father and had proposed reasonable means of sustaining it, such as regular in-person visits, regular telephone contact, and daily e-mail communications.

Fred Wells may claim that the move interferes with the parent-child relationship:

- Fred's time with Sammy will be reduced from regular weekly contacts, totaling about 20 weeks a year, to eight weeks per year;
- Sammy will not see relatives on a regular basis;
- Fred will no longer engage in activities on a weekly basis with Sammy.

But time is not the only factor courts use in assessing bad faith. The courts have permitted moves where they affect the time a parent has with the child but where the relationship can be sustained through other means. *Feldman v. Feldman.* Courts are more suspicious of the moving parent's motive where there has been a history of interference with the relationship between the objecting parent and the child. *Marshall v. Marshall; Davis v. Davis.* Unlike the situations in those cases, Joan has been supportive of the father-son relationship and has proposed means of supporting the relationship despite the distance between Fred and Sammy. Applicants should detail what Joan has done and has offered to do in support of the father-son relationship:

- Joan has kept a photo of Sammy and his father in Sammy's room ever since the separation and has not interfered in the time Sammy spends with his father.

- If the move is permitted, Joan has offered that Fred may make tapes of books for Sammy to listen to, Fred may call Sammy whenever he wants, Fred and Sammy can communicate daily by computer conferencing and later, when Sammy is older, by e-mail.

- Joan will have Sammy send his father packets of his schoolwork every week.

- She will also record Sammy's activities and send them to his father.

- She will take Sammy to visit his father in person eight weeks a year and when Sammy is older, he can fly on his own for these visits.

Fred may also claim that the move is in bad faith because it is motivated by Joan's jealousy over Fred's remarriage to someone she dislikes:

- Joan will not talk with Fred's new wife, Kathleen.

- Joan is jealous of Kathleen or of Fred's remarriage or both.

Joan will rebut this evidence by showing that her desire to move to take the position in Irish Studies is part of a lifelong dream expressed long before Fred remarried.

Applicants should argue to the court that the sort of evidence Fred introduced is insufficient to show bad faith and is rebutted by Joan's history of pursuing her career goal.

IV.   Conclusion: Applicants should persuade the court that Joan has met her burden by offering a legitimate reason for the move and that therefore she is entitled to a presumption in favor of the petition. While Fred has attempted to rebut that presumption by offering evidence of bad faith and evidence that the move is not in the best interests of Sammy, Joan has effectively rebutted such evidence. In light of the case law in Franklin, Joan is entitled to remove Sammy.

July 2002 Multistate Performance Tests
and Point Sheets

State v. Tweedy

FILE

LIBRARY

Office of the District Attorney

DeSoto County
83645 Washington Street
DeSoto, Franklin 33123
(901) 555-1294

TO: Applicant

FROM: Shirley Clay Scott, Assistant District Attorney

RE: Tweedy, James A.

DATE: July 30, 2002

I have been asked to recommend whether we should prosecute James A. Tweedy. The District Attorney has stated his belief that the case will be difficult to try and that it is unlikely that a conviction can be obtained. I, however, believe that this case is worth pursuing and want to seek a felony indictment against Mr. Tweedy for two counts of endangering the welfare of a child under Penal Code § 4304.

Please prepare for my signature a two-part memorandum to the District Attorney. The first part should persuade the District Attorney that we have sufficient admissible evidence to prove all the elements necessary to obtain a conviction. You may assume that we can avoid any hearsay problems that might arise. I know that additional facts may facilitate prosecution, but in this first part you should address only the question of whether we have enough evidence to proceed based on what we *already* know.

In the second part of the memorandum, which should be brief, identify any conflicting or incomplete facts in the File that we will need to further investigate or clarify to facilitate prosecution. Recommend the investigative steps this office should take to develop these additional facts.

INCIDENT NO. 02-3105	**DeSoto Police Department Incident Report**			Date of Statement 7/17/02
NAME (LAST, FIRST, MIDDLE) OF PERSON GIVING STATEMENT Tweedy, James A.		DOB/AGE 8/3/76	RESIDENCE PHONE None	BUSINESS PHONE None
STREET ADDRESS 1376 Archer Ave, Apt. 27		CITY DeSoto	STATE Franklin	ZIP CODE 33123
STATEMENT TAKEN BY (NAME/BADGE) Mary Lou Higgerson #1361		IN PRESENCE OF		

On the evening of July 16, 2002, and the early morning hours of July 17, officer called to the scene of a fire to investigate possible criminal neglect. Two minor children (the older child three (3) years of age and the younger twenty (20) months) were left in their apartment unattended while father, James A. Tweedy, participated in a social evening with friends.

Before leaving, Tweedy put the children in the bedroom. According to his statement, he secured the bedroom door by inserting two table knives between the door and the jamb. In addition, he locked the main door to the apartment. Tweedy claims he spoke to neighbor, Mrs. England, who had consented to watch out for the children in his absence.

According to another neighbor, Glen Poshard, at approximately 12:05 a.m. a fire started in the building, possibly originating as a result of a defective television set in Tweedy's apartment. Tweedy returned to premises at 3:00 a.m. at which point investigating officer briefly interviewed Tweedy before Tweedy left for the hospital to see if he could find the children.

Firefighter Albert Malone informed officer that unknown visitor to the building, learning from a neighbor that the youngsters were trapped in the bedroom, attempted to remove them but was prevented from doing so by the manner in which the bedroom door had been fastened. Firefighters, upon entry, found the children apparently dead in the bedroom of the apartment.

Signature

INCIDENT NO. 02-3105	**DeSoto Police Department Incident Report** **Addendum**	Date of Statement 7/18/02

NAME (LAST, FIRST, MIDDLE) OF PERSON GIVING STATEMENT Wirthin, Harry P.	DOB/AGE 9/2/46	RESIDENCE PHONE 555-5678	BUSINESS PHONE same

LOCATION OF INCIDENT 1376 Archer Ave, Apt. 22	CITY DeSoto	STATE Franklin	ZIP CODE 33123

STATEMENT TAKEN BY (NAME/BADGE) Mary Lou Higgerson #1361	IN PRESENCE OF

Addendum to Incident Report dated July 17, 2002.

I spoke with Harry P. Wirthin, owner and superintendent of the building occupied by James Tweedy and family. He stated that Tweedy was typical tenant. Only problem was that 4 years ago a small electrical fire occurred in Tweedy's apartment. Apparently, Tweedy's wife, who is now deceased, left a curling iron on in the bathroom and it overheated causing a short that started a fire. No one was in the apartment at the time.

Mr. Wirthin did indicate that on at least two prior occasions he knew the children were left alone in the apartment. He also indicated that the neighbor two floors up, a Mrs. England, occasionally watched the children. I spoke with Mrs. England who indicated that on one or two occasions she had watched the children. She indicated that she had been asked to watch them on the night in question, but that she declined.

A check of DeSoto Licensing & Inspection records indicates that Mr. Wirthin has been cited on 5 occasions within the last 5 years for code violations related to wiring problems in the building. All citations resulted from complaints from tenants about faulty wiring.

Signature

INCIDENT NO. 02-3105	**DeSoto Fire Marshal Report** **DeSoto, Franklin**	DATE OF INVESTIGATION 7/17/02

An investigation was conducted on the above-referenced date into the fire at 1376 Archer Ave, Apt. 27.

Cause of fire was electrical problem located in defective television set. This conclusion was easily reached with examination of set and surrounding area. There existed little actual fire damage. Damage was limited to television set and curtains located near the set. Internal part of television set received extensive damage.

Smoke and water damage in contrast was extensive. Level of smoke commensurate with high use of synthetic materials in apartment.

NAME (LAST, FIRST, MIDDLE) OF PERSON MAKING REPORT Gatton, Phil	TITLE Deputy Fire Marshal	BUSINESS PHONE 555-8463	
STREET ADDRESS OF INVESTIGATION 1376 Archer Ave, Apt. 27	CITY DeSoto	STATE Franklin	ZIP CODE 33123
Signature			

OFFICE OF THE DESOTO COUNTY MEDICAL EXAMINER
Marsha Ryan, J.D., M.D.
Chief Medical Examiner
9765 Garwin Street
DeSoto, Franklin 33123

July 22, 2002

TO: Shirley Clay Scott, Assistant District Attorney

FROM: Marsha Ryan, Chief Medical Examiner

RE: Alma & Fred Tweedy

I got your voice mail concerning the autopsies on the Tweedy children. The autopsies are complete, and I'll send you a copy of the report. The important details, however, are pretty straightforward.

Fred: White male, approximately three years old. General health was good. No evidence of any disease process. Cause of death was smoke inhalation resulting from fire.

Alma: White female, approximately twenty months old. General health was poor. Evidence of congenital heart malformation, which if remained undetected would be life threatening. Cause of death was smoke inhalation resulting from fire.

Let me know if you need anything else.

Transcript of Interview of James Tweedy

by Officer Higgerson

July 22, 2002

Officer: Thank you for coming down, Mr. Tweedy. The night of the fire was horrible and I understand your difficulty in answering all my questions then.

Tweedy: Well, of course, I wanted to get to the hospital as soon as possible, but it was too late.

Officer: Yes, I know. I'm sorry. Now, Mr. Tweedy, I want to state on the record that you do not have to talk with me. Anything you say can and will be used against you. You have the right to be represented by a lawyer. If you cannot afford to hire a lawyer, one will be appointed to represent you.

Tweedy: I know my rights.

Officer: And you are willing to talk to me?

Tweedy: Yes.

Officer: Why did you leave the children alone?

Tweedy: I didn't.

Officer: What do you mean?

Tweedy: I asked Mrs. England to watch them. She said she would be happy to.

Officer: But she didn't come down to the apartment, did she?

Tweedy: Not right when I asked, but she said she'd be down there in a few minutes, after she finished her dishes.

Officer: Then why did you jam the bedroom door the way you did?

Tweedy: This is not a safe neighborhood. The landlord doesn't keep the place in the best shape and I could not trust the locks on the door to the apartment. Look, I did what I could. I even left the TV on to make people think I was home.

Officer: But, it was the bedroom door jamb that you stuck the knives into.

Tweedy: Well, I couldn't very well do that on the outside door.

Officer: Was it your habit to leave the children unattended?

Tweedy: No.

Officer: Had you ever done it before?

Tweedy: Like I said, I didn't do it this time. I'd asked Mrs. England to watch them.

Officer: Mrs. England denies being asked.

Tweedy: Well, she's lying. Obviously she's afraid that she's going to be blamed. In fact, rather than sitting here and accusing me, you should be asking her why she didn't do what she said she would.

Officer: Mr. Tweedy, were you drinking the night of the fire?

Tweedy: I went to a club that night. Yes, I had a couple beers. I was not drunk. I'm sorry, I think I should talk to an attorney.

Franklin Penal Code

§ 4304. Endangering Welfare of a Child

(a) Offense defined. A parent, guardian, or other person supervising the welfare of a child under 18 years of age commits an offense if he knowingly endangers the welfare of the child by violating a duty of care, protection or support.

(b) Grading. An offense under this section constitutes a felony of the third degree.

Franklin Rules of Evidence

Rule 401. Definition of "Relevant Evidence"

"Relevant evidence" means evidence having any tendency to make the existence of any fact that is of consequence to the determination of the action more probable or less probable than it would be without the evidence.

Rule 402. Relevant Evidence Generally Admissible; Irrelevant Evidence Inadmissible

All relevant evidence is admissible, except as otherwise provided by the Constitution of the State of Franklin, by Act of the Franklin Legislature, by these rules, or by other rules prescribed by the Franklin Supreme Court pursuant to statutory authority. Evidence which is not relevant is not admissible.

Rule 403. Exclusion of Relevant Evidence on Grounds of Prejudice, Confusion, or Waste of Time

Although relevant, evidence may be excluded if its probative value is substantially outweighed by the danger of unfair prejudice, confusion of the issues, or misleading the jury, or by considerations of undue delay, waste of time, or needless presentation of cumulative evidence.

Rule 404. Character Evidence Not Admissible To Prove Conduct; Exceptions; Other Crimes

(a) Character evidence generally. Evidence of a person's character or a trait of character is not admissible for the purpose of proving action in conformity therewith on a particular occasion, except:

(1) Character of accused. Evidence of a pertinent trait of character offered by an accused, or by the prosecution to rebut the same;

(2) Character of victim. Evidence of a pertinent trait of character of the victim of the crime offered by an accused, or by the prosecution to rebut the same, or evidence of a character trait of peacefulness of the victim offered by the prosecution in a homicide case to rebut evidence that the victim was the first aggressor;

* * * *

(b) Other crimes, wrongs, or acts. Evidence of other crimes, wrongs, or acts is not admissible to prove the character of a person in order to show action in conformity therewith. It may, however, be admissible for other purposes, such as proof of motive, opportunity, intent, preparation, plan, knowledge, identity, or absence of mistake or accident, provided that upon request by the accused, the prosecution in a criminal case shall provide reasonable notice in advance of trial, or during trial if the court excuses pretrial notice on good cause shown, of the general nature of any such evidence it intends to introduce at trial.

State v. Miller

Franklin Supreme Court (1992)

Appellant, Rachel Miller, was convicted under Franklin Penal Code § 4304, endangering the welfare of a child, following a non-jury trial. Miller was thereafter sentenced to two years' probation. This appeal ensued.

The relevant facts are straightforward and thoroughly tragic. On the evening of November 18, 1989, Miller, with her 22-month-old son, Clarence, visited Antonio Green, the father of the child. Green and Miller are not husband and wife. Green resided in a three-story rooming house. A restaurant was located on the first floor of the premises. Eugenia Orr lived on the second level and Green occupied the top floor.

Father, mother, and child met at a neighborhood tavern and then returned to the rooming house. Earlier in the day, Green had accompanied Orr on a shopping trip; father, mother, and child went directly to Orr's apartment to examine that day's purchases. Miller was not well acquainted with Orr. After some time, Miller went upstairs to Green's room, leaving the child in Orr's apartment in the care of Green because the child was playing with his father's new shoes. When the child tired of this activity, Green took him upstairs to Miller and then returned to the Orr apartment.

Miller washed and changed the child and prepared him for bed. Green's room contained a double bed. Nearby was an electric space heater, which turned out to be in a damaged condition but was then operating. Miller put the child in the bed and then lay down with the child until he fell asleep. Once her son was asleep, Miller decided to go down to the first-floor restaurant to buy some juice for the child. She left Green's apartment with the child asleep in the bed, the space heater operating, and the door to the hallway stairs open. She also left her sweater in the apartment.

When Miller stopped on the second floor en route to the restaurant, Green asked Miller if she would "go clubbing" (visiting bars or nightclubs) with him. She declined, explaining that she had to watch the child and that she was tired and not dressed for the occasion anyway. While she was on the first floor, Green yelled down to her through the common hallway, repeating his request and saying that Orr had agreed to watch the child. Miller agreed to accompany him. She asked Green to bring down her sweater and did not return upstairs. Green brought her the sweater. He had, in fact, not spoken to Orr about watching the child and Orr did not do so.

Green and Miller left the rooming house at approximately 1:00 a.m. and visited two clubs. During this time, they were joined by friends. One of these friends was called as a witness and testified that Miller continually fretted about the child. Returning to the rooming house after 3:00 a.m., Green and

Miller discovered police and fire trucks in the street outside and the building ablaze. The only death resulting from the conflagration was Miller's infant son, who died of smoke inhalation and burns. The space heater was determined to be the cause of the fire. Green was convicted of various criminal charges in connection with the child's death. Miller was convicted of endangering the welfare of her child.

We must consider whether the evidence was sufficient to uphold the verdict of the trial court. We must accept all the evidence and all reasonable inferences that may be drawn from that evidence upon which the factfinder could have based its verdict. If the evidence, viewed in the light most favorable to the state, is not sufficient to establish guilt beyond a reasonable doubt of the crime charged, then the conviction should be overturned.

Miller claims that the evidence presented at trial was insufficient to prove the intent element of the crime with which she was charged. Under Penal Code § 4304, a parent or other person supervising the welfare of a child commits a felony if he or she *knowingly* endangers the child. Section 302(b) of the Penal Code defines knowingly:

> (2) A person acts knowingly with respect to a material element of an offense when:
>
> > (i) if the element involves the nature of his conduct or the attendant circumstances, he is aware that his conduct is of that nature or that such circumstances exist; and

> > (ii) if the element involves the result of his conduct, he is aware that it is practically certain that his conduct will cause such a result.

It is clear that § 4304 contemplates endangerment either by act or by omission to act. In *State v. Cardwell* (1986), this court established a three-pronged standard for testing the sufficiency of evidence of the intent element under § 4304:

> We hold that evidence is sufficient to prove the intent element of the offense of endangering the welfare of a child when the accused is aware of his or her duty to protect the child; is aware that the child is in circumstances that are reasonably likely to result in harm to the child; and has either failed to act or has taken actions so lame or meager that such actions cannot reasonably be expected to be effective to protect the child from physical or psychological harm.

If proof fails on any one of these prongs, the evidence must be found insufficient.

Employing this test, the *Cardwell* court found sufficient evidence of intent where a mother was aware that her child was being subjected to sexual abuse by the stepfather and took wholly ineffectual remedial actions. Specifically, she wrote letters to the stepfather expressing outrage and warning that she would not tolerate such conduct and she made an aborted attempt to move the child to a relative's house.

On the other hand, in *State v. Louie* (1990), this court found insufficient evidence to convict a husband and wife where they knew that their 13-year-old daughter was engaging in sexual activity with an adult and became pregnant against the express warnings of a physician. *Louie* differed from *Cardwell* in that the parents did not allow the child to remain in a potentially dangerous situation; they simply failed to stop the child from surreptitiously seeking out sexual activity. The court was unwilling to extend culpability, noting that parents could not know everything about their child's activities nor was § 4304 intended to punish parents merely because their child becomes pregnant.

Here, the trial court, sitting as factfinder, determined that when Miller left with Green to go clubbing, she was aware that her infant son was in the third-floor room with the space heater on. The court found that by failing to question Green's statement that Orr would watch the child, Miller has evidenced the requisite intent for purposes of § 4304. We have difficulty in finding that the evidence is sufficient to satisfy the *Cardwell* tripartite test. It is undisputed that appellant was aware of her duty to protect her child. However, merely leaving the child alone is insufficient to establish the requisite intent. We cannot find as a matter of law that she was aware that she had placed her child in circumstances that were likely to result in harm to the child or that her failure to check on the alleged babysitting arrangements was unreasonable under *Cardwell*.

The trial court specifically credited Miller's

testimony that she believed Green when he told her that Orr was watching her child. The logical inference based on this finding is that Miller was not aware that she had left her child unattended. There was no evidence presented at trial that Green was an inherently dishonest person or that Miller had cause to disbelieve him. The trial court has based Miller's culpability under § 4304 not on the fact that Miller knowingly left her child alone, but rather that she should not have been so gullible as to believe Green. Undeniably, Miller may have exercised poor judgment on the night in question, and perhaps she is guilty of reckless or negligent conduct in connection with her son's death. However, this is not sufficient for a finding of guilt under § 4304. If Miller in fact believed that her son was in the care of another, she did not knowingly place him in circumstances that were reasonably likely to result in harm, and her conduct cannot be adjudged criminal.

Judgment reversed. Appellant discharged.

State v. Shoup

Franklin Supreme Court (1993)

Joseph C. Shoup was tried by jury and was found guilty of homicide by vehicle while driving under the influence of alcohol. Shoup asserts that the trial court committed reversible error by refusing to give the instruction requested by the defense on the issue of causation.

On January 3, 1990, at about 8:00 p.m., appellant was operating an automobile on Oak Street, a narrow alleyway located in the town of Vienna. The passengers in appellant's vehicle were Michelle Shoup, his wife, who was seated in the front passenger seat, and Jean Moll and John Rush, who were in the back seat. Appellant was observed failing to stop for three consecutive stop signs, and the speed of his vehicle was estimated to be approximately 50 to 55 miles per hour.

Appellant drove through the intersection of Oak and Williams Streets without stopping at the stop sign. His vehicle collided with a large dump truck parked in the alleyway near a loading dock at a garment factory. The site of the accident was about 30 to 35 feet from the intersection.

Upon being summoned to the scene of the accident, Charles Harris, the Police Chief for the town of Vienna, observed that appellant smelled strongly of alcohol and that there were several beer cans on the floor of the vehicle. All of the vehicle's occupants were transported for medical treatment. Appellant's

wife suffered massive internal injuries and died shortly after being taken by helicopter to Cardinal Medical Center. Appellant was taken to Ashland State Hospital, where, at 9:30 p.m., blood samples were drawn at the request of Chief Harris for the purpose of determining appellant's blood alcohol level. Two blood tests measured appellant's blood alcohol content at 0.176% and 0.175%.

At trial, the defense contended that the legal cause of Michelle Shoup's death had been the illegal parking of the dump truck with which appellant's vehicle collided. Police Chief Harris testified that there had been a no parking sign posted at the loading dock where the dump truck was parked. However, according to Chief Harris, this sign had been placed there by the garment factory and not by the town. Therefore, he was without legal authority to issue tickets for illegal parking at that location. Other testimony established that, despite poor lighting conditions, the dump truck could be seen from the intersection at Oak and Williams Streets. Additionally, both Jean Moll and John Rush described appellant's driving prior to the accident as erratic.

Causation is an essential element of a criminal charge, which the State must prove beyond a reasonable doubt. The tort concept of proximate cause plays no role in a prosecution for criminal homicide. Rather, the State must prove a more direct causal relationship between the defendant's conduct and the victim's death. However, it has never been the law of this State that criminal responsibility must be confined to a sole or immediate cause of death. Criminal responsibility is properly assessed against one whose conduct was a direct and substantial factor in producing the result even though other factors combined with that conduct to achieve the result. Thus, a defendant cannot escape the natural consequences of his act merely because of foreseeable complications.

In this case, a jury could find that appellant's conduct was a direct and substantial factor in bringing about the death of Michelle Shoup. The evidence disclosed that, while intoxicated, appellant drove his vehicle down a narrow, dimly lit alleyway, erratically and at a high rate of speed, failing to stop at three consecutive intersections where stop signs had been posted. Moreover, the evidence suggested that had appellant obeyed the stop sign at the intersection of Oak and Williams Streets, he would have been able to observe the dump truck parked in the alleyway. The fact that the dump truck was parked in the alleyway undoubtedly contributed to the accident. Appellant's conduct started an unbroken chain of causation that directly and substantially led to his wife's death. Because the fact that another vehicle may have been parked in a hazardous manner was a foreseeable circumstance, appellant is not relieved from the natural consequences of his conduct.

Affirmed.

State v. Tweedy
DRAFTERS' POINT SHEET

In this performance test item, applicants are employed in the Office of the District Attorney. Their task is to write a persuasive memorandum to convince the District Attorney that there is enough evidence to prosecute James Tweedy on two felony counts of endangering the welfare of a child and to identify additional facts that would be helpful.

On the night of the incident, James Tweedy, a single parent of two minor children, put the children to bed, secured the bedroom door by jamming two table knives in the door jamb, locked the main door to his apartment, and went out to a night club, leaving the children alone. He claims that he asked Mrs. England, a neighbor, if she would watch the children, and he claims that she said she would. Mrs. England is reported at one place in the record to have said she declined and in another place to have said that she was not asked to watch the children on this occasion.

While Tweedy was away, a fire started in a defective television set he had left on in his apartment. An unidentified visitor to the building went into Tweedy's apartment in an attempt to rescue the two children but was unable to get into the bedroom because of the way the door had been secured. The children died of smoke inhalation.

The File contains the police incident reports, the fire marshal's report, a letter from the county medical examiner assigning the cause of death, and a transcript of a police interview with Tweedy. The Library contains the "endangering" statute, excerpts from the Franklin Rules of Evidence, and two cases.

The following discussion covers all of the points the drafters intended to raise in the problem. Applicants need not cover them all to receive passing or even excellent grades. Grading decisions are within the discretion of the graders in the jurisdictions.

1.   **Overview:** The applicants' work product should be persuasive in tone and the format should be similar to that of an office memorandum.

The problem breaks down into four logical components:

- A recognition that a conviction under the "endangering" statute requires that the accused have "knowingly" violated a duty to care for the children;

- A recognition that the accused's acts or omissions must be the direct and substantial cause of the deaths of the children;

- Application of the available facts, with the conclusion that there is enough evidence to obtain a conviction (Subsumed in this component is the requirement of a showing of adequate, competent, and admissible evidence.); and

- Identification of specific additional facts to be obtained and/or clarified, and the investigative steps that should be taken to do so. Applicants should recognize these as *additional* and not as already known facts that can be used to convince the DA that there is enough evidence to obtain a conviction.

No particular format or order of discussion is required. It must be discernible from the answers that the foregoing components are covered, but whether the applicants discuss them separately and discretely or whether they mix their discussions of the facts and the law is not important. Either format is acceptable.

2.   **The Elements of the Crime:** Applicants are expected to analyze § 4304 of the Franklin Penal Code, "the endangering statute," and recognize that a showing of causation is necessary.

- Section 4304 contains the following elements to the crime:

  - The offender must be a parent, guardian, or other person supervising the welfare of the child.

    - Tweedy was the father of the children.

  - The child must be under 18.

    - The Medical Examiner's letter shows that the children were 3 years old and 20 months old.

  - The offender must have the "duty of care, protection or support."

    - Tweedy, as the children's parent, had such a duty.

  - The duty to care for the children must be "knowingly" violated. This is the problematic intent issue.

    - The applicants must look to *State v. Miller* for a definition of "knowingly" and the standard for testing whether conduct was knowing.

- Causation, in the criminal sense, must be shown to be direct and substantial as opposed to proximate causation in the tort sense.
- The discussion in *State v. Shoup* is relevant to this issue.

3.   **Application of the Available Facts:** Here, applicants should apply the available facts to each of the elements of the crime and argue how the facts suffice to prove each of the elements.

- The statutory definition of "knowingly" is given in *State v. Miller*.
    - Applicants should recognize that the element of the crime to which the "knowingly" standard is applied is Tweedy's violation of his duty of care or protection.
- The known facts are to be applied to the three-pronged test set forth in *State v. Miller*:
    - <u>Tweedy was aware of his duty to protect the children</u>.
        - He is presumed as parent to know that he has a such a duty toward his children.
        - His actual knowledge of his duty is shown by the following provable facts:
            - The police incident report and the police interview both record admissions by Tweedy that he asked Mrs. England to watch the children. This admissible evidence demonstrates that he knew he had a duty not to leave them home alone.
            - He admits having jammed the bedroom door with the table knives because it was not a safe neighborhood and the locks on the door to his apartment could not be trusted. This admission is also admissible evidence that he knew he had to protect the children.
            - He left the television set on to make it appear as if he were at home—another piece of admissible evidence that he knew the children should be supervised.
            - He admits in the police interview that in the past, when he had gone out without the children, he had asked Mrs. England to watch them. This admission is corroborated by Mrs.

England's statement to the investigating officer and is also admissible evidence of his awareness of his duty.

- <u>Tweedy was aware that the children were in circumstances that were reasonably likely to result in harm</u>.

  - All of the foregoing facts go equally to prove this element; i.e., his jamming the door, having asked Mrs. England in the past to babysit when he left without the children, and leaving the television set turned on also tend to prove that Tweedy was aware that leaving the children home alone was a threat to their welfare. The facts are therefore generally relevant and admissible under the Franklin Rules of Evidence, Rules 401 and 402.

  - The problem, however, is that these facts are not directly relevant to the issue of whether Tweedy knew that the danger to which the children were exposed was the danger of fire.

    - It is implicit in the two cases cited internally in *State v. Miller* (*Cardwell* and *Louie*) that the requisite awareness must be somehow related to the danger that resulted in the harm.

  - Accordingly, there is a need for evidence of Tweedy's specific awareness of the fire danger. This part of the case is problematic.

  - The only *currently available* evidence that Tweedy was aware of the danger of fire (and more particularly, an electrical fire) was that four years earlier Tweedy's now deceased wife had left a curling iron plugged in and it had shorted, causing a fire in the same apartment.

  - Applicants must find a way to make this fact admissible as to Tweedy's knowledge that there was a danger of fire. (See *infra* for *additional* facts to be investigated that may help prove this knowledge.)

- Evidence Rule 404(b) should furnish a clue to the applicants that evidence of the prior fire should come in to show Tweedy's knowledge of the danger of fire.
  - Starting the earlier fire is not an "other act" within the meaning of 404(b) because it was not his act. It was his wife's act.
  - Admission of the evidence of the earlier fire would be sought not to show that Tweedy was responsible for the fire but, rather, merely that he knew about it as a "similar happening."
- Applicants should recognize that admissibility of the fact of the earlier fire will be contested at trial. Nevertheless, they should argue that it will be admitted to show Tweedy's knowledge of the specific danger of fire. This evidence, together with the evidence of his knowledge about ensuring the physical welfare of his children, will suffice to convict.
- The actions Tweedy took to carry out his duty were so "lame or meager" as to be ineffectual.
  - It is disputed whether Tweedy asked Mrs. England to babysit that evening and whether, if he did ask, she agreed or declined to do so.
  - Nevertheless, even if Tweedy is to be believed, he admitted to police that he left the children in the apartment knowing that it would be some time before Mrs. England would join them.
    - This is distinguishable from the situation in *State v. Miller*, where the defendant did reasonably believe that a neighbor was watching the baby when she left to go "clubbing."
    - Given his knowledge of the earlier fire, his actions were antithetical to the protection of the children:

leaving before Mrs. England arrived to be with them; jamming the bedroom door shut in such a way that no one could get in to rescue them in the event of an emergency; and leaving the television set on, thus risking another electrical fire.

- <u>Tweedy's actions were a direct and substantial factor in the deaths of the children.</u>
  - According to the fire marshal's report, the fire was caused by an electrical problem in the defective television set.
    - But for Tweedy's having left the TV set on, the fire would not have occurred.
    - Even though the fire itself was not extensive, smoke resulted from "high use of synthetic materials in the apartment." Under the reasoning of *State v. Shoup*, the smoke from the fire was a "foreseeable circumstance" that did not relieve Tweedy of liability.
  - Moreover, the way Tweedy secured the bedroom door prevented entry or escape.
  - All of the foregoing facts, taken together with the fact that Tweedy left the children just so he could go out drinking, should suffice to obtain a conviction.

4.   **Additional Facts and Investigative Steps:** The materials in the File suggest that many more facts that will help in the prosecution can be obtained and/or clarified:

- The investigating officer should be contacted to ascertain which is correct: the statement in the incident report that Mrs. England was asked but declined to babysit, or the statement in the interview transcript that Mrs. England denies she was even asked.
- Mrs. England should be contacted and asked about whether she was asked and agreed to babysit on the night of the fire as well as about past occasions when she babysat or when she was asked but declined to babysit. She should also be asked

whether she knows of occasions when she had declined, but Tweedy had nevertheless gone out and left the children alone.

- In view of the fact that the outside door to the apartment was locked, Mrs. England should be asked whether she has a key.

- An investigator should interview the neighbor to whom Firefighter Albert Malone had spoken and also try to find the "unknown visitor" (see Police Incident Report), to ascertain why the jammed bedroom door prevented rescue.

- The building owner should be contacted to ascertain what he knows about the prior fire in Tweedy's apartment and the "two prior occasions [when] he knew the children were left alone in the apartment."

- An investigator should follow up on the five citations for code violations relating to wiring problems to determine whether any of them related to Tweedy's apartment and whether Tweedy was one of the tenants who complained about faulty wiring. In this connection, all the complaining tenants should be interviewed.

  - Was notice of the code violations sent to the tenants so that Tweedy can be deemed to have known about them?

In re Al Merton

FILE

LIBRARY

Locher, Lawson & Klein, P.A.
Attorneys and Counselors at Law
6714 Tulsa Cove
Munster, Franklin 33448

To: Applicant
From: Catherine Locher
Date: July 30, 2002
Subject: Al Merton's Will

Al Merton came in earlier today to talk about updating his will. I've attached a transcript of my interview with him. I've also charted his family tree insofar as it is relevant to our task.

Mr. Merton is going to have heart surgery tomorrow. He is apprehensive and wants us to draft a new will in accordance with the wishes he expressed when I interviewed him. He will come in and sign the will later today.

Eventually, we may need to draft additional documents necessary to carry out Mr. Merton's testamentary scheme, but the main thing now is to get the will done in time for Mr. Merton to execute it before his surgery. I would like you to complete the following tasks:

1. Draft the introductory clauses and all dispositive clauses for Mr. Merton's new will. Follow our firm's Will Drafting Guidelines and set forth the clauses in separately labeled paragraphs, using the headings set forth in the guidelines. Do not concern yourself with the definitional and boilerplate clauses.

2. I'm particularly concerned about how you deal with Stuart Merton and the gifts of the corporate stock. Once you draft the provisions regarding those issues, please explain why you drafted them the way you did.

Another associate is researching the tax implications, so you need not concern yourself with them.

Locher, Lawson & Klein, P.A.

MEMORANDUM   September 8, 1995

To: All Attorneys
From: Robert Lawson
Re: Will Drafting Guidelines

Over the years, this firm has used a variety of formats in drafting wills. Effective immediately, all wills drafted by this firm should follow this format:

PART ONE: Introduction.

1.   Set forth the first of the introductory clauses with a statement declaring it to be the testator's will and the name and domicile of the testator.

2.   Include an appropriate clause regarding the revocation of prior testamentary instruments.

3.   Include a clause naming the testator's immediate family members and identifying their relationship to the testator (parents, siblings, spouse, children, grandchildren, nephews, and nieces).

PART TWO: Dispositive Clauses (to be set forth in separate subdivisions or subparagraphs by class of bequest.) See the attached excerpt from *Walker's Treatise on Wills* for the definitions of the different classes of bequests. Bequests should be set forth in the following order, using the appropriate heading:

1.   Specific bequests

   a. Real property

   b. Tangible personal property

   c. Other specific bequests

   d.   Any other clauses stating conditions that might affect the disposition of specific bequests

2.   General bequests

3.   Demonstrative bequests

4.   Residuary bequests

PART THREE: Definitional Clauses. Clauses relating to how words and phrases used in the will should be interpreted.

PART FOUR: Boilerplate Clauses. Clauses relating to the naming of fiduciaries and their administrative and management authority, payment of debts and expenses, tax clauses, attestation clauses, and self-proving will affidavits.

Walker's Treatise on Wills

CLASSIFICATION OF BEQUESTS:

Section 500. All bequests under wills are classified as either (1) specific, (2) general, (3) demonstrative, or (4) residuary.

Section 501. A *specific* bequest is a bequest of a specific asset.

Section 502. A *general* bequest (typically a gift of money) is a bequest payable out of general estate assets or to be acquired for a beneficiary out of general estate assets.

Section 503. A *demonstrative* bequest is a bequest of a specific sum of money payable from a designated account. To the extent that the designated account is insufficient to satisfy the bequest, the balance is paid from the general funds of the estate.

Section 504. A *residuary* bequest is a bequest that is neither general, specific, nor demonstrative and includes bequests that purport to dispose of the whole of the remaining estate.

Merton Family Tree

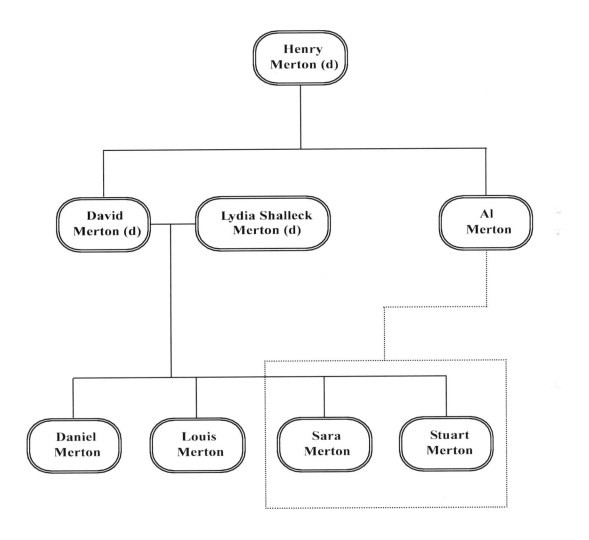

Transcript of Interview with Al Merton

July 30, 2002

* * * *

Q: What brings you here today?

A: Tomorrow I will have open heart surgery and I'm thinking some about death. The surgery is very risky, plus I lost my father last year.

Q: Sounds like a scary time for you.

A: I can't think about anything else. My will is more than 20 years old and so much has happened since it was drafted, I'm sure that it needs to be revised. When my father passed away, I inherited his office supply business, and I need to figure out how to deal with it in case I die. I know I've left everything to the last minute. I just couldn't force myself to deal with this task.

Q: Did you bring your old will with you?

A: Yes. I also brought my father's.

Q: Tell me more.

A: When my brother David and his wife died three years ago in an auto accident, I became responsible for their two youngest children, the twins, Sara and Stuart. At the time their parents died, the twins were 17 years old.

Q: What do you mean you were responsible for them?

A: Well, there was no one else to take care of them so I adopted the twins. I was reluctant to adopt Stuart because he has always been trouble. About a year ago, he left home and I only hear from him when he wants money. David also had two older children, Daniel, who is 27 and has become very wealthy in the software business, and Louis, who is 25 and somewhat irresponsible. There was no point in adopting them.

Q: Tell me about the business you inherited from your father.

A: At least 40 years ago, my father, Henry Merton, inherited from his own father Merton Office Supply and the Lincoln Street land and building where the business is located. Dad incorporated the business, but he retained ownership of the Lincoln Street Property in his individual capacity. The rental income he received from the corporation for the Lincoln Street Property supported him when he retired.

Dad had two children, David and me. I earned a Ph.D. in business strategy and joined the faculty of Franklin College 30 years ago. My brother began working at Merton Office Supply 26 years ago, shortly after earning his B.B.A. in marketing.

Q: And David is the brother who died?

A: Yes. David and his wife Lydia died three years ago without a will. Although their debts effectively wiped out most of their assets, they left a trust holding $75,000 in life insurance proceeds for each child. Each child began receiving the income at age 18 and will receive the principal at age 25. Daniel and Louis have already received their $75,000.

Q: Do you have children of your own?

A: Nope, I never married or had kids. My students at the college keep me young.

Q: Can you tell me about your resources?

A: Well, there is Dad's business, Merton Office Supply Corporation. I brought an appraisal that was done in the year after Dad died. I think it is very accurate. There is a net profit of around $100,000 on sales of $3 million.

Q: I want to learn a lot more about the business, but tell me what else you own.

A: I inherited the Lincoln Street land and building that are leased to the office supply corporation. I also have a savings account of about $50,000 and a stock portfolio worth a little more than $2.5 million. I also own my house in Highland, worth around $450,000.

Q: Now can you tell me about the business?

A: Dad would have left the business to my brother David because he worked there for his whole life and ran it after Dad retired, but that was not to be. I inherited it from Dad and have been running it, but I really want to go back to teaching and the important pro bono work I was doing in Franklin College's small business program. Since David died, Sara has become more interested in the business and has worked there after school and in the summers. Neither of David's two older kids ever had any interest in the business. Sara really seems to have a head for it and is majoring in business in college. She will graduate at the end of this semester. I am reluctant to sell the business as long as she has an interest in running it, and it really may be that her interest in it is a way of dealing with the death of her father when she was so young. The older boys just want me to sell it. Indeed, I have an unsolicited offer of $900,000 for the Lincoln Street Property already.

Q: So let me see if I understand. There are twins, age 20, one of whom is interested in the business and the other of whom is not. There are two older boys—one is wealthy and the other?

A: Ahh, Louis. Louis has yet to graduate from college after six years and can't seem to focus. He just switched to his fourth major and his grades are terrible. He took part of the insurance money and bought a fancy car. I don't think he will ever amount to very much, and I am sure he will want a lot of money if he can get it without hard work.

Q: What about Sara's twin, Stuart?

A: It is heartbreaking, but I have given up. He hung around with a bad crowd, and I know they were into drugs and motorcycles. I tried but couldn't reach him, and now he is out of contact. I think that if I left him anything it would only exacerbate his worst behaviors, and so I can't in good conscience give him anything in my will.

Q: So you want to permanently disinherit him?

A: Yes, but if he turns around, then I may change my mind. Besides, he'll get his share of the proceeds from his parents' life insurance.

Q: And have you thought about what you want to do with your assets?

A: I am torn. My father wanted the business to continue in the family. I want to go back to teaching. Only one of the kids, Sara, could conceivably carry on the business. Louis and Stuart would sell it and waste the money, and Daniel doesn't need another penny. Also, the college has been my home for the last 30 years and I want to support it. I also need to protect Sara until she can support herself and, if she really wants to run the business, I need to give her a chance. To do that, the assets of the business plus the Lincoln Street Property must be kept intact, but it would be unfair to leave the whole thing to Sara and cut out the others completely.

Q: So . . . ?

A: I need some advice about how to do it. I want to give the three kids other than Stuart an equal share of the business but be sure that Sara has the power to make the decisions she will need to make in order to be successful. I would like her to be able to have all of the votes and for the three of them to share in the profits, but if either Louis or Daniel won't agree to give her the power, then that person's shares should go to Sara.

Q: There is such a thing as a voting trust, and I think it might be useful here. We can't create a voting trust in a will, but we can attach enough conditions to the gifts of the corporate stock to Sara, Daniel, and Louis to lay the groundwork for the trust. We can formalize the voting trust later.

A: That's fine. That's exactly what I want you to do. Sara's going to need at least 15 years to make a success of the business.

Q: Do you know if the articles of incorporation of Merton Office Supply say anything about voting trusts?

A: I just looked at them yesterday, and they say nothing at all about voting trusts.

Q: Okay. What would you like to do with the rest of the property?

A: I want to leave Franklin College $1 million in assets to endow the small business program and name it for my dad—The Henry Merton Small Business Assistance Program.

Q: There is still a sizable amount left. What would you like to do with it?

A: Well, I want to pay whatever taxes I owe. Then, I want to leave Sara some money so she can finish college—say $25,000, which should be paid first out of whatever is left in my savings account. Then, I want to leave Sara, Louis, and Daniel $100,000 each. If there is anything left, I want to leave it to the Franklin College Faculty Development Fund.

Q: Is there anything else?

A: Well, both the land and the building that comprise the Lincoln Street Property are absolutely essential to the successful operation of Merton Office Supply. Is there some way to make sure they remain linked?

Q: Well, the simplest thing would be to give the Lincoln Street Property to the corporation.

A: That sounds okay.

Q: All right. Anything else?

A: No, I think that covers it.

Q: In light of how you are feeling about your surgery, we will put a priority on revising your will so that you can sign it before you go to the hospital. In the long run, you will need to have a more sophisticated estate plan that includes tax planning, but for now let us get to work and get this done. Can you come back late this afternoon, and we will have it ready?

A: Okay. I'll be back later.

Last Will and Testament

Henry Merton

I, Henry Merton, a resident of Griffin County, Franklin, do make, publish and declare this my last will and testament. I revoke all wills and codicils previously made by me. I am widowed and have two adult sons, Al and David, and two grandchildren, Daniel and Louis.

Article One. I bequeath my real property to my son David. If my son David predeceases me, I bequeath my real property to my son Al. If both sons predecease me, I bequeath my real property to Franklin College.

Article Two. I bequeath my stock in Merton Office Supply Corporation to my son David. If my son David predeceases me, I bequeath said stock to my son Al. If both sons predecease me, I bequeath said stock to Franklin College.

Article Three. I bequeath the sum of $10,000 to my secretary Mary Jones if she survives me.

Article Four. I leave all the rest, residue, and remainder of my estate in equal shares to my sons David and Al or to the survivor of them.

Article Five. I appoint my son David to serve as my personal representative. If he is unable or unwilling to serve as personal representative, I appoint Franklin State Bank to serve. I direct my personal representative to pay as soon as practicable all of the following sums: all debts owed by me at my death; the expenses of my last illness; the expenses of my funeral; any unpaid charitable pledges, whether or not these are enforceable; and the costs of administering my estate.

Date: ___July 21, 1978___   Signed: _____

Witnesses: _____

          _____

          _____

Last Will and Testament
Al Merton

Introduction

A. I am Al Merton, a resident of Griffin County, Franklin. This is my last will and testament.

B. I revoke all wills and codicils previously made by me.

C. My father is Henry Merton. I have one brother, David, and two nephews, Daniel and Louis.

Article One. I bequeath all my real property to Franklin College.

Article Two. I bequeath all other property owned by me at my death to those individuals who would inherit my property under the laws of Franklin if I died intestate.

Article Three. I appoint my brother David to serve as my personal representative. If my brother David is unable or unwilling to serve as my personal representative, I appoint Franklin State Bank as my personal representative. I direct my personal representative to pay, as soon as practicable, all of the following sums: all debts owed by me at my death; the expenses of my last illness; the expenses of my funeral; any unpaid charitable pledges, whether or not these are enforceable; and the costs of administering my estate. My personal representative shall have the power to sell property as needed for the payment of debts and expenses and to distribute property to those individuals who take under Article Two.

Date:_____September 19, 1980_____   _____

                                                                                    Al Merton

Witnesses: _____

                   _____

                   _____

Appraisal of Merton Office Supply Corporation
by Expert Appraisals LLC
October 24, 2001

Executive Summary

Merton Office Supply Corporation (MOSC) has operated at the same Lincoln Street location since its founding as an unincorporated business in 1917. Henry Merton, the second owner, incorporated the company in 1946 and, until his death, owned all 150 of the issued and outstanding shares of stock. He retained individual ownership of the Lincoln Street land and the building on that land. Henry's executor valued the MOSC stock at $800,000 and the land and the building (i.e., the Lincoln Street Property) at $1,000,000. On Henry's death, his son, Al Merton, inherited Henry's corporate stock and the Lincoln Street Property. Al now owns all 150 shares.

MOSC has not responded well to the challenges posed by large chains and the Internet. Because Henry did not expand into larger quarters, open additional stores, or even join a buying cooperative, MOSC foregoes economies of scale with respect to inventory buying, insurance rates, and other costs. The existence of competitors limits its ability to increase prices.

Last year's $100,000 profit on sales of $3 million would have been wiped out if Al Merton had received a salary as his father and brother had before him. Neither his brother David nor his father Henry received a salary reflecting anywhere near the amount of effort required to run this business.

MOSC's assets consist only of the inventory, the lease on the Lincoln Street Property, and the corporate name. Potential purchasers of the stock would discount the price offered unless they could be guaranteed a long-term lease option on the Lincoln Street Property. Without that guarantee, Al Merton would be fortunate to receive even $800,000 for his stock. With the guarantee of a long-term lease, the value of the stock would be $1.1 million. If he sold the business and the land and invested in no-risk certificates of deposit, Al Merton could easily earn 5% per year on the sale proceeds. Unless he is willing to undertake significant expansion activities, MOSC's value will not grow at even that conservative rate.

Franklin Probate Code

Article One. Succession

§ 101. Definitions.

* * * *

(e) Lineal Descendant. An adopted person is a lineal descendant of the adopting parent and is not a lineal descendant of his or her biological parents.

* * * *

Article Two. Wills

* * * *

§ 206. Pretermitted Heirs.

(a) Surviving Spouse. If the decedent's will fails to provide for a surviving spouse who marries the decedent after the will is made, the surviving spouse shall receive an amount equal to what he or she would have received if the decedent had died intestate. This provision shall not apply if the surviving spouse waived that share in a valid prenuptial or postnuptial agreement.

(b) Surviving Children. If the decedent's will fails to provide for children born or adopted after the will is made, each omitted child shall receive the share that he or she would have received had the decedent died intestate. This provision shall not apply if language in the will indicates that the omission was intentional.

* * * *

Franklin Corporations Code

* * * *

§ 102. Stockholders' Rights.

(a) Each owner of a corporation's common stock shall be entitled to one vote per share owned when electing the board of directors. No stockholder shall have any right to manage the corporation solely by virtue of his or her status as a stockholder.

(b) One or more stockholders can voluntarily limit their voting rights by transferring those rights to a trustee under a voting trust. No voting trust agreement shall be valid unless it is in writing, deposited with the corporation at its registered office, and subject to inspection by both stockholders and holders of the beneficial interests in the trust. No voting trust shall be established for more than ten years unless the articles of incorporation authorize a longer term.

(c) Dividends or other distributions made with respect to a class of stock shall be made on a per-share basis. All distributions made with respect to shares that are subject to a voting trust shall be made to the beneficial owner. All distributions made with respect to shares held in any other type of trust shall be made to the trustee.

* * * *

Barry v. Allen

Franklin Supreme Court (1992)

This case arises out of Paul Barry's attempts to protect his daughters' disparate interests. Lisa Barry appeals the lower court's determination that a voting trust was void *ab initio*.

Paul Barry founded Eon Corporation 30 years ago. Eon issued only voting common stock.

Paul had three children, Lisa, Dorothy, and Judy. Only Lisa ever worked for Eon. As Paul contemplated retirement, he considered methods of ensuring that Lisa would retain operating control.

Paul could have bequeathed all of his shares to Lisa. Because the shares represented virtually all of his intangible personal property and because he had no tangible personal or real property, he would have effectively disinherited Dorothy and Judy. His attorney suggested using a voting trust for the shares.

When Paul retired, he transferred 150 shares to each daughter and retained 150 shares for himself. Lisa, Dorothy, and Judy transferred their shares into a voting trust. Each signed a trust agreement that provided for voting all of their shares according to Lisa's wishes for the next 15 years and that bound subsequent takers of these shares.

As president, Lisa operated the company successfully. Eon continued to pay the $300 annual per-share dividend that it paid before Paul's retirement. Paul and his daughters each received $45,000 in each of the next five years.

When Paul died, he bequeathed his remaining shares equally to each daughter conditioned upon their agreement to transfer those shares to the voting trust. The shares of any daughter who did not agree would be divided equally between the ones who did. All three daughters agreed. Two years later, Lisa decided that Eon should cease paying such large dividends and instead should use corporate profits to expand the company. The board cut the dividend to $3 per share.

Dorothy and Judy concluded that Lisa was acting in her own interests, rather than those of the entire family. Only the trust prevented them from electing a board that might be more amenable to their wishes.

In the eighth year of the trust, Dorothy and Judy sued to have the voting trust dissolved because it was not limited to a 10-year term, as provided in Franklin Corporations Code § 102(b). The corporation's articles do not specifically mention voting trusts.

Lisa argues that her father's primary goal was preserving her control, which he could have achieved in a number of ways. She claims the trust is valid for at least 10 years because the language in § 102(b) that mandates invalidity does not appear in the sentence limiting the term of such trusts. This court must decide whether § 102 voids the voting trust *ab initio* or operates only to limit it to a 10-year term.

Paul could have carried out his plan in several ways. For example, he could have recapitalized the corporation and transferred voting stock only to Lisa. That action would have avoided the requirements applicable to voting trusts.

Alternatively, he could have bequeathed the remaining stock on the condition that the daughters agree to vote for an amendment of the articles of incorporation to validate the 15-year voting trust. That conditional bequest could also have provided that any daughter who failed to vote for the amendment would be divested of her shares, with a gift over to Lisa. There are few limits on the conditions a testator can place on bequests in a will.

We cannot determine which of Paul's goals *vis-à-vis* his children governed his actions. Even if we could, we will not validate the voting trust merely because he could have accomplished the same goal using a different means. Paul chose a voting trust, and we must determine its validity under § 102.

At common law, courts invalidated voting trusts because they separated the voting power from the ownership of the stock. Because statutory authorization changes the common law rule, many courts will not enforce a voting trust unless it strictly complies with the statutory language. We interpret the last sentence of § 102(b) as validating voting trusts exceeding 10 years only if the corporate articles authorize a longer term.

We agree with the trial court that the voting trust was void *ab initio*.

We affirm.

In re Estate of Henry K. Tourneau

Franklin Court of Appeal (1920)

This case presents the problem of whether the bequest to the testator's wife of one-fifth of the residuary estate is burdened by the conditions set out in Paragraph Five of the will. This paragraph reads:

> Five: With respect to my interests in the corporation known as Tourneau, Inc., and as a condition precedent to turning over my stock interests in such business to my brother and sisters as hereinabove set forth, I direct that such beneficiaries enter into a voting trust agreement in favor of my brother, Pierre S. Tourneau. The voting trust agreement shall give to my brother the full voting rights for a minimum of ten (10) years with respect to the stock interests of all of the beneficiaries. The voting trust agreement shall further provide that, if my brother dies prior to the expiration of the voting trust agreement, the voting trust shall cease, and the stock certificates shall be delivered to the beneficiaries thereof.

Paragraph Five clearly shows the intention of the testator to give his brother the voting rights to the stock in question for the specified period.

The cases cited by the siblings challenging the will under the proposition that the condition precedent is illegal under the Franklin Corporations Code do not involve the right of a testator who owns stock in a corporation to impose conditions precedent upon a bequest of such stock. That the testator has the right to impose conditions is unquestioned. The donee must take the gift with the condition imposed or not at all, so long as the condition does not offend public policy or statutory enactment.[1] We hold, therefore, that the bequest is valid.

---

[1] The same result would be reached with a condition subsequent, as long as there was an express gift over to another person if the condition were breached.

In re Al Merton
DRAFTERS' POINT SHEET

On the day before he is scheduled to undergo open heart surgery, the client, Al Merton, meets with the supervising partner in the firm about getting his will updated. He is concerned that he might not survive the surgery and wants to set his affairs in order.

The task for the applicants is to draft the introductory and dispositive clauses of a will in accordance with the wishes expressed by Mr. Merton in his interview with the partner. In addition, applicants must deal with Stuart Merton (the adopted son whom Mr. Merton wants to disinherit) and the disposition of the corporate stock and explain why they have dealt with these issues as they have. The applicants are also told to follow the instructions in the firm's Will Drafting Guidelines, which are included in the File.

The File contains the wills of Henry Merton, from whom Al Merton inherited the Merton Office Supply Corporation ("MOSC") and associated property, and the latest will of Al Merton himself. These documents are in the File to give the applicants some idea of what a will looks like and the sort of language that might be used to express a disposition of property. The two wills are sufficiently different from the one the applicants are assigned to write so that the exercise does not become one of simply copying from the wills of Henry and Al Merton.

The File also contains an excerpt from a treatise, *Walker's Treatise on Wills*, explaining the classifications of bequests to aid the applicants in placing Mr. Merton's bequests in the proper order in the new will. It also contains an appraisal of MOSC. The appraisal furnishes some background information regarding the corporation's assets, the number of shares owned by Mr. Merton, and the history and future prospects for carrying on the business but is otherwise irrelevant to the task. Finally, the File contains a family tree to assist the applicants in keeping the parties straight.

The Library contains some relevant, definitional statutes on descent of property and basic corporations law, including a provision regarding voting trusts, which is relevant to Mr. Merton's desire to vest control of MOSC in Sara, one of his adopted children.

The Library also contains two cases, including *Barry v. Allen*, a Franklin case that stands for the proposition that a voting trust cannot last longer than 10 years unless certain conditions exist. The applicants should use that case in molding the will language regarding the establishment of a voting trust.

The following discussion covers all of the points the drafters intended to raise in the problem. Applicants need not cover them all to receive passing or even excellent grades. Grading decisions are within the discretion of the graders in the jurisdictions.

Overview: There are two things the applicants are required to do:

(1) Draft the introductory and dispositive provisions of a new will for Mr. Merton. In doing so, applicants must follow the instructions in the firm's guidelines and adhere to Mr. Merton's wishes as expressed in the transcript of the interview.

The will should include numbered paragraphs setting forth the provisions in the order prescribed in the guidelines. That organization will require the applicants to determine the character of each bequest as defined in the excerpt from *Walker's Treatise on Wills* and to order them according to the guidelines.

The provisions should be stated concisely and written in the structure and format of a will.

(2) Follow the dispositive provisions regarding the disposition of the MOSC stock with a short explanation of why the dispositive language says what it does. This part of the exercise offers the applicants the opportunity to state in narrative, expository form what the language they have drafted means and why. They must also explain how they have dealt with Stuart Merton, and why, irrespective of whether they included language about Stuart in the will *(see infra)*.

Graders can decide for themselves how much weight, if any, to ascribe to artful exposition and facial format.

PART ONE - The Introductory Clauses: This should be a fairly easy task. The Will Drafting Guidelines are clear. These clauses should recite that:

- The document is Mr. Merton's will;
- He is a resident of Griffin County, Franklin; this comes from his prior will and information contained in the interview.
- His immediate family consists of the two adopted children, Sara and Stuart, and his two nephews, Daniel and Louis.
- He revokes all prior wills and codicils.

PART TWO - The Dispositive Clauses: The order of bequests should follow the directions set forth in the guidelines. First the specific bequests: real property (of which the only one is the land and the building comprising the Lincoln Street Property); tangible personal property (none); and other specific bequests (the stock in MOSC).

The guidelines also tell applicants that they are to set forth "any other clauses stating conditions that might affect the disposition of specific bequests." It is unclear whether such clauses should be part of the dispositive clauses themselves or whether they should be separate clauses referring back to the dispositive clauses. Either way will work, but it will be more efficient if the applicants state the conditions in the dispositive clauses themselves.

Then, in sequence, applicants should set forth the general bequests (gifts of money to Sara, Daniel, and Louis, and to Franklin College for the Henry Merton Small Business Assistance Program); next, the demonstrative bequest to Sara to be paid from the savings account; and, finally, the residuary bequest.

At some point in the exercise, they must also deal with Mr. Merton's desire to disinherit Stuart.

SPECIFIC BEQUESTS

- **Real Property—Disposition of the Lincoln Street Property:** The interview and the business appraisal make it clear that the Lincoln Street Property consists of the land and the building and that it is not among the assets of MOSC. In order to "link" the Lincoln Street Property with the business, Mr. Merton has decided simply to will the Lincoln Street Property to MOSC. Thus, the applicants should simply draft a clause giving the land and buildings to MOSC.

    - NOTE: It would be erroneous to mention Mr. Merton's residence in this section because it falls into the residuary bequest.

- **Other Specific Bequests—Disposition of the Corporate Stock:** Under the facts, Mr. Merton wants to leave "an equal share of the business" to Sara, Daniel, and Louis and have them all share in the profits but wants to ensure that Sara retains the power to "make the decisions" for at least 15 years. This will require, as the supervising attorney put it, laying the groundwork in the will for the later creation of a voting trust. Drawing upon the wishes Mr. Merton expressed in the interview, § 102 of the Franklin Corporations Code, and the holdings in *Barry v. Allen* and *In re Estate of Tourneau*, the applicants should draft language reflecting that:

    - Sara, Daniel, and Louis are each to receive one-third (or 50 shares) of the MOSC stock;

    - Sara is to have the right to vote all shares, a goal that is to be accomplished by the later creation of a voting trust;

- Accordingly, Sara, Daniel, and Louis must agree that their respective shares will be placed in a voting trust for up to 15 years and that Sara is to have the sole right to vote the shares.
  - They will also have to agree that, if MOSC's articles of incorporation do not provide that a voting trust can last for more than 10 years (which they appear not to), the articles will be amended so to provide. (See *Barry v. Allen*, *In re Estate of Tourneau*, and Franklin Corporations Code § 102(b).)
  - If either Daniel or Louis should refuse to agree to these conditions, the shares of the corporate stock that each would receive under the will would go to Sara.
  - This would be the "gift over" that appears as a requirement in *Tourneau*.
- The applicants might also draft language specifying that Mr. Merton wants all three to share in the profits. However, omission of such language is not fatal because the statute (§102(c)) provides that dividends paid on account of stock in a voting trust shall be paid to the beneficial owners (Sara, Daniel, and Louis). If applicants omit such language they should cover it in their explanations.
- **Explanation:** Applicants should explain that the language used in the dispositive provisions is intended to make sure that Sara retains the right to run the business for up to 15 years even though all three of them will share in the profits (and, unless applicants have explicitly included "share-the-profits" language, they must explain that sharing results automatically by operation of § 102(c)); that, although each beneficiary is getting one-third of the stock, it is on the condition that they all agree to put it into a 15-year voting trust giving Sara the sole power to vote the stock; that the beneficiaries must agree that the articles of incorporation may be amended to carry out that intent; and that if either Daniel or Louis refuses to agree to these conditions, that beneficiary will lose his shares to Sara.

- It should be implicit in applicants' treatment of this subject that they understand that a bequest of the corporate stock conveys ownership of the assets of the corporation, i.e., the inventory, the lease, and the corporate name (see the appraisal of the corporation). Applicants who attempt to bequeath these assets separately have missed the point and should receive reduced credit.

- It should also be implicit that applicants recognize that this bequest falls into the category of "other specific bequests" as opposed to a bequest of "tangible personal property," i.e., stock in a corporation is not tangible personal property in the ordinary sense of the word. *See Barry v. Allen.*

GENERAL BEQUESTS

- **The general gifts of money or estate assets:** There are two categories of such gifts: the bequest of $100,000 each to Sara, Daniel, and Louis; and the gift of $1,000,000 to Franklin College to endow a specific entity.

  - The gifts of $100,000 each to Sara, Daniel, and Louis can be stated in a single dispositive paragraph (e.g., "I give Sara, Daniel, and Louis $100,000 each.") or in separate paragraphs reciting the gift for each of them.

  - The gift of $1,000,000 out of general estate assets to Franklin College should recite that it is to endow the small business program and is conditioned on the program's being named after Mr. Merton's father: The Henry Merton Small Business Assistance Program.

DEMONSTRATIVE BEQUEST

- **The gift to Sara to be paid from the savings account:** This is a demonstrative bequest because its payment is to be made from a designated fund—the savings account.

  - The language of the bequest should state that the gift is to be paid first out of the savings account and that it is a separate bequest to furnish money to enable Sara to finish college.

RESIDUARY BEQUEST

- **The gift of the remainder of the estate:** The language of this clause should recite clearly that the remainder of the estate goes to the Franklin College Faculty Development Fund (e.g., "the rest, residue, and remainder" or "all my property not otherwise disposed of by this will.")

  - Note that the residue also contains Al Merton's home, which is realty. It is not disposed of as a specific bequest because Mr. Merton did not direct that it be given to the Faculty Development Fund separately and distinctly from the residue.

DISINHERITING STUART

- **The intent to disinherit Stuart:** At some point in the exercise, applicants will have to deal with Mr. Merton's desire to disinherit Stuart. It can be done either at the beginning or at the end of the document.

  - It can be accomplished by an express statement in the will that Mr. Merton wants to disinherit Stuart. (e.g., "It is my intention that my adopted child, Stuart Merton, take nothing under my will.") It can also be accomplished by saying nothing in the will, inasmuch as Stuart had been adopted several years before Mr. Merton's visit with the partner and therefore he is the legal equivalent of a child in being before the will was written. Better applicants will definitely opt to make the express statement rather than leave it open to interpretation.

  - **Explanation:** This is the only point in the exercise, other than a reference in the introductory clause, where the fact that Mr. Merton adopted Sara and Stuart is called into play. As to Sara, it makes no difference because she is a named beneficiary and takes under the terms of the will, irrespective of the adoption.

    - With regard to Stuart, applicants should discuss whether he would be a pretermitted heir if he is not provided for in the will. Under Franklin Probate Code § 101(e), Stuart is deemed for all purposes to be Mr. Merton's lineal descendant. Section 206 raises the issue of pretermission, and it is abundantly clear that Stuart would not be pretermitted because he was not adopted after the will was made.

Applicants should make it clear that they understand this. An applicant who explains that he or she has included language expressly disinheriting Stuart because, otherwise, Stuart could claim as a pretermitted heir shows a lack of understanding. If, on the other hand, an applicant chooses to leave the will silent as to Stuart, it is essential that he or she explain why, i.e., that there is no need to mention him because the will was made after Stuart became a child of Mr. Merton and, therefore, Stuart is not pretermitted.

GVP Non-Disclosure Agreement

FILE

LIBRARY

Blevin, Edmonds & Victor, P.A.

BEV.pa

Attorneys & Counselors at Law
1000 Commercial Boulevard
Webville, Franklin 33883

www.bevlaw.org
bev@paris.com
(555) 349-0890

TO: Applicant
FROM: Tom Edmonds
RE: *GVP Non-Disclosure Agreement*
DATE: August 1, 2002

We represent General Vision Processing, Inc. (GVP), a closely held research and development company. Dr. Nabeel Adsani, GVP's President and Chief Executive Officer, is a former Professor of Computer Science at the University of Franklin. He developed a breakthrough discovery known as the *iChip™*, and GVP has a patent pending.

Dr. Adsani is exploring a strategic alliance with MicroSystems (Micro), a high tech incubator company that acquires leading edge technologies, evaluates whether there is a market for them, and spins off new companies to produce them. Micro and GVP are evaluating whether the *iChip™* is something on which the two companies should collaborate to create applications for use in computerized transportation safety systems.

In undertaking this strategic alliance, GVP realizes that it needs to disclose confidential information about the *iChip™* to Micro. Therefore, GVP faces both substantial risks and benefits in this collaboration. A non-disclosure agreement (NDA) is one mechanism GVP can use to reduce the risks associated with disclosures made during this alliance.

Dr. Adsani is concerned that the "boilerplate" NDA proposed by Micro fails to adequately protect GVP from unauthorized use and disclosure of its trade secrets. You can glean from the transcript of my interview with Dr. Adsani the points that he is worried about. I have reviewed Micro's proposed NDA and excerpted several provisions. I would like your help in preparing an opinion letter to Dr. Adsani. Other members of the team are working on other aspects of the proposed NDA. I want you to analyze the NDA and focus on the following three concerns expressed by Dr. Adsani:

1.   Restrictions as to the persons or entities (receiving parties) to whom disclosure can be made;

2.   The conditions or limitations that should be placed on the disclosures to those receiving parties; and

3.   GVP's ability to enforce its rights as a third-party beneficiary against persons or entities who obtain confidential information but who are not signatories to the GVP/Micro NDA.

Write the portion of the opinion letter that analyzes whether and how effectively the excerpts from Micro's proposed NDA address from GVP's perspective each of those concerns and whether the existing language adequately protects GVP.

In addressing each of the three concerns I've set forth above

- Examine each paragraph of the NDA provision by provision;
- Explain why particular language protects or fails to protect GVP's interests, including how the language of each provision relates to the concerns and suggestions Dr. Adsani expressed during the interview;
- If particular language fails to protect GVP's interests, suggest a solution using the materials in the File and the authorities in the Library.

You need not rewrite the entire NDA, but you do need to explain in narrative form the points you believe we should be concerned about and the changes you would suggest. For example, I noted the following about the preamble: "The preamble as written suggests that Micro is seeking protection for its own confidential information as well as GVP's. As Dr. Adsani said in the interview, he is not interested in protecting Micro's trade secrets. If the language is left as is, it might unwittingly impose some obligations on GVP. The language should be changed to make clear that Micro is the party that wishes to evaluate the technology and that it is GVP's confidential information that needs the protection."

I want you to analyze the rest of the NDA excerpts in the same manner. You should identify and recommend any and all changes you believe are necessary. I will decide which ones to communicate to Dr. Adsani. Please avoid conclusive, non-explanatory statements of the ultimate facts, such as: "The NDA does not adequately define to whom Micro may disclose information and it should be clarified."

Transcript of Interview

Adsani: Thanks for squeezing me in, Tom. I know you have a full schedule.

Edmonds: No problem, Nabeel. How are things at GVP?

A: Terrific, Tom. Do you remember those two young software engineers I hired? You drafted the various protective agreements we had them sign.

Q: Sure. What were their names?

A: Andrew Sutton and Charles Cato, who graduated from my old department at the University of Franklin. They developed software for the *iChip* that has it doing things even I wasn't sure it would ever do.

Q: Like what?

A: Well, they've got the *iChip* measuring the blinking of a person's eyelids.

Q: What's the practical application of that?

A: The *iChip* can now monitor when a person is dozing off. Properly packaged and placed on the dashboard of commercial trucks, it will warn drivers who have become inattentive. The National Transportation Safety Board ranks an effective warning device for dozing truck drivers as one of its top highway safety goals.

Q: That's impressive!

A: And that's not all. They have the *iChip* tracking the white lines on highways, warning drivers when they're drifting out of their lane and in danger of a collision.

Q: What's the next step?

A: Well, I was leaning toward raising more venture capital so I could fully develop these applications for the emerging market for transportation safety systems. But then I got a call from J.P. Shaw who wants to talk seriously about a strategic alliance between our companies. That changed everything.

Q: How does the call change things?

A: Her call changes things because Shaw is the vision engineering inspiration at MicroSystems, a leading edge company that exploits new technologies. As head of New Vision Products at Micro, Shaw has at least a couple dozen patents. More important, she's the one who first developed Perception Tracing, a theory that changed the direction of computer vision research. It emphasizes the perception aspect of sight instead of concentrating on the understanding process.

Q: I hope I don't need to understand the nuances of Perception Tracing theory to advise you!

A: You don't, Tom. Suffice it to say that every computer vision engineer who graduates from a leading technology university today is exposed to the theory. The GVP *iChip* is premised on Perception Tracing. That's one of the reasons Shaw is investigating a partnership with us.

Q: Tell me more about Micro's interest in the *iChip*.

A: Micro's Transportation Safety Division has two breakthrough products. *InterSect* is a system that controls traffic lights by estimating vehicle traffic and maximizing green light time. *LaneTrac* is a device mounted on the dashboard that signals a driver who is veering out of the traffic lane.

Q: So, that's the link with the *iChip*?

A: Right. Shaw wants to find out if the *iChip* is a more efficient system than Micro's. If it is, then Micro will propose a strategic alliance between the two companies to enhance Micro's existing products and to develop new products, like the driver drowsiness detector.

Q: What does GVP gain from a strategic alliance with Micro?

A: A ton! Micro will front most, if not all, of the product development costs. Micro also has existing relationships with the tier one auto parts manufacturers. That means that GVP/Micro's products will have a clear path directly into the market. Moreover, Micro is a well-known and well-respected company. Partnering with Micro gives GVP instant credibility.

Q: Are there risks associated with a strategic alliance?

A: Many, and they're high. Our *iChip* patent is pending, and we copyrighted our software source code. But as we get into technical demonstrations of the *iChip*, showing what it can do and how it's done, we're bound to reveal some of our trade secrets and our know-how. My greatest fear is that Shaw is on a fishing expedition, trying to learn as much as possible about the *iChip*, then dumping GVP. If that happens, the next thing we know, we'll see subtle but important improvements in

Q: Micro's products based on GVP technology. But it'll be almost impossible to trace them back to the confidential information we provided to Micro.

Q: There's that and there's also the possibility that GVP and Micro will create an alliance but somewhere down the road, following successful or unsuccessful technology development, the relationship sours. If Micro and GVP split, won't Micro's employees have some understanding of GVP's trade secrets and know-how?

A: Well, you can't purge their minds of what they've learned from us, although I'd sure like to if I could! How about making Micro return the information, the documents, we've given them? And, of course, I'd want to get back the evaluation of the *iChip* itself. Can you do these things?

Q: We certainly can put together a non-disclosure agreement that will afford you as much protection as possible.

A: Oh- I nearly forgot to mention that Shaw sent us Micro's non-disclosure form. She said it's their standard agreement whenever they're evaluating technology.

Q: Let me take a quick peek at it.

A: Here's what I'm most concerned about. Can we limit how Micro can use the confidential information we give them and to whom they can disclose it?

Q: Let me get some more details. Exactly what will you reveal to Micro?

A: The *iChip* is a board about the size of a business card consisting of a .25 micron chip with a built-in microprocessor. We'll demonstrate to Micro how the *iChip* can measure and analyze eye blinking as well as track the left and right lane markers.

Q: Will the demos reveal any trade secrets or know-how?

A: Some. I hope not too much. But the Micro engineers will have dozens of follow-up questions about everything, from the architecture of the chip to programming protocols.

Q: Is there a way to limit the people associated with Micro who have access to GVP's information?

A: I'm not sure. I want Micro to give the *iChip* a full examination. So I want GVP information to go to those at Micro who have the knowledge and expertise to do a full and fair evaluation of the technology's potential. That may go beyond Micro's employees. All high tech companies draw on outside consultants as independent contractors. I'm sure Micro will use consultants on the review of *iChip*. I'd sure like to be able to find out ahead of time what consultants they're using and when they're using them.

Q: OK, we'll think about that issue. Anything else?

A: There's a huge employee turnover in the technology field. Competitors are always trying to pick off engineers from other companies. What do we do if a Micro employee who has received GVP confidential information leaves and ends up with a competitor of both Micro and GVP?

Q: Well, Micro has an interest in protecting itself against the loss of trade secrets. They're sure to have Micro employees under a non-disclosure agreement, just as you do at GVP.

A: Maybe, but I'm not interested in protecting Micro's trade secrets. I'm nervous about relying on Micro to protect GVP's rights. Can we be more proactive if a Micro employee leaves after having access to GVP data?

Q: I'm sure there's a way to empower GVP to act on its own to preserve its trade secrets. Is that it?

A: Micro has a pattern of spinning off successful divisions as independent companies. In its annual SEC report, Micro said it plans to transform its Transportation Safety Division into a public company in which it holds a significant interest. Micro's plans, however, are dependent on its ability to acquire or develop more sophisticated technology to support its products. Could that be a problem?

Q: It could be. We'll evaluate GVP's alternatives and make a recommendation on how best to protect your interests if Micro makes such a move.

A: Great. I want to protect our confidential information but I don't want to scare Micro off. I've always wanted to work with J.P. Shaw, and this may be my only chance. I've heard she plans to retire soon.

Q: I'm sure we can come up with language that will balance your desire to create an alliance with Micro and your need to guard GVP's confidential information. When I have had a chance to review the entire NDA, we'll get together and go over it line by line.

A: Thanks, Tom. I appreciate your assistance.

Excerpts from the Non-Disclosure Agreement (NDA)

Drafted and Proposed by MicroSystems

* * * *

This agreement is intended to allow General Vision Processing (GVP) and MicroSystems (Micro) to evaluate the feasibility of possible cooperation in the development of GVP's *iChip*™ technology (hereinafter referred to as the "Project") while protecting their confidential information against unauthorized use or disclosure.

IT IS AGREED AS FOLLOWS:

1. CONFIDENTIAL INFORMATION means any item or information, including electrical/electronic schematic and circuit diagrams, documentation, specifications, formulas, manufacturing processes, know-how, computer programs, technology, technical descriptions and other technical and economic data, records and information pertaining to the Project that is disclosed by GVP (hereinafter the DISCLOSING PARTY) to Micro (hereinafter the RECEIVING PARTY) under this Agreement, whether disclosed orally, in writing, or in any other form, provided it is clearly and conspicuously marked or designated in writing by the DISCLOSING PARTY as being CONFIDENTIAL INFORMATION or if originally disclosed orally, it is confirmed in writing as CONFIDENTIAL INFORMATION by the DISCLOSING PARTY within ten (10) calendar days after oral disclosure.

2. During the term of this Agreement, the RECEIVING PARTY undertakes to apply to all CONFIDENTIAL INFORMATION the same degree of care with which it treats and protects its own proprietary information against public disclosure. The RECEIVING PARTY further undertakes to restrict its use of CONFIDENTIAL INFORMATION to the Project. However, the RECEIVING PARTY reserves the right to disclose the CONFIDENTIAL INFORMATION to persons working as employees of an Affiliated Company, provided the RECEIVING PARTY shall ensure that such persons comply with the provisions of this Agreement. For the purpose of this Agreement, an Affiliated Company shall mean any company, owned or controlled, directly or indirectly, now or hereafter, by the RECEIVING PARTY.

3. Information is not considered CONFIDENTIAL INFORMATION if the RECEIVING PARTY can prove that such information is
  a) in or passes into the public domain other than by breach of this Agreement; or,
  b) known to the RECEIVING PARTY prior to disclosure by the DISCLOSING PARTY; or,
  c) disclosed to the RECEIVING PARTY by one having the full right to disclose it; or,
  d) independently developed by an employee of the RECEIVING PARTY; or,
  e) approved for release by written authorization of the DISCLOSING PARTY; or
  f) required to be disclosed as a result of a Court order or pursuant to government action.

* * * *

AL Limited v. Glass Glo Corporation

United States Court of Appeals for the Fifteenth Circuit (1995)

Per Curiam: This interlocutory appeal was certified by the district court after it dismissed, for failure to state a claim, one of the claims in a suit by AL Limited against Glass Glo Corporation.

AL Limited, a United Kingdom corporation, owns the worldwide rights to the "Aluglas Process," a coating system by which a thin layer of metalized aluminum is applied to products such as greeting cards, gift wrappings, and labels. Part of the Aluglas Process is patented, but major portions of the process are trade secrets. AL has consistently taken great care to protect its trade secrets, principally by the use of non-disclosure agreements between it and its licensees.

AL licensed the Aluglas Process to Prodicom, a Mexican company that used the process to manufacture its products and was familiar with all aspects of the process, including AL's patent and trade secret information. The licensing agreement between AL and Prodicom contained a non-disclosure provision that prohibited Prodicom from disclosing any "confidential information," which was defined in the agreement, to any person or entity without the express, prior written consent of AL. Moreover, any such disclosures were to be made under terms at least as restrictive as the non-disclosure terms of the AL/Prodicom agreement.

Robert Faris, chief executive officer of Glass Glo Corporation, a Franklin corporation, was interested in evaluating whether the Aluglas Process could be applied beneficially to the products manufactured by Glass Glo. He met with officials of Prodicom and requested that he be permitted to examine Prodicom's manufacturing methods using the Aluglas Process. Prodicom communicated with AL and received approval to allow Faris to receive formulas, documentation, and other information vital to the use of the process. All the information Faris sought fell within the definition of "confidential information" as defined in the AL/Prodicom agreement. The condition upon which AL agreed to let Prodicom disclose to Faris, however, was that Faris and Glass Glo first enter into a non-disclosure agreement with Prodicom restricting Faris' and Glass Glo's right to disclose information relating to the Aluglas Process to the same extent that Prodicom was prevented from disclosing such information.

Consequently, Prodicom and Faris, on behalf of Glass Glo, entered into a written agreement defining "confidential information and trade secrets" consistent with the definitions in the AL/Prodicom agreement and containing a non-disclosure clause that stated: "Prodicom reveals the confidential information and trade secrets ('information') relating to the Aluglas Process upon the express undertaking of Glass Glo Corporation that it receives the information from Prodicom in confidence and that it will not disclose any of the information to any person or entity [other than certain specified scientific and engineering personnel of Glass Glo] for any purpose whatsoever without first obtaining the written consent of Prodicom." The Prodicom/Glass Glo agreement did not mention or otherwise refer to AL Limited.

Faris later concluded that the Aluglas Process was not suited to Glass Glo's purposes and decided not to use it. However, one of the members of Glass Glo's board of directors was the chief executive officer of Shining Light, Inc., a manufacturer of ornamental papers. Believing that Shining Light might be able to use the Aluglas Process and without getting Prodicom's approval, Faris turned over to Shining Light the files and materials he had obtained from Prodicom.

When AL discovered Faris' disclosure to Shining Light, AL sued Glass Glo on a number of claims, including one for breach of the Prodicom/Glass Glo nondisclosure agreement. AL asserted that it was an intended beneficiary of the Prodicom/Glass Glo agreement.

It is ancient law in Franklin that, to succeed on a third-party beneficiary theory, a non-party to an agreement "must be the intended beneficiary of the contract, not merely an incidental beneficiary to whom no duty is owed." *Lawrence v. Fox* (Franklin Supreme Court, 1895). More recently, the Franklin Supreme Court, applying principles declared in the Restatement (Second) of Contracts, stated, "essential to the status as an intended

beneficiary are circumstances indicating that the promisee intends to give the beneficiary the benefit of the promised performance." *Goldman v. Belden* (Franklin Supreme Court, 1995).

The non-disclosure agreement that Faris signed makes no reference to a licensing agreement between AL and Prodicom, nor does it purport by its terms to run to the benefit of AL. Mere mention of the Aluglas Process in the Prodicom/Glass Glo agreement does not satisfy the requirement that the contract must expressly identify the intended third-party beneficiary and provide that the promises of the promisee run to that intended beneficiary.

The contract upon which AL sued Glass Glo does not satisfy these requirements. Accordingly, the court below did not err in dismissing this cause of action for failure to state a claim.

We affirm.

Celeritas Technologies v. Rockwell International Corporation

United States Court of Appeals for the Fifteenth Circuit (1998)

In July 1993, Michael Dolan filed a patent application for a "de-emphasizer" apparatus to increase the rate of data transmission over analog cellular telephone networks. The resulting patent, assigned to Celeritas, was issued in January 1995.

In September 1993, Dolan and other officials of Celeritas met with representatives from Rockwell to demonstrate their proprietary de-emphasis technology. Rockwell entered into a non-disclosure agreement (NDA) with Celeritas which provided that Rockwell "shall not disclose or use any Proprietary Information except for the purpose of evaluating possible business arrangements between Celeritas and Rockwell."

The agreement also provided that proprietary information "shall not include material which . . . was in the public domain on the date hereof or comes into the public domain other than through the fault or negligence of Rockwell . . . or information independently developed by Rockwell or Rockwell's employees who had no access to the Information disclosed hereunder."[2]

In March 1994, AT&T began to sell a modem that incorporated de-emphasis technology. In that same month, Rockwell informed Celeritas it would not license the use of Celeritas' proprietary technology and concurrently began a development project to incorporate de-emphasis technology into its modem chip sets. In January 1995, Rockwell began shipping its first prototype chip sets that contained de-emphasis technology.

Celeritas' subsequent suit against Rockwell on breach of contract resulted in a jury verdict in its favor and a judgment in excess of $57 million.[3] Rockwell's motion for judgment as a matter of law was denied by the district court. Rockwell appeals.

Rockwell argues the de-emphasis technology disclosed to Rockwell was already in the public domain before Rockwell used it, specifically when AT&T began selling its modems. Rockwell asserts that the technology was "readily ascertainable" because "any

---

[2] The full text of the clause setting forth the exclusions from proprietary information reads as follows:

"Such Information shall not include material which Rockwell can by reasonable proof: (1) Show was in the public domain on the date hereof or comes into the public domain other than through the fault or negligence of Rockwell; (2) Show was contained in a written record in Rockwell's files prior to the date of receipt from Celeritas; (3) Show was lawfully obtained under circumstances permitting its disclosure and use;

---

(4) Show was disclosed by Celeritas to others on an unrestricted basis; and (5) Demonstrate was independently developed by Rockwell or Rockwell's employees who had no access to the Information disclosed hereunder."

[3] The term of the confidentiality agreement was designated "perpetual" as opposed to a set number of years in duration. Permanent confidentiality signifies that the parties assigned high value to the information that was to be disclosed to Rockwell and supports the amount awarded to Celeritas by the jury. *See Stamats v. Concord Tech* (Franklin Supreme Court, 1991).

competent engineer could have reverse-engineered the AT&T modem." Rockwell further argues that any confidentiality obligation under the NDA regarding de-emphasis technology was extinguished once the Celeritas patent was issued in January 1995.

Substantial evidence supports the jury's conclusion that Rockwell breached the NDA. The jury implicitly found the information given to Rockwell by Celeritas was covered by the NDA. Unrebutted testimony established that Celeritas disclosed to Rockwell implementation details and techniques that went beyond the information disclosed in the patent. Accordingly, Rockwell's reliance on the issuance of the Celeritas patent is misplaced.

There was substantial evidence on which the jury could find that Rockwell used Celeritas' proprietary data to develop its modem chip sets. Significantly, when Rockwell initiated its de-emphasis development program it did not erect an organizational barrier to protect the confidential information of Celeritas. In place of a "clean room,"[4] Rockwell assigned the same engineers who had learned of Celeritas' technology under the NDA to its own de-emphasis development project.

The jury also found that the technology had not been placed in the public domain by the sale of the AT&T modem. Franklin law appears somewhat unsettled regarding whether a trade secret enters the public domain when it is "readily ascertainable" or whether it must also be "actually ascertained" by the public. Because the judgment is supportable under either standard, we need not attempt to resolve this issue of state law. Suffice it to say that substantial evidence supports a finding that the technology implementing the de-emphasis function in the modem was not "readily ascertainable."

Accordingly, the court did not err in denying Rockwell's motion for judgment as a matter of law regarding its breach of the NDA.

Affirmed.

---

[4] A "clean room" involves a development team working under a set of strict written procedures to control the transfer of data from other research efforts to the team, thereby protecting the development team from exposure to confidential information or trade secrets of third parties. *See* K. Copenhaver, *Structuring, Negotiating & Implementing Strategic Alliances* (PLI 1997).

Nilsen v. Motorola, Inc.

United States District Court (D. Franklin 1997)

In mid-1987, Joseph Nilsen, the president of Innovation Center, Inc., approached Motorola about an alliance to produce electronic ballasts, devices used to power fluorescent lamps. Nilsen offered Motorola an "exclusive licensing of proprietary technology that permits the development of electronic ballasts at substantially reduced cost as compared with the least costly of presently available electronic ballasts."

In September 1987, Nilsen and Motorola executed a non-disclosure agreement (NDA) to establish the terms under which Nilsen would provide confidential information to Motorola. Essential provisions of the NDA included these:

• "Confidential Information" was defined as "any device, graphics, written information, or information in other tangible forms that is disclosed, for evaluation purposes, to Motorola by [Nilsen] relating to [electronic ballasts] and that is marked at the time of disclosure as being 'Confidential' or 'Proprietary.' "

• Information disclosed orally or visually and identified at the time of such disclosure as "Confidential" was to be considered as "Confidential Information" only if reduced to tangible form, marked "Confidential," and transmitted to Motorola within 30 days of such oral or visual disclosure.

• "Confidential Information" was explicitly defined to exclude "any information which: (a) is or becomes publicly known through no wrongful act on Motorola's part; or (b) is, at the time of disclosure under this Agreement, already known to Motorola without restriction on disclosure; or (c) is, or subsequently becomes, rightfully and without breach of this Agreement, in Motorola's possession without an obligation restricting disclosure; or (d) is independently developed by Motorola without breach of this Agreement; or (e) is furnished to a third party by [Nilsen] without a similar restriction on the third party's rights; or (f) is explicitly approved for release by written authorization of [Nilsen]."

• Motorola undertook "to apply to all 'Confidential Information' the same degree of care with which it treats and protects its own proprietary information against public disclosure but no less than reasonable care."

• Motorola also agreed that "Disclosure of confidential information is limited to Motorola employees and Motorola is not to disclose the 'Confidential Information' to any third party" nor was it to "use the 'Confidential Information' for any purpose" other than "evaluation purposes, which evaluation is to be completed within two months from [September 1, 1987]."

• In the event of termination, Motorola undertook to deliver to Nilsen all of the

'Confidential Information' it had received from Nilsen, or to certify its destruction, at Nilsen's option.

Within a short time after executing the NDA, Motorola wrote to Nilsen "to confirm the various 'to-dos' that you agreed to address during our meeting last Monday....

> 2. Review your documents and determine whether any of them should have been stamped 'confidential.' Our mutual intent is to specifically identify 'confidential information.' "

Motorola reminded Nilsen of this "to do" item a number of times.

From September 1987 to May 1988, Motorola personnel evaluated its possible entry into the electronic ballast business. Nilsen provided Motorola personnel with a prototype ballast in a "black box"[1] that Motorola used as a test device. He later built another prototype based on a set of Motorola performance specifications.

During that same period, Motorola engaged two non-Motorola employees as consultants. David Bergman, a marketing specialist, and William Alling, an electronics specialist, were asked to prepare a report detailing financial

and technical objectives for Motorola's potential entry into the electronic ballast industry. Motorola shared with Bergman and Alling all the material Nilsen had provided to Motorola from the onset of their relationship. Based on the Bergman-Alling report, Motorola decided to "put on hold" the decision whether to enter the electronic ballast business and wrote to Nilsen informing him of that decision.

In 1990, Motorola reconsidered the Bergman-Alling report and concluded that Motorola should go forward with the business, using Nilsen's technology.

Over the next several months, Nilsen and Motorola engaged in what can only be described as "arm's-length bargaining." Motorola offered Nilsen several compensation packages and business models. Nilsen rejected all of them as inadequate. In light of the "significant gap" between them, Motorola sent Nilsen a letter in November 1990 terminating their discussions. Motorola later returned to Nilsen all documents that Motorola had received, but retained an "archive copy" for Motorola's files that included documents that Nilsen had failed to mark "confidential."

Once discussions with Nilsen were terminated, Motorola communicated with Carl Stevens, an engineer who had developed his own "Super Ballast," a design that he had earlier licensed to Calmont Technologies. Motorola hired Stevens as its chief engineer and executed a Licensing Agreement for the exclusive use of his electronic ballast

---

[1] A "black box" is a unit whose internal structure is unknown but whose function can be documented. The internal mechanics of a device do not matter to the engineer who uses the unit to evaluate the device's function. A memory chip, for example, can be viewed as a black box so that its function can be ascertained without disclosing its structure. Many people use memory chips and even design them into computers, but generally only the memory chip designer needs to understand the chip's internal operation.

technology. Stevens and other Motorola engineers participated in the improvement of electronic ballast design until December 1993, at which time Motorola completed its final design and proceeded to production.[2] Nilsen thereafter filed suit, claiming Motorola breached the non-disclosure agreement it had with him.

Before this case proceeds to a jury trial, one matter that must be decided is whether, as a matter of law, Motorola breached its contractual obligations of limited disclosure under the NDA when it revealed confidential information provided by Nilsen to third parties. Construction of the parties' written agreements is, of course, a question of law for this Court and not one of fact for the jury.

As a preliminary matter, however, this Court concludes that there was no implied duty imposed on Motorola to maintain the confidentiality of any of Nilsen's documents that he himself had failed to designate as "confidential." The "to-do" list (*supra*) afforded Nilsen the full opportunity to stamp his documents as "confidential." Since he failed to stamp a number of documents, he cannot now contend that the trade secret concept extends to any implied duty stemming from his delivery to Motorola of any information that had not been marked as "confidential."

Franklin courts have repeatedly held that any disclosure believed to be proprie-

tary—including previous disclosures that had not been so marked—must be in written form and stamped "confidential" (e.g., *In re Andrea Dumon* (Franklin Supreme Court, 1994)). Motorola, therefore, was under no duty to maintain the confidentiality of any of Nilsen's disclosures (whenever made) that were not so marked.

Nilsen also contends that, as a matter of law, Motorola violated the NDA when it provided information marked as "confidential" to Alling and Bergman, who were not employees of Motorola. Motorola presses the view that the section of the NDA that reads "Disclosure of Confidential Information is limited to Motorola employees" and "Motorola is not to disclose the 'Confidential Information' to any third party" should be interpreted expansively. It contends that customary business practice in situations where companies are evaluating technologies and commercial opportunities includes passing the information on to non-employee consultants and experts for review and analysis. Therefore, argues Motorola, the clause in the NDA must be read to allow it to share the confidential information it received from Nilsen with non-employees who had a "need to know" in order to provide Motorola with essential advice.

Courts have traditionally held that non-disclosure agreements restricting dissemination of confidential information to employees of the receiving party permitted disclosure to legal counsel (*Matters v. Siddown Corporation* (Franklin Court of Appeal, 1980)), and other professionals normally engaged by the receiving company

---

[2] Discovery during the course of this litigation has uncovered several of Nilsen's disclosures, designated as "confidential" per the NDA, in Stevens' files.

(e.g., technical consultants, *Otone, Inc. v. Chambers* (Franklin Supreme Court, 1984)). More recently, however, the Franklin courts have concluded that an NDA clause restricting disclosure of information to employees "is a very clear expression that the intent of the parties was employees only and not employees and others to whom the Disclosing Party might have foreseen that the Receiving Party would make disclosures." *Den-Tal-Ez, Inc. v. Siemens Capital Corp.* (Franklin Supreme Court, 1993). That interpretation is all the more appropriate here, where the clause not only restricts disclosure to employees but goes on to explicitly prohibit disclosure "to any third party."

The parties had the opportunity to craft conditions under which confidential information could have been revealed by Motorola to third parties who were providing assistance in the evaluation of the data it received from Nilsen. They could have, for example, allowed disclosure to those with "a need to know"; or to those individuals specifically identified; or to third parties who were under a confidentiality agreement the terms of which were at least as restrictive as the terms of the Nilsen-Motorola agreement; or, on an *ad hoc* basis, to those third parties approved in advance by Nilsen. These options and more were available to the contracting parties and would have permitted at least some disclosure to third parties.

Motorola and Nilsen, however, did not avail themselves of such options. Instead they agreed to a flat ban on the disclosure of "'Confidential Information' to any third party." Therefore, the Court concludes, as a matter of law, that Motorola breached its duty under the NDA when it disclosed confidential information to the third parties identified above.

GVP Non-Disclosure Agreement
DRAFTERS' POINT SHEET

In this test item, the applicants' firm represents General Vision Processing, Inc. (GVP), the developer of an electronic device known as the *iChip*. GVP is about to enter into an arrangement with Microsystems (Micro), by which GVP will give Micro access to the *iChip* so Micro can evaluate whether the *iChip* can be used to enhance its computerized transportation safety systems. GVP's immediate concern is the protection of the trade secrets and know-how (confidential information) that it will necessarily have to disclose to Micro in the course of Micro's evaluation of the *iChip*.

Micro has supplied its standard form non-disclosure agreement (NDA), and Dr. Nabeel Adsani, GVP's President and Chief Executive Officer, is concerned that this "boilerplate" agreement may not adequately protect GVP from the unauthorized use and disclosure of GVP's trade secrets and confidential information. Dr. Adsani has expressed his concerns in an interview with the supervising partner.

The File contains the instructing memorandum from the supervising partner, a transcript of the interview with Dr. Adsani, and selected excerpts from Micro's NDA. The Library contains three federal court opinions that bear upon different aspects of the problem. Using these materials, the applicants are instructed to write part of an opinion letter to Dr. Adsani.

The following discussion covers all of the points the drafters intended to raise in the problem. Applicants need not cover them all to receive passing or even excellent grades. Grading decisions are within the discretion of the graders in the user jurisdictions.

Overview: No particular format is prescribed for the applicants' work product. It should be a narrative exposition that can be incorporated into an opinion letter being prepared by the supervising partner, written in language suitable to communication with a non-lawyer. The applicants are told specifically to focus their analysis of Micro's NDA on three concerns:

- The NDA's restrictions as to the persons or entities (receiving parties) to whom disclosure can be made;

- The conditions or limitations that should be placed on disclosures to those receiving parties; and

- GVP's ability to enforce its rights as a third-party beneficiary against persons or entities who obtain confidential information but who are not signatories to the GVP/Micro NDA.

Applicants are to explain whether the excerpted parts of Micro's NDA provide GVP with adequate protection on the foregoing issues. If applicants answer "yes," they should explain how the NDA provides adequate protection. If they answer "no," they should explain why and indicate the changes they would recommend to address GVP's concerns.

In the interview, Dr. Adsani says, "I don't want to scare Micro off." In other words, he doesn't want to require changes to the NDA that will make the confidentiality burden on Micro so onerous that Micro will refuse to go forward with the deal. Nevertheless, applicants should push the envelope and let the partner decide, after consultation with Dr. Adsani, which suggestions to adopt and which ones to reject.

There are a number of ways in which applicants can organize their answers. The best way is probably to analyze each of the paragraphs in the NDA, in serial order.

The Preamble: The preamble is adequate as an introductory statement of the purpose of the agreement.

- It identifies the parties and the technology (i.e., the *iChip*);
- It states that the purpose is to protect the use and disclosure of confidential information.

An applicant might suggest that the "project" be defined a bit more carefully, e.g., " exploring the feasibility of possible cooperation in the development of GVP's *iChip* technology for use in transportation safety products being developed by Micro."

As currently written, the preamble suggests that Micro is also seeking to protect its own confidential information. It would not be out of order for an applicant to suggest that the thrust of the language should be changed to make it clear that Micro is the party that wishes to evaluate the technology and that it is *GVP's* confidential information that is sought to be protected. It might also help in ascribing the proper relationship of the parties to identify Micro as the "Receiving Party" and GVP as the "Disclosing Party" in the preamble rather than later on.

Paragraph 1: The language of this paragraph adequately defines "confidential information."

- It clearly states that it pertains to the litany of subjects potentially to be disclosed by the Disclosing Party, GVP, to the Receiving Party, Micro.

- Applicants can analogize to the definition found in the *Nilsen* case and conclude that the definition in Micro's form NDA is sufficiently broad to cover any conceivable type of tangible and intangible information given by GVP regarding the *iChip*.

- In *Celeritas*, the court rejected the claim that the confidentiality obligation was extinguished once a patent was issued, finding that the information furnished by the disclosing party went far beyond that which could have been gleaned from the patent documents.

  - To guard against a similar claim by Micro, a perceptive applicant might suggest an expansion of the definition of "confidential information" by including a recitation to the effect that the information that will be disclosed by GVP on this "project" includes information that cannot be obtained from GVP's patent application. This might be helpful later on if Micro asserts that it obtained the information from GVP's patent documents.

Other parts of this paragraph of Micro's form NDA are problematic in two respects:

  - The proviso that information must be "clearly and conspicuously marked or designated in writing" by GVP as being confidential information places a burden on GVP; and

  - The obligation that GVP "confirm [ ] in writing . . . within ten (10) calendar days" information that was communicated orally is too restrictive.

- The clue for the applicants that these points are issues to deal with is found in *Nilsen*, where the court refused to find a breach of the agreement because the disclosing party had failed to mark certain documents.

  - Applicants should suggest changes that will ease the burden on GVP and make it less likely that mere oversight by GVP will let something fall between the cracks. For example:

    - The agreement could recite that *all* information communicated by GVP in connection with the "project" shall be deemed confidential unless otherwise designated; or

    - It could require Micro to maintain a log of all information communicated by GVP, to identify that which has not been "marked or designated" confidential, and give periodic notice to GVP so that GVP might have the option of so marking or designating it.

- The clue for this approach is also found in *Nilsen*.

- In any event, the 10-day limitation is too short.

- The time for marking and designating should be lengthened to, perhaps, 30 days or to a period more consistent with when it can reasonably be expected that GVP could react to the notice.

Paragraph 2: This is the paragraph that needs the most work. In their comments, applicants should address each of the following concerns expressed by the client in the interview:

- How to ensure that Micro's employees observe and are bound by the NDA;

- How to protect information disclosed to people (e.g., outside consultants) "associated with" Micro;

- How to take into account the risks associated with turnover in Micro's workforce;

- How to protect the information in the likely event that Micro spins off its Transportation Safety Division into a separate entity; and

- How to protect the information if GVP and Micro are not able to make a deal and they end up going their separate ways.

- The first sentence in this paragraph requires Micro to apply to GVP's confidential information "the same degree of care with which it treats its own proprietary information against public disclosure."

- The language should go beyond that and set a base standard, e.g., "but not less than reasonable care."

- The clue for this change is found in the court's recitation of the provisions of the NDA in *Nilsen*.

- The next sentence, the one that restricts Micro's use of the confidential information to the "project" (i.e., the evaluation of the *iChip* for use in Micro's traffic safety products), appears adequate to protect GVP from having Micro use the information for other purposes, especially if the definition of the "project" is augmented as suggested above.

- There is no language specifically stating that Micro will limit access to GVP's confidential information to Micro employees and others assigned or retained to work on the "project." This deficiency goes directly to several of the concerns expressed by Dr. Adsani, i.e.:

- How to ensure that Micro's employees observe and are bound by the NDA.
    - To address this concern, language should be inserted into the NDA that either requires all Micro employees who work on the "project" to subscribe to the Micro/GVP NDA as signatories or, if that is impractical because of the numbers of such employees, that requires them to execute separate NDAs specifically acknowledging that the NDAs are for the benefit of GVP.
    - The latter approach would satisfy the third-party beneficiary requirement set forth in *AL Limited v. Glass Glo Corporation*.
- How to protect information disclosed to people "associated with" Micro (e.g., outside consultants).
    - Dr. Adsani recognizes that Micro is likely to want to use outside consultants to assist in the evaluation of the *iChip* but says he would like to know ahead of time who they are and when they would be used. To address this concern and avoid the problem encountered in *Nilsen*, the NDA should specifically provide that Micro may disclose confidential information to such consultants but under strict controls, e.g.:
        - The information should be disclosed only to outside consultants who have a need to know (see *Nilsen*);
        - The outside consultants should be identified to GVP before any confidential information is communicated to them, with GVP having the right to object;
        - GVP should be told what information will be disclosed to the consultants and for what purposes;
        - All documents and other tangible forms of information disclosed should be marked confidential and a log maintained by Micro, with a copy to GVP;
        - At the conclusion of the consultancy, all information communicated to the consultants in written or other tangible form, including archival copies, should be returned to Micro; and
        - All outsiders should be required to execute NDAs at least as restrictive as that between GVP and Micro, specifically recognizing that GVP is the third-party beneficiary of those agreements.
- How to take into account the risks associated with turnover in Micro's workforce.

- Anticipating the reality that employees who have worked on the "project" will leave Micro's workforce and others will enter,
  - Micro should be obligated to require all new employees to subscribe to or sign NDAs;
  - The NDAs signed by all employees assigned to the "project" should provide that they will preserve the confidentiality of the information in perpetuity (*cf. Celeritas*) and that when they leave they will not take with them any of the written or otherwise tangible confidential information.
    - These agreements, too, should recognize that GVP is the third-party beneficiary.
- How to protect the information in the likely event that Micro spins off its Transportation Safety Division into a separate entity.
  - An eventual spinoff appears to be a certainty, and Micro's form NDA deals somewhat with this eventuality. However, the form language does not go far enough.
  - Under Micro's form NDA, Micro reserves the right to disclose the confidential information to employees of the "Affiliated Company" and undertakes to require those employees to comply with the GVP/Micro NDA.
    - To address Dr. Adsani's concerns, the GVP/Micro NDA should provide that, in the event of a spinoff,
      - Micro will require the new entity (not just the employees of the new entity) to execute an NDA incorporating all the protections that exist in the GVP/Micro NDA;
      - The employees of the new entity who are assigned to work on the evaluation of the *iChip* will be required to either execute NDAs or subscribe to the one entered into by the new entity; and
      - In all events, the new NDAs must specifically make GVP the intended beneficiary. *See AL Limited v. Glass Glo Corporation.*
- How to protect the information if GVP and Micro are not able to make a deal and they end up going their separate ways.

- In expressing this concern during the interview, Dr. Adsani himself suggests the solution, i.e., require Micro to return to GVP all the documents and other tangible forms of information, including the *iChip* itself.
- Accordingly, the NDA should include such a requirement.
- It should also include a requirement for Micro's "certification of destruction" of documents and other things that have not been returned. *Nilsen.*

- In addition, in the event GVP and Micro are unable to work out a deal, the NDA should contain a provision stating for how long the information should remain confidential once the "project" has concluded.

  - As suggested in *Celeritas*, it may depend on the value of the information, but it would not be out of order for an applicant to suggest that the NDA should provide for perpetual confidentiality. Presumably, if GVP were unable to make a deal with Micro, GVP would want to offer the opportunity to others. In that event, Micro's continued confidentiality would be necessary.

- Along these same lines, an applicant might want to suggest that there be an agreed-upon timeframe within which the evaluation of the *iChip* must take place, i.e., when the "project" must end. (See the NDA in *Nilsen*, which included such a provision.)

  - This would prescribe the period during which GVP would be required to make disclosures and make it easier to manage the flow of information.

Paragraph 3: This part of the NDA attempts to articulate categories of information that are not considered "confidential," and, while an applicant might suggest removing them completely from the NDA, the likelihood is that Micro would insist on this language or similar language for its own protection.

Subparts a, b, and d of this paragraph require the applicants' scrutiny. Subparts c, e, and f need not be altered.

- Subpart a excludes information that is "in or passes into the public domain other than by breach of this agreement."

  - This might be a good place for applicants to suggest inserting language to the effect that the information disclosed by GVP is above and beyond that which is contained in the patent application. This would prevent Micro from asserting that it obtained it information from the public domain, i.e., the patent application. (*Cf. Celeritas*.)

- The exclusions in subparts b (information that was known to Micro before GVP disclosed it) and d (information that was independently developed by a Micro employee) are related.
  - Recall that in the interview, Dr. Adsani pointed out that Micro is in the process of developing two "perception tracing" products—*Intersect* and *LaneTrac*—which might make efficient use of the *iChip*.
  - This suggests that certain research and development work has been underway at Micro and that there is a potential for claims by Micro that it already knew certain things disclosed by GVP and that those things were independently developed by Micro. (These problems are suggested in *Celeritas* and *Nilsen*.)
  - To prevent disputes arising from such claims, applicants might suggest that:
    - Micro should be required to disclose to GVP the status of its "perception tracing" research and development efforts on the *Intersect* and *LaneTrac* products so it can be ascertained whether and what *iChip*-type information may already be known to Micro.
      - GVP would agree to receive the information under a non-disclosure obligation.
    - Micro should be required to identify to GVP all Micro employees who have worked on the "perception tracing" aspects of *Intersect* and *LaneTrac* and to describe the status of their research and development so it can be ascertained whether any of them have "independently developed" any of the *iChip* information.
      - Again, GVP would agree to receive this information under a non-disclosure obligation.
      - Applicants should recognize that this proposal will present two risks: (1) that GVP will be polluted by Micro's confidential information, and (2) that Micro might be so turned off by the requests that it will balk at the deal.
    - Micro should be required to establish a "clean room" (*see Celeritas*) so that Micro employees who have been working on Micro's products will not be exposed to GVP's information.
    - Likewise, Micro should be required to agree that employees and outside consultants it assigns to work on the *iChip* evaluation project (*cf. Nilsen*) shall not

be allowed to work on Micro's *Intersect* and *LaneTrac* projects for the duration of the evaluation period and perhaps even for a number of years into the future.

82961605R00163

Made in the USA
Columbia, SC
22 December 2017